Historic Amusement
Parts of Baltimore

To David,
with love.
from Mom

Historic Amusement Parks of Baltimore

An Illustrated History

JOHN P. COLEMAN

McFarland & Company, Inc., Publishers

Jefferson, North Carolina

All photographs are from the author's collection
unless otherwise noted.

Library of Congress Cataloguing-in-Publication Data

Coleman, John P., 1962–
Historic amusement parks in Baltimore : an illustrated history / John P. Coleman.
p.   cm.
Includes bibliographical references and index.

ISBN 978-0-7864-7814-9 (softcover : acid free paper) ∞
ISBN 978-1-4766-1648-3 (ebook)

1. Amusement parks—Maryland—Baltimore.   I. Title.
GV1853.3.M32.C65 2014   791.06'87526—dc23   2014027225

British Library cataloguing data are available

Front cover: *left to right* Rosalie Elbon, Evonne Fear, and Nancy Earnhartt
enjoy a spin on the Whip during a June 1948 schoolchildren's outing
(courtesy of Hearst Newspaper LLC/*Baltimore News American*)

Printed in the United States of America

McFarland & Company, Inc., Publishers
Box 611, Jefferson, North Carolina 28640
www.mcfarlandpub.com

This book is dedicated to my wife, Marilynn, and
our three children—Joshua, Kyle, and Emily.

It is also dedicated to my mother, Catherine Coleman,
whose childhood stories of Glen Echo Amusement Park
helped lead me to a lifelong interest in amusement parks.

Table of Contents

Acknowledgments

This book could not have been completed without the help of the following individuals; to all of you, I thank you very much.

Richard Parsons and Jason Domasky, Baltimore County Public Library.

Adam Youssi and James Long, Historical Society of Baltimore County.

Donna Hunt and Maryland Public Television allowed me to browse the files from the *Things That Aren't There Anymore* PBS documentary that celebrated several of Baltimore's old amusement parks.

Dr. Robert Headley, University of Maryland Library, author of *Motion Picture Exhibition in Baltimore*, was kind enough to share his detailed database on Baltimore's theaters, which contains references to dozens of old newspaper articles on Baltimore's parks. He patiently copied and forwarded to me several dozen newspaper articles that were helpful in researching this book.

Ann Hanlon and Megan McShea, University of Maryland Library, searched for and forwarded to me many photocopies of old amusement park images from the *Baltimore News American* archives and were instrumental in helping me obtain quality scans of many of the photographs appearing in this book. I received several old newspaper clippings from the library as well.

Marge Murphy and Jay D. Smith of the Hearst Corporation helped me obtain permission to use *News American* archive photographs from the University of Maryland Library.

Sandy Levy, Zach Dixon, Pat Leader, and staff, especially Paul McCardell diligently combed the *Baltimore Sun* archives, forwarded clippings on several of Baltimore's old amusement parks, and helped forward copies of old amusement park photographs from the *Sun* photograph archives.

David Prencipe, Ruth Mitchell, Mary Markey, and Chris Becker from the Maryland Historical Society played a key role in reproducing several rare photographs from the outstanding MHS archives. The MHS's vertical files were a welcome find as well. Thanks also to Francis O'Neill for helping dig up the old maps depicting several of Baltimore's old parks.

Jeff Korman, Enoch Pratt Library, was kind enough to get me oriented during my visits to the library. Access to the vertical files was extremely beneficial to the success of this project.

Elizabeth Stewart, former Research Historian, Maryland Commission on African American History and Culture (Banneker-Douglass Museum), took the time to forward detailed information on Carr's Beach and Highland Beach. Jonie Jones from the Banneker-Douglass Museum was kind enough to review the museum's files on Carr's Beach.

Adam Paul, who helps maintain the "Ghosts of Baltimore" website, was instrumental in helping me find the location of the old Cannstatter Park/Frederick Road Park site.

Thanks to Chris Haley at the Maryland State Archives in Annapolis.

Harriet Stout, Chesapeake Beach Museum, spent several hours detailing the history of the old Chesapeake Beach Amusement Park and allowed me to review their large collection of old postcards and photographs, several of which are included in this book. Harriet and Kristen Scott copied and forwarded many photographs from their archives, which really enhanced the Chesapeake Beach chapter.

The knowledgeable crew at the Baltimore Streetcar Museum, especially Charles Plantholt, Bob Janssen, the late Harry Gesser, Denis Falter, Kenneth Spencer, and the late Rev. Edwin Schell, were extremely helpful in uncovering various old photographs, articles, journals, and the like during my research visit to the museum library.

Gilbert Sandler was kind enough to pass along some fond memories of Carlin's Park.

Mary Kate O'Donnell, Historical Society of Kent County, supplied me with several pieces of information on Betterton Beach.

The late Haywood Mayo forwarded some valuable information on Carr's Beach to assist with that chapter.

The helpful staff at the Dundalk/Patapsco Neck Historical Society and Museum provided me with several photographs from Bay Shore and River View parks.

A special thanks goes to Tom Rebbie, president and CEO of the Philadelphia Toboggan Coasters, Inc. Tom allowed me to access their extensive company archives and granted me permission to use several outstanding photographs from Liberty Heights/Carlin's Park and Frederick Road Park.

Dark ride and Funhouse Enthusiast (DAFE) Club member Joel Styer helped me navigate the extensive Philadelphia Toboggan Coasters, Inc., archives and scanned several rare PTCI amusement park photographs for me.

Dr. Edward Heir and his wife, Susan, donated copies of postcard images from Carlin's Park.

Kudos to Mike Taylor for his permission to use his excellent photographs of Gwynn Oak Park taken after the park had closed.

Paul M. Blitz, historian at the Essex Middle River Heritage Society, shared some of Hollywood Park's history with me.

Russ Sears, who specializes in historical Baltimore memorabilia, allowed me to use reproductions of items from his vast collection of unique Baltimore artifacts.

The late Bill Betts, who was curator of the Tolchester Beach Museum in Rock Hall, provided me with historical facts on the old Chesapeake Bay resort. During a visit to the museum, he allowed me to order several reproductions of fascinating Tolchester Beach photographs. Bill also forwarded additional photographs and letters from the museum to help complete the Tolchester Beach chapter. I am very grateful for his help on this project.

Jim Abbate, long-time member of the National Amusement Park Historical Association (NAPHA), graciously searched his personal files and forwarded several rare photographs from Baltimore's old amusement parks.

Fred Dahlinger Jr. took the time to review my manuscript in its early stages and provided invaluable assistance in formatting this book. Fred is a well-known authority on circuses, traveling shows, amusement parks, and world's fair midways. He has written three books and more than 60 articles on these topics. I can't thank him enough for his time and efforts on this project.

Former Gwynn Oak Park employee Bob Thorn was kind enough to share his fascinating collection of Gwynn Oak memorabilia. Bob took the time to walk me around the Gwynn Oak Park site and pass along many fond childhood memories of this favorite playground.

A big thanks to the many Baltimore residents who took the time to relate their memories of the good times they spent at the old amusement parks, especially Jo Ruth, Stan Rosenstein, Allan Plimack, the late Charlie Echols, Harry Young, Betty Cook, Joan Kilmon, and Bob Thorn.

Last, I'd like to thank my wife and several other family members for their support, and for their valuable assistance on this project, especially my brother Joe Coleman and my sister Pat Coleman. A special thanks is owed to my brother Tom Coleman, who introduced me to several individuals who contributed memories or park memorabilia to this book. Tom also acquired several unique amusement park items in his travels around the Mid-Atlantic region for use in this book. For this, I am truly grateful.

Preface

When asked what initiated my strong interest in amusement parks, I find I'm not able to provide a brief response. It may be partially due to my mother's stories of her childhood visits to her local amusement park—Glen Echo Park in Washington, D.C. Visits, incidentally, that may or may not have taken place during regular school hours (she wouldn't say). It may have been my faint memories of a spin on the kiddie boat ride and the miniature train on a visit to Marshall Hall Amusement Park on the Potomac River. It may also be attributed to the thrills I experienced at the King's Dominion theme park during several visits, starting when that park opened in 1975. It could also be the family's annual drive up to Hersheypark with the promise of exciting rides and the potential for winning stuffed animals and other prizes for siblings at the midway games that awaited.

I can think of two triggers that specifically prompted me to start researching the history of amusement parks. In late summer of 1977, I took a Sunday drive with family to Marshall Hall Amusement Park in Charles County. At that time, a $3 admission fee entitled you to ride as many of the rides that remained in operation, as many times as you liked. But the park had been dying for several seasons, and the rides and buildings were not in good shape. The park had no chance to compete with the new theme parks in Virginia (Busch Gardens and King's Dominion), nor with Hersheypark. Certainly it was not the same Marshall Hall that my parents had taken me to just ten years earlier. However, the visit to the forlorn park had an impact on me, and I began to clip out and collect any newspaper and magazine articles on amusement parks that I ran across. About a year later, while thumbing through a copy of Tim Onosko's excellent book on amusement parks, *Funland U.S.A.*, at the local library, I realized that there were many old amusement parks still in operation in the United States. These seemed to coexist nicely with the explosion of the theme parks whose news-making thrill rides were contorting guests in ways not previously thought possible. This soon led to many attempts on my part at mailing inquiries to nearly all of the amusement parks across the country, seeking history and information.

A vacation with my wife and kids to Baltimore in 2005 gave me the inspiration to take some of the newspaper articles, photographs, postcards, and other memorabilia, I had accumulated over the years and attempt to document many of the amusement parks that Baltimoreans had frequented in years past. This book is the result of several years of part-time research and writing. I've tried to include as many of Baltimore's significant amusement parks as possible in this book. While many German culture beer gardens and social gathering places gradually developed into amusement parks around the turn of the century, I haven't necessarily included chapters on the festival parks and social club establishments like Arion Park, which was located off of Wilkens Avenue, and Schuetzen Park, which was near North Avenue at Gay Street. However, both share an interesting history and deserve to be researched and documented further. Some of the parks, like Chesapeake Beach and Carr's Beach, which also drew large crowds from both Washington and Annapolis, are outside of the Baltimore city limits. But they're included in this volume because they were near enough for many Baltimoreans to make the trip.

While a challenge, researching the old amusement parks was thoroughly enjoyable. Visits to the vertical files at the Maryland Historical Society, the Maryland Rail Heritage Library and the Enoch Pratt Free Library helped me to narrow down the parks that should be considered for inclusion in the book. Trips to the excellent museums on or near the Chesapeake Bay—the Tolchester Beach Revisited Museum and the Chesapeake Beach Railway Museum—offered a multitude of photographs to pore over. A journey to Philadelphia Toboggan Coasters, Inc., outside of Philadelphia, to complete research on two Baltimore parks uncovered a treasure trove of information and rare photographs. Journals and ledgers from the inception of the company in the early 1900s contained detailed notes and letters, many written by their on-site designers and builders at amusement park sites across the country.

I did run across other works on this subject while searching for information over the last several years. Jason Rhodes put together an excellent book on the history of Maryland's amusement parks, while Fr. Kevin Mueller's *Bay Shore Park: Fun on the Chesapeake* is a revealing history of that long-time Baltimore institution. In addition, an excellent volume on the town of Bay Ridge on the Chesapeake Bay, which includes a detailed history of the Victorian amusement resort that operated there, was written by Jane McWilliams and Carol Patterson in 1986.

The intent of my book is to document the history of the many amusement parks and beach resorts that Baltimoreans frequented over the years. My plan was to elaborate on the park owners, the development of the parks, and the challenges faced, the rides and attractions, and the factors that led to the closing of these special places. I hope all will find something in this volume that will bring back a fond memory or two.

Introduction

Just mention the name of an old Baltimore amusement park to any native Balti-morean, and you'll get a similar reaction. The eyes light up, and a smile invariably spreads across the face. You can easily be drawn into an extended conversation on the subject, with fond remembrances of almost forgotten parks flowing freely. The breezy steamer trip down the Chesapeake to Tolchester Beach; the wicked Mountain Speedway roller coaster at Carlin's, or a moonlight dance at Gwynn Oak's ballroom are often recalled. Some old-timers have faint memories of long-departed Baltimore playgrounds like Hollywood Park and River View Amusement Park at Point Breeze. And yet, there are other parks, obscure places like Frederick Road Park and Luna Park, which have gone virtually unnoticed for decades and whose names would most likely not be rec-ognized today.

This book is an attempt to highlight many of the Baltimore area's old amusement parks. The intent is to raise awareness and revisit how Baltimoreans spent their leisure time at these fascinating places. It's a bit of a challenge to present the history of each of the parks in fine detail, especially the older defunct parks. In general, the traditional amusement park tended to be overlooked and somewhat unappreciated in some circles. Some parks did not receive much press coverage in the local newspapers of the time, and when they did, it tended to be negative publicity. However, included in this book are thoughts from Marylanders who were kind enough to pass along some of their fondest memories, accompanied by many old photos and postcard images. Reproduc-tions of assorted park memorabilia which help tell the story of each unique place are offered here as well.

The American amusement park itself can be traced back to the 1860s, when a small number of picnic groves and resorts began to offer primitive rides and diversions for the curious public. The first enclosed modern amusement park is considered to be Chicago's Chutes Park, opened by aquatic legend Captain Paul Boyton in 1894. Prior to 1894 Boyton was famous for building a rubber suit with air chambers that allowed him to float on the water and use a paddle to propel him to his destination. He navigated several notable bodies of water inside his novel invention, giving exhibitions around the globe. No doubt influenced by the hugely successful World Columbian Exposition held in Chicago the previous year, Boyton's park offered various amusements within an enclosed space that could be enjoyed for the price of admission, carrying on the "midway" concept unveiled at the recent world's fair.

Boyton would go on to greater success the following summer by opening Sea Lion

Park at Coney Island. This park helped establish Coney Island as the premier entertainment spot for the masses as the wildly spectacular Steeplechase Park, Luna Park, and Dreamland would open over the next decade, thrilling millions where the sand meets the sea. Coney's success would lead to an explosion in the number of amusement parks around the country and in the number of companies building amusement devices to satisfy the publics' demand for thrills. The number of amusement parks peaked in the early 1920s, with the depression years sharply reducing the number of profitable parks.

Business would pick up after World War II, when the introduction of "Kiddielands" to attract families with children helped to reinvigorate the reputation of the amusement park industry. The industry had a somewhat tarnished and worn image after years of neglect following the depression and wartime restrictions. Walt Disney's dissatisfaction with a visit to a local rundown amusement park gave him the inspiration to develop a place where children of all ages could enjoy simple amusements, in a clean and friendly environment. His Disneyland opening in 1955 would signal the beginning of the new theme park era, with large parks being developed in subsequent years by Six Flags, Anheuser-Busch, and the Marriott Corporation, among others.

Like nearly all major U.S. cities in the late 19th and early 20th centuries, Baltimore had several amusement parks open to the public. They could be grouped together into a few distinct classifications of parks and included the excursion park, trolley park, and picnic park. The excursion park was one typically reached by steamboat, sailing out of the Baltimore harbor. By the mid–1800s, many steamboat excursions on the Chesapeake were available to Baltimoreans; with popular destinations such as Philadelphia, Cambridge, Easton, and various ports in Delaware. Sightseeing and simple picnic pleasures awaited excursionists on these early trips. In the late 1800s and early 1900s, Tolchester Beach, Betterton Beach, and Chesapeake Beach were some of the more popular amusement resorts frequented by Baltimore excursion groups.

The trolley park was considered to be a park reached primarily by customers via the trolley system. During this period, the popularity of the electric trolley was in full swing in many American cities. Typically the traction companies were charged a flat monthly fee for the electricity they expended. Being that the trolleys were used primarily during the weekdays to provide transportation for city-dwellers to and from work, the traction companies began to consider how to stimulate ridership on the weekends. They soon realized that a desirable destination at the end of the trolley line would entice people to patronize the lines on weekends. A typical early trolley park would have been placed a fair distance from the center of the city so people could escape the sweltering heat during the hot summer months. A site on or near a body of water, with ample shade trees, cool breezes and sufficient picnic facilities were the common traits of an ideal trolley park. Gwynn Oak Park was a classic example of the early trolley park.

Sadly, the Baltimore of today can't claim itself as home to a major amusement park. The much-loved Enchanted Forest was closed down in the 1980s, preceded by the demise of Gwynn Oak Park in the early 1970s. Various factors contributed to the demise of Baltimore's old amusement parks. Changing social habits, shifts in the transportation industry, and escalating property values all played a role in park closings during the last century. Some were originally located in what was then considered the outskirts of the city but would soon be engulfed by the inevitable expansion of a blossoming Baltimore. Another amusement park nemesis was fire, as countless blazes hindered park development over the years. (Most early amusement park structures were built of wood and other cheap materials that were highly susceptible to fire.) Nearly every Baltimore park suffered at least one blaze during its lifetime. The explosive growth of the large regional theme parks that occurred in the early to mid–1970s would be the final nail in the coffin and pushed many of the smaller traditional amusement parks across the country into oblivion.

One is hard-pressed to experience an amusement park visit today without arriving via automobile, as the days of riding an open-air streetcar or taking a moonlit cruise to a distant beach park are all but gone. I hope this volume will provide many people, including Baltimoreans, a fond look back at these memorable places, a look back to a time when getting there was half the fun.

1

Bay Ridge

Bay Ridge made its debut as the Chesapeake Bay's newest excursion resort in June of 1880. Located about 4 miles from Annapolis at Tolly Point, it was owned by the Chesapeake Steam Navigation and Hotel Company, in which Annapolis resident James Vansant was a major influence. A large three-story hotel was erected and awaiting guests for the summer opening. It afforded guests comfortable stays, with a wide porch surrounding the first two levels of the structure, which was located high on a bluff overlooking the bay. The resort was served by the Weems Transportation Company, which operated steamers that departed Baltimore's Light Street wharf for the two and one-half hour cruise down the bay. A bandstand, pavilion, and bathhouse were situated near the water. Early offerings at Bay Ridge included bathing, a dance pavilion, swings, and a merry-go-round.[1]

Improvements were gradually made to the scenic resort. A new two-story building was erected for the 1881 season. The first floor housed a bowling alley, while the upper level contained servants' quarters and billiard tables. The lower floor of the large hotel was renovated to remove some of the partitioned areas that had housed a barber shop and barroom the first season. A sizable dining area took over the open space, allowing up to 500 guests to enjoy dinner during the evening. An ice house, capable of holding up to 150 tons of ice, was built in time for the summer season. One of the few complaints from the resorts' inaugural season was the lengthy and uneven walk for excursionists from the steamboat landing to the hotel. This was adequately addressed during the off-season by the laying of wood planking on the long path, with an accompanying overhead awning to protect guests from the elements.[2] (A second pier, located in front of the hotel would be erected for the 1885 season, affording guests a much shorter walk.) The *Theodore Weems* and the *Louise* made the trek from Baltimore twice daily.

For the 1883 season, the steamer *Shadyside* made the Bay Ridge run. This vessel had a capacity of 800 passengers and could reportedly make the trip in under two hours.[3] The *Louise* would be reassigned to make the bay voyage from the harbor to Tolchester Beach that season. Bay Ridge was managed by Dr. G.O. Glavis, who booked the Naval Academy Band to play daily concerts for guests.

Mr. Jerome Durham would lease Bay Ridge for the 1884 season. He encountered trouble, however, with the Bay Ridge ownership, which evidently had agreed to an additional lease with the competing Tolchester Beach Company, giving them exclusive control of the only steamboat landing at Bay Ridge for the sum of $7,000. Durham cried foul, asserting that the Tolchester Company had no intentions of operating excursions to Bay Ridge and that this was an attempt to prevent him from doing so. To quell rumors of a plan to stop the steamer *Georgeanna* from docking at Bay Ridge, the Anne Arundel County sheriff was called in to keep order. The steamer was allowed to dock at Bay Ridge, to Durham's relief, but the crowds were noticeably smaller than would be normally expected.[4] Majority owner Hamilton Disston met with several businessmen from Philadelphia, Baltimore, and Washington in September to discuss potential improvements to the resort. A railroad reaching Bay Ridge from Annapolis was one of the ideas raised.[5]

Looking to expand on its blossoming excursion business, the Bay Ridge Company sought to find additional space for a steamboat berth in the harbor. When they could not find sufficient space near Light Street, they explored the option of building a new pier in the harbor at Calvert Street before the 1886 season was underway. The city council had agreed to lease a small, 30-foot parcel of the wharf at Calvert Street to the Bay Ridge Company, but this drew immediate opposition from the local merchants, especially those in the fruit and produce lines of work. They felt that Baltimore's growing trade business should take priority over the steamboat excursion business. At that time, the thriving melon business saw approximately forty vessels a day arrive at the Pratt Street wharf, each carrying around two thousand melons. Merchants felt it would be an outrage to squeeze out any more of the coveted wharf space to appease the Bay Ridge Company.[6]

The steamer *Bay Ridge* transported a large party of dignitaries to the resort in June of 1886 to witness the large number of improvements in evidence. A new restaurant was open for business, complete with electric lighting, which was claimed to be the largest dining pavilion in the U.S.; and a bathhouse to serve 500 bathers was erected. An opera house was constructed to please the music lovers, as well as a new novelty—the gravity railroad. This early roller coaster, believed to be the first to operate in Maryland, was ready to thrill the more adventurous. Lake Ogleton (named for former Maryland governor Benjamin Ogle's Ogleton property) was completed to offer boating and fishing for guests. T.J. Hurley, president of the Bay Ridge Company, gave a short speech and announced the upcoming grand opening of the Bay Ridge and Annapolis Railroad, which would provide the resort with rail connections to Washington and Baltimore via the Baltimore and Ohio and Pennsylvania systems later that year.[7] This rail line would also be instrumental in the development of other summer communities on the Annapolis Neck like Highland Beach and Arundel on the Bay.

The steamer *Columbia* was overhauled for the 1889 season to the tune of $25,000; this included new upholstery to offer guests a more comfortable voyage. Perhaps the most unique attraction to ever operate at Bay Ridge debuted that summer—the Sprague Electric Railway. At approximately 2.5 miles in length, the railway ran along a path near the water's edge and terminated at the hotel, providing a scenic route for all. Various stations were erected along the railway loop so riders could jump on or off the car, a ride costing one dime. A new steam carousel with a capacity of sixty guests was purchased, and the bathhouse capacity was expanded as well. A new harbor pier, number #10, was constructed near Conway Street to handle the anticipated increase in excursion fares.[8]

Bay Ridge's large restaurant pavilion was 200 feet long. The restaurant itself could hold up to 1,600 diners at one time. The ground level offered tables for picnickers, as well as souvenir and refreshment stands, the billiards room, and other attractions (collection of the Maryland State Archives).

Bay Ridge and other Annapolis-based resorts faced stiff opposition in June of 1890, when pastors of several area churches implored their congregations not to patronize the bay resorts on Sundays. This tended to be a running battle over many years for various businesses and their practice of operating on Sunday. The new steam carousel would be destroyed in a fire the following July, though. The machine had been built by C.W.F. Dare of New York, had an initial cost of $4,000, and was complete with two band organs, one of which was steam powered. Fortunately, insurance would cover nearly the entire loss.[9] An important announcement was made just before the 4th of July that summer, as several railroads announced a rail line consolidation in Baltimore. A line of railroads reaching from Annapolis to Ocean City, Maryland, was to be ready that summer, complete with bridge crossings at the Nanticoke and Choptank rivers. This endeavor included the five-mile-long Bay Ridge line, the one-mile line from Bay Ridge to Claiborne on the Eastern Shore; the Baltimore and Eastern Shore Road (approximately 57 miles long) stretching from Claiborne to Salisbury; and the Wicomico and Pocomoke Road (approximately 31 miles), which extended from Salisbury to Ocean City.[10]

The Catholic Young's People's Association, also known as the United Catholic Literary Association, held a large reunion at Bay Ridge in June of 1891. Over 3000 excur-

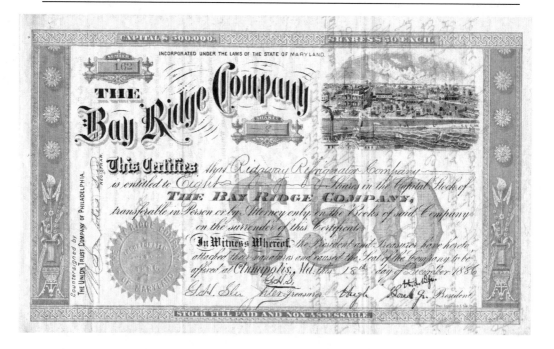

Copy of a stock certificate from the Bay Ridge Company from December of 1886 (courtesy Russ Sears Collection).

sionists crowded the decks of the *Columbia*. The club members saw an excellent vaude-ville show, participated in baseball games and enjoyed the switchback ride, as well as a spin on the new merry-go-round.[11] Bay Ridge's proprietors were charged with violating the Sunday liquor law during the summer of 1892, a charge evidently stemming from a previous incident between a Bay Ridge guard and a group of Annapolis citizens. Park management soon announced that "no disorderly persons will be allowed on the grounds" and that "all boats are prohibited from landing hereafter at the wharf except by permission of those in charge."[12] The switchback/gravity railroad was extended to nearly a half-mile in length for the season.[13]

The unique and historically significant bay village of Highland Beach was actually born out of an unpleasant incident at Bay Ridge in 1892. A black man seeking to have dinner with his wife was refused entrance to Bay Ridge. The man happened to be the son of famed abolitionist Frederick Douglass—Major Charles Douglass. Undeterred, Major Douglass soon purchased 40 acres of farmland that was adjacent to Bay Ridge with the intention of building a resort that could be enjoyed by blacks. Highland Beach was con-sidered by many to be the first African–American summer resort in the United States.[14]

Improvements in place for the summer of 1893 at Bay Ridge included a new bicycle racing track and 125 new bathhouses. Professor Fred Lax's Fifth Regiment Band and Charles G. Wright's band provided popular music for guests beginning in June.[15] Edward R. Schumacher, owner of the carousel that appeared at the park in 1891 to replace the machine lost to fire, lost a judgment to the New York Carousal Manufac-turing Company in April of 1894. Schumacher had failed to make the payment due on the carrousel, claiming that the company's failure to deliver the attraction prior to the beginning of the season had seriously damaged his business. A superior court jury awarded the New York company $522.[16]

"Grand Army Day" was held in early August of 1894. Army veterans and their families were treated to a full day of food, fun, and sporting events. The *Columbia* transported 3500 guests during two treks down the bay. Foot races, sack races, a bicycle race, and a baseball game were part of the athletic contests. The most elusive swine was declared the winner of the greased pig contest and remained at large when all participants began boarding the *Columbia* for the cruise back home.[17] Another exciting attraction was added to Bay Ridge in June of 1895, when the large seventy-five-foot Ferris wheel was erected at a cost of $10,000.[18]

General infrastructure improvements were made at Bay Ridge for the 1896 season. In an effort to improve the dining areas, the kitchen was relocated from the basement of the café to the upper floor, and the dining room was moved closer to the hotel. A new sewage system was dug, and the old bandstand was replaced with a more modern structure.[19] Bay Ridge hosted a Christian Endeavor Day in July. More than twelve hundred excursionists made the bay voyage, and another four hundred rode the rail from Washington, D.C., to enjoy the day at the resort. No dancing was evident on the boat or at the park, but many enjoyed the simple pleasures of Bay Ridge. Many attendees had recently participated at the Christian Endeavor convention held in Washington. Representatives from many neighboring states including Virginia, Pennsylvania, and Delaware made the journey, some traveling from as far away as Michigan.[20]

Various social and fraternal groups participated in excursions to Bay Ridge over the years. St. Leo's Gymnasium and Literary Association held their annual field day in June. Over 2800 crowded aboard the *Columbia* for the 1897 season excursion, each wearing a colorful club ribbon. Track events including the 100-yard dash, high jump, broad jump, pole vault and shot put were held.[21]

The new Bay Ridge Electric Park and Steamboat Company was successful in reaching a five-year lease agreement for additional pier space in the harbor in November of 1898. Space on the new Bay Line Piers, numbers 10, 11, and 12 near Light Street, was obtained to handle the large crowds anticipated for the upcoming summer. Significant landscaping additions were planned, with extensive electric lighting being installed. The hotel and café were renovated and additional bathhouses constructed.[22]

The huge expenditures for the 1899 season at Bay Ridge was perhaps the most aggressive expansion in the resort's history. Resort manager W.H. Herzog announced that fifty new attractions, part of an investment of over $100,000 in improvements, would be in place for the June 10 opening. The feature attraction was the new London Steeple (also called the Coney Island Steeple), a half-mile-long steeple chase gravity ride. Believed to be erected by the Tilyou family of Coney Island, New York, fame, the thirty-six-horse ride cost a hefty $30,000. It allowed for one or two "riders" to mount the back of a mechanical horse, which was lifted to the top of an incline. Once released, riders raced over various dips and curves propelled via gravity alone. A similar steeple chase ride was the signature attraction of George C. Tilyou's recently opened Steeplechase Park, a wildly popular draw at Coney Island. Other attractions scheduled to debut included a miniature railroad, the Electric Stairway and the Tumbling Barrels, installed by C.G. Hawkins of Philadelphia, and a new merry-go-round delivered by G. W. Hill, also of Philadelphia, which included two pipe organs at a total cost of $6,000. Other exciting additions included the New Bijou Theatre and Wargraf Building, constructed by Edward De Corsie at the cost of $3,000, the $5,000 recreation pier at the German Village, and Professor Sweet's Movable Wax Figures. Spectacular shows like Hatch's Oriental Company of Dancing Girls, Professor J. Peters' Marvelous Illusions, and a gypsy camp complete with snake charmers were booked for the highly anticipated season.[23]

Quite a lot of money was spent to overhaul the *Columbia* prior to the 1899 opening, which frequently made the Bay Ridge run under the careful eye of Capt. John Thomas. A roof garden was added to the top deck of the steamer, where continuous music could be enjoyed on both legs of the trip. Guests could choose from concert, dance, or vaudeville orchestra numbers while sailing on the *Columbia*.[24] Perhaps the Bay Ridge Improvement Company (of which the Baltimore and Ohio Railroad was a major stockholder) allocated a bit too much in expenditures for the 1899 season. Soon finding it too expensive to maintain and operate the huge *Columbia,* a decision was quickly reached on July 17 that summer to sell the steamer to the Cape May and Delaware Navigation Company. The *Columbia* would be moved to New York, soon to begin making the trip between Long Branch, New York, and New York City. Disappointed excursionists who arrived that morning and realized they could not board the *Columbia* were offered transportation via train to Bay Ridge on the Annapolis and Short Line. Herzog announced plans for a replacement steamer, the *John S. Morgan,* owned by Samuel O. Stokes, to make the Bay Ridge run. Captain Isaac Kirby, formerly skipper of the *Jane Moseley,* would be at the helm of the new side-wheeler. It was just under 200 feet in length and could maintain a speed of 12 knots, with a capacity of between 1200 and 1500 passengers.[25] The novel Electric Railway would be removed this summer; it had not operated since being damaged during a winter storm a few months earlier.[26]

Despite the wide variety of events and attractions at Bay Ridge, excursion business was beginning to wane. In April of 1900, the Bay Ridge Improvement Company announced the sale of the resort to the Chesapeake Chautauqua Assembly, a group of individuals from Pennsylvania led by the Rev. Dr. C.C. McLean, for the price of $10 a share. The assembly planned to rename Bay Ridge "Brighton." McLean's grand plans included group studies of the Chautauqua Literary and Scientific Circle, where students could earn diplomas after four years of courses. McLean noted that "the grounds will also be used for the excursions of churches, Sunday-schools, and all moral and respectable organizations, who will have the privilege of giving lectures and concerts."[27] Formal opening would be Decoration Day (May 30), but no Sunday excursions would be permitted.

The formal opening of the Chesapeake Chautauqua drew around 600 people. Dr. McLean declared "this will be a moral, religious place where you will have all that will amuse and entertain, with a restraining moral influence that will be a blessing. There is no resort on the Chesapeake having the advantages of this. This is a place where men may come with their wives and children and feel they are safe. No liquor will be sold on the ground unless on a doctor's prescription in case of sickness. There will be no Sunday desecration here. Our objective is not to make money, but to establish a school."[28] It was thought that a summer school could be operated on the same principles as those recently established at Ocean Grove, New Jersey and Chautauqua, New York. The dance pavilion was converted for classroom use and also expanded to provide sleeping quarters.

An interesting incident occurred in June of 1900, when it was reported that the steamer *Columbia* had been "stolen" while anchored for repairs at Erie Basin, near Buffalo, New York. Two tugboats reportedly made their way into the basin after dark and took off with the *Columbia* while the watchmen assigned to guard the large vessel were distracted for a drink with "a pleasant-mannered stranger, who for two days had cultivated their acquaintance."[29] Evidently, *Columbia*'s former owners, the Baltimore and Ohio Railroad, strongly felt that the conditions of the sale were not met by the buyers; and, not wishing for a lengthy court dispute over possession of the ship, the railroad decided to take action on its own. The tugboats turned over the pirated steamer to B&O representatives at the St. George Marina in New York.

The conversion of Bay Ridge to the Chesapeake Chautauqua did not go over well with the general public, and the doors would be closed at the resort in 1903. A fire destroyed the old Bay Ridge Hotel in March of 1915; however a new hotel, the Bay Ridge Inn, would open in 1915 for those wishing a quiet bay getaway. In February of 1922, the Bay Ridge Realty Corporation purchased the title to the 387 acres of land that the Bay Ridge resort had operated on. The owners successfully developed the land, and a thriving summer community was born. The Loffler and Baur families purchased the Bay Ridge Inn and soon opened Baur's Beach, a popular family resort that would flourish in the postdepression era. With the threat of war brewing, the beach resort was sold to B.B Wills, a man with extensive experience in the resort trade. The popular Bay Ridge Beach, as it was also known, was sometimes referred to as "Tahiti on the Chesapeake," for its colorful thatched-roof huts and palm décor.[30]

The Bay Ridge summer colony became a suburban year-round community in the 1960s. Bay Ridge Beach would host large summer outings for local corporations and organizations, including Crown Cork and Seal, the Sixth District Democratic Club, the Real Estate Board of Baltimore, and the Home Builders Association. A large children's playground, pony rides, cart rides, the accommodating picnic groves, and, of course, the beach were the prime attractions at Bay Ridge Beach. Picnics would typically include crabcakes, softdrinks, horseshoes, and baseball games for company employees to enjoy.

2

Bay Shore Park

Bay Shore Park's early beginnings can be traced to a land purchase in early to mid–1905 by the United Railways and Electric Company of Baltimore, the local trolley company. In October of that year, the company announced that they were aggressively pursuing development plans for that 30-acre tract of land, which was to be transformed into a first-class amusement resort. The intent was to build ridership on the trolley line. Architects Simonson and Pietsch, who had previously designed various structures for Baltimore's River View Park, were hired to develop plans for the proposed park buildings. In February of 1906, the final drawings were divulged to the public. Among the unique buildings were a three-story restaurant, a two-story dance pavilion, a bath-house, a music pavilion, and a carousel pavilion.[1] A total of nine buildings were to be erected, with the construction work contracted out to Henry S. Ripple & Sons and Charles L. Stockhausen in March. It was hoped that the work could be completed by May 1, 1906.[2]

Located on what was known as Black Marsh on the Chesapeake Bay, Bay Shore Park was directly across the water from what would later become the Bethlehem Steel plant. This spot carried some historical significance as well, as it was the landing site of the British forces during the Battle of North Point in the War of 1812. One of the eagerly awaited attractions at the new resort was the 1000-foot pier, sections of which were to be covered to offer shelter from the sun and poor weather. Fishing, picnicking, and strolls out over the bay were envisioned on what was thought to be the longest pier in Baltimore. Michael J. Fitzsimmons, who had managed River View Park for the past few seasons, signed a lease with United Railways in May of 1906 to operate Bay Shore Park.[3] The park was to open in late spring of that year, but rainy weather hindered construction. The bathhouse, bowling alley, and dance pavilion were all complete by mid–June, but the restaurant and remaining buildings still had additional work to be tackled. One of the major problems encountered was in laying the new rail bed across Black Marsh. The roadbed sank about half a foot over night at one point, as the soft ground could not support the weight.[4] The revised opening date of July 4 came and passed with Bay Shore still not ready.[5]

Finally, on August 11, the park opened to rave reviews. River View's Royal Artillery Band was allowed to appear at Bay Shore's grand opening after much haggling between Fitzsimmons and Bay Shore architect Otto Simonson and contractor David Evans. (Fitzsimmons was reluctant to allow the band to leave River View, with which he was still affiliated). An "informal inspection" of the park was carried out the day before its opening. The streetcar *Lord Baltimore* left from the corner of Baltimore and Holiday streets at 5:00 p.m. with a party of 20 notables. What awaited them at Bay Shore was described by the guests with one word—"magnificent."[6] For this first season, the United Railways Company decided to offer a 10-minute trolley car schedule for trips to Bay Shore Park. The first trolley of the morning would leave Howard and Franklin streets at 7:00 a.m., with cars running every 10 minutes thereafter. The last trolley would leave the park around 11:20 p.m.

Extending the railway from Sparrow's Point to Bay Shore added a great benefit to Fort Howard, one of the main defensive positions protecting the city of Baltimore at that time. "It is believed that the building of the Bay Shore extension should be of considerable interest to the Government, which has recently increased the garrison at Fort Howard, the convenience of which must be greatly subserved by the road, which will have a station within 100 yards of the fort gate. As originally planned, the (rail)road was to have been constructed partly on Government property, but in view of the necessity for concealing some important features of the plan of defense, the Secretary of War decided that the public should not be given promiscuous admission to the reservation by the railway."[7] In a letter to the garrison commander, Colonel Thorp, President Hood of United Railways communicated his thoughts on the arrangement: "I think as an engineer, and an old soldier, that the effectiveness of the garrison in preventing landing by an enemy to pass the fort by or to take it in the rear would be materially enhanced by having the railway roadbed across Shallow Creek and extending northwardly one and one-half mile to Black Marsh, for use in handling troops upon the most direct line, as they would thus be relieved of the necessity of passing around

A postcard view of the popular dance pavilion.

the head of Denton Creek, but of Shallow Creek as well—that is, they would place both of these obstructions behind them by using this 1,200 foot crossing." Hood would go on to state "the railways company would stand ready at any time to place the transportation facilities of its system at the service of the Government, for the quick handling of troops in any number. It is often being called on to handle 30,000 passengers to and from a single resort in a few hours, while it has a record of handling something over 700,000 persons in 20 hours."[8]

An early postcard depicting views of the bowling alley. At 60 feet wide and 108 feet long, it housed 10 modern alleys offering both ten-pin and duck-pin bowling.

Bay Shore's ornate three-row carousel was created by master carver Gustav Dentzel. It was in place during the park's first season of operation (courtesy Dundalk-Patapsco Neck Historical Society).

Bay Shore Park quickly earned a solid reputation as a first-class family amusement resort. No alcohol was allowed on the premises, in contrast to some other local parks in operation. It was also believed that the steep round-trip fee of 30 cents for the trolley ride from the city would help to keep out any potential troublemakers.[9] Park-goers to Bay Shore's opening weekend encountered serious unexpected delays due to power outages that crippled the United Railway's streetcar lines twice on a busy Saturday. The first accident snarled the busy afternoon "rush" for approximately two hours; the source of the problem was believed to be a problem with wiring at the Westport Station of the Consolidated Gas and Electric Light Power Company, from which United purchased their power. The second incident occurred in United's Pratt Street powerhouse around 11:00 p.m. which prompted the power to be shut off in order for repairs to proceed. Large crowds of passengers, particularly those at the amusement resorts, were stranded at various points throughout the city. Overcrowded stations and the heat exacerbated the situation. Trolleys did not begin to run again until after 1:00 a.m., with some riders not reaching their homes until 4:00 a.m. A large public outcry was heard the following day, many placing the blame directly on United Railways directors. Demands were leveled at United to establish more efficient methods and procedures in dealing with interruptions in passenger service.[10]

Baltimoreans would soon begin to make the scenic ride to Bay Shore in large numbers, though. A *News-American* writer described an early trolley ride to Bay Shore:

"It is doubtful if there is any trolley ride about Baltimore as attractive as that from Sparrow's Point to the Bay Shore, through fertile farmlands that skirt the track, the fields rich with ungarnered fruit or waving with unharvested grain. Farmhouses, the doors of which are filled with women and children, to whom the clang of the trolley bell is as yet a novelty, are rapidly passed. Through half-cleared woodland and along country roads speeds the car, and the Bay breaks into view."[11]

With its rushed late-season opening however, the park's full lineup of attractions wasn't quite ready for patrons. The long concrete pier that extended into the bay was not yet finished, and several of the amusement devices had not been completed. Management of United Railways continued to fine-tune Bay Shore over the winter months, battling poor weather to build a powerhouse to illuminate the grounds and to act as an auxiliary to the Pratt Street plant and the station at Highlandtown. A deep artesian well was also dug to provide fresh spring water.[12] Plans were submitted by Bay Shore architects Simonson and Pietsch prior to the 1907 opening to construct a new amusement building, motion picture theater, and soda and candy pavilion.[13] When guests returned in May of 1907, they were welcomed to a fully operational beach resort. Early diversions at Bay Shore Park included a skating rink, penny arcade, photo gallery, row boats, 10-lane bowling alley, and baseball diamond. Highly regarded conductor Giuseppe Aiala directed the band in the large concert hall for a few seasons before returning to his previous position at River View Amusement Park. Carefully tended lawns and gardens, viewed by guests strolling on the gravel walks, were a big part of the park's appeal. The 1000-foot long pier had large covered pavilions that sheltered guests from the sun while allowing the cool sea breezes. Men could shoot billiards or practice their aim on the rifle range. The Mansion House offered several excellent dining areas where just 75 cents bought a seafood feast. Nearby, the large ornate fountain was a popular gathering spot.

Rides to experience during the park's early years included the Figure–8 roller coaster and a carousel. The aptly named Figure–8 was a standard roller coaster design at that time. Trains would negotiate a fairly tame course in the shape of a figure eight before returning riders to the station. A three-row carousel with hand-carved figures from the workshop of Gustav Dentzel stood near the bay. Dentzel, a German immigrant who learned the craft from his father, was considered to be a master carver of carousel figures.[14]

Other midway attractions that were soon added included a miniature train, a Circle Swing ride, and Pike's Peak. Additional rides that were added were the Thingamajig, a roller coaster; a miniature Ferris wheel, the Whip, and the Whirl-a-Drome. The sandy beach offered plenty of room for bathers. The Tour of the Seas attraction, touted as just the second of its kind in operation (the first having debuted at the recent Jamestown Exhibition), was developed by a Baltimore man who recreated the set of a battleship within a 50-foot diameter building. Guests entering the Tour of the Seas experienced a realistic sea voyage on the deck of a battleship.[15]

A February 1907 article in the *Street Railway Journal* documented the layout of Bay Shore Park, including detailed drawings of several park structures, including the dance and music pavilions. The latter was capable of holding upwards of 2000 people and measured 122 ft. × 144 ft. The bathhouse, which was situated along the shoreline, was an impressive two-story building complete with offices and changing rooms. The two-story dance pavilion housed a billiard room on the first level, with the dance floor on the second level. The bowling hall was situated just next to this building and offered ten alleys for duck-pin and ten-pin play. William F. Corcoran, the popular tenor, performed with Signor Ailia's orchestra in the summer of 1907.

A trip to Bay Shore Park via trolley was a thing to remember. The park's trolley station could handle up to four streetcars at a time. The cars on the #26 streetcar line fondly referred to as the "Red Rocket," offered a fast, jolting ride from downtown. Streetcar motormen recall "the cars being so full and moving at such a decent clip, that if something was on the track, they just hit it."[16] Last call at the end of a long fun-filled day came at 1:00 a.m.

Bay Shore's 1908 opening saw the park crowded by nearly 5000 visitors. Guests enjoyed the sounds of Ricci's Premier Concert Band during afternoon and nighttime performances. The famous tenor John Nestor, thought to be the top band singer in the country, appeared at the weekend concerts during the opening weekend.[17]

Acrobats, aeronauts, and daredevils were all the rage at amusement parks and other public gathering places during this time. Bay Shore was no exception. Arthur C. Holden, the "death looper" (and noted high-diver) appeared here in July of 1909. Although he had the occasional accident, his act consisted of a bicycle ride down a steep incline that ended with a vertical loop.[18] Holden would also dive from a height of over 90 feet into a five-foot-deep pool. Another interesting act that performed at Bay Shore that summer was Captain Hinman and his lifesaving dogs. Hinman would wade well out into the bay waters and feign drowning, whereupon his dogs would paddle out into the water and pull their master ashore.[19]

Much preparation was underway at the park over a month in advance of the 1910 season opening. A new ride installation—the Tipsy Automobile, or Joy Ride—featured a standard-sized automobile which sat on a set of casters rather than wheels. "The automobile is hauled to the top of a long incline by means of moving platforms. When it gets to the top, it is allowed to roll down the incline, which is set at various angles. The quarter wheels of the automobile, which are exactly like the outer wheels of a bedstead, move in different directions as the auto goes down and the occupants of the car are tossed here and there."[20] Also, the Wizard's Cave attraction opened in the former Tours of the Seas building. Additional tables and benches were added to the picnic grove, and Signor Quitano's Royal Italian Concert Band was booked to perform concerts each afternoon and evening.[21] A thrilling act to appear that summer was Develo, riding his bicycle in the "cage of death."

The Boston Ladies' Orchestra was onboard for the 1911 season opening at Bay Shore. The all-woman orchestra had appeared at Bay Shore in 1909, with Belle Yeaton Renfrew conducting. Large crowds enjoyed the park's offerings and the notable seafood suppers, a highlight of the visit to the park's restaurant, which was managed by J. Duncan Rose.[22] Children arriving for a visit during the 1912 season were entertained by the new pony track. Bay Shore's 1913 weekend opening coincided with Decoration Day (Memorial Day). Free Japanese bird kites were distributed to each child during a special hour, followed by a unique kite-flying exhibit. The late–May opening of the park for the 1914 season saw several thousand dollars in improvements to the park's appearance. Farson's Orchestra was booked for the summer to perform in the large pavilion.[23] Sadly, the 1915 season was marred by a tragic accident, when the carousel operator was caught in the machinery after pulling the starting lever. He was rushed to the hospital via a United Railways streetcar, but the attending physicians could not save him.[24] (Another incident on the park's carousel in August of 1917 resulted in a broken ankle for a woman thrown from the ride. She filed suit against United Railways for $10,000 for the injuries suffered.[25])

Bay Shore's blossoming resort continued to attract large numbers of patrons, who at times overwhelmed the streetcar line to Bay Shore. One exasperated writer vented his frustration towards United Railways in a letter to the *Sun* editor in the summer of 1916:

> At Bay Shore last Sunday night, this writer along with his wife and child, waited half an hour, while men, women, and children fought and pushed and tussled to get on the few cars that did come along, city-bound. Seeing that the only way to get home was to do as the others were doing—use force—the writer fought his way to the inside of a car—the fourth one that came along during that long wait of half an hour—and succeeded through sheer strength in obtaining a seat for his wife. This performance is repeated every Sunday night at Bay Shore. It has been so for two or three years. Last Sunday night the crowd there exceeded all records, I am told. Yet the United made no effort whatever to handle it. Some fine day somebody is going to be killed in that crush, and then it will cost the company considerably more than

Guests are taking in the view from near the end of the pier. The park's carousel can be seen on the beach in the background (from the Maryland Rail Heritage Library, courtesy Baltimore Streetcar Museum).

a bit of foresight would. The cars coming cityward were packed to suffocation, despite the overcrowding "rule."[26]

The increase in patrons prompted the park to erect an addition to the crowded bathing pavilion that summer. A new bathhouse was added for the 1917 season that reportedly could handle up to 8000 swimmers a day.

United Railways had to deal with the occasional minor "controversy" over the years. In 1918, Baltimoreans protested the increase in what was already considered to be an excessive passenger fare to Fort Howard and Bay Shore. At that time, two fares were required to reach Bay Shore when other locations of equal distances required only one fare.[27] Being the only practical means for many to reach the popular saltwater bathing spot, the streetcar journey by 1920 offered a wide variety of sights. "The route to it is an interesting one, since the Baltimore Courthouses, Post Office and City Hall are passed, and the excursionist glimpses the ancient Shot Tower, the Church Home and Infirmary, where Edgar Allan Poe breathed his last, the Johns Hopkins Hospital, and the wide stretch of Broadway. The car passes through Sparrows Point, with its giant steel plant, and the bugles of Fort Howard are heard within a stone's throw of the park."[28]

Guests in fine attire stroll along the picturesque path in front of the landmark fountain (from the Maryland Rail Heritage Library, courtesy Baltimore Streetcar Museum).

Bathers and the exciting Sea Swing, c.1920, with the pier in the background (courtesy Hearst Newspapers LLC/*Baltimore News-American*).

Bay Shore advertised for its 1920 season by stating that the park had been remodeled and enlarged, with many new amusements added, including a new dance floor, and a roller coaster, frequently referred to as a racer dip. A popular claim regarding the excellent restaurant was publicized on occasion: "Just arrange to eat one of Rose's Famous Seafood Dinners at Bay Shore. You'll say it's the nearest I've had to real good old-fashioned home cooking in many a long day."[29] An impressive fireworks display was presented on July 4th, with the bay serving as a backdrop for the large show. Night bathing became one of Bay Shore's popular offerings that summer.

Extensive changes were made at Bay Shore Park prior to the summer of 1921. A new 200-foot bathers-only pier was constructed. It allowed an alternative to wading out far from the shore, with wide steps provided at different locations for both young and old to enter the bay. A new boardwalk was erected that extended from the bathhouse to the large pier. Benches facing the water offered a cozy spot to watch bathers or keep an eye on the children. Several sets of plans were drawn up to give the long pier a facelift. It was decided that the large pier would be renovated to contain a new flower garden. Two pagodas were erected on it surrounded by trees and flowers. Several new benches were added, as well as a soda fountain, which was placed at the far end of the pier.

To provide a more intimate setting for couples wishing to dance, management decided to create a dance pavilion at the head of the long pier, in the carousel building. The carousel was moved to the large building that formerly served as the dance hall. A dance floor was installed, and the building was decorated and screened in to keep out the pesky mosquitoes. Dancers could now also enjoy a spectacular view of the water. Upgrades to the amusements included the addition of airplanes replacing the old ride vehicles on the Circle Swing, and a new building housing the shooting gallery. Also, a Crazy House funhouse attraction and a new Balloon Racer game were added to excite the crowds. To help tired mothers manage the kids, a new playground with slides, sandboxes and other diversions was installed in a section of the picnic grove. With the increasing popularity of the automobile, Bay Shore tripled its parking capacity by tearing out part of the midway and expanding the parking lot. The access road to Bay Shore was paved to allow for a smoother drive on to park property.[30]

Annual group outings at amusement parks provided a constant source of excitement for Baltimoreans. The Chesapeake and Potomac Telephone Company held its annual outing at Bay Shore for a time. The August outing in 1921 attracted nearly 2500 employees who stepped away from work for a day and forgot their troubles. Various contests and events were held; including the sack race, the three-legged race, and the tug-of-war. The women could compete in a ball throw and nail-driving contests. The "fat man" race was just that, the hefty winner being awarded a case of "near beer" for his exhausting efforts. The day was capped off with a baseball game between Washington, D.C., and Baltimore workers.[31]

Bay Shore expanded its beach front area in May of 1922 by creating a new beach, trucking in tons of sand from Rehoboth Beach, Delaware. This new area was on the site of the former bathhouses. Much painting was done and many decorations were added to help revitalize the park for visitors. Even the carousel horses were spruced up with the addition of new tails and manes.[32] Those park-goers looking for water thrills could brave the new Sea Swing ride. Bathers sat in a harness-type seat and were spun in circles, skimming the top of the bay waters. A new sliding board was added during the summer as well. An authentic streetcar was added to the children's playground area for the kids to play in. The Jolley Trolley (or Monkeyshine Railroad) allowed kids to pretend they were the streetcar conductor and to clang the bell.

Several flaps over proper bathing attire would arise during the early 1920s. The one-piece bathing suit for girls was banned at popular beach resorts like Coney Island and Atlantic City. However, they were allowed at most Baltimore beaches as long as discretion was used. George Tucker, Bay Shore's assistant superintendent, related that they did not have rules governing swimsuits: "Though we have no garment restrictions, we expect the girls to use the ordinary precautions in the design of their suits. One-piece suits will be tolerated if they do not prove objectionable."[33]

The Bay Shore Athletic Club was admitted to the South Atlantic Association of the Amateur Athletic Union (AAU) in July of 1923. This allowed for the park to hold sanctioned swim and dive meets. A large crowd numbering nearly 4000 spectators witnessed a water exhibition about a week later. A variety of women's swimming and diving stars, including world record-holders and Olympic athletes, presented a wide variety of strokes and fancy dives for the appreciative crowd.[34] The growing popularity of these outdoor exhibitions was further strengthened in August of that summer when nearly 10,000 people crowded Bay Shore Park to watch a second exhibition of swimming and diving events presented by national and local champions.

Bay Shore unveiled some additional water-based attractions for the 1924 season. Innovative horseshoe floating chairs, along with tube floats and water wings, were now available to bathers. Fishing and crabbing facilities were added to the long pier, and a boat launch ride was introduced as well, offering a six-mile round-trip cruise to a mid-channel lighthouse. The Toboggan waterslide was added for the more adventurous.[35] The bathhouses were upgraded with additional lockers and locker rooms, and the park purchased hundreds of new bathing suits to rent out to swimmers.[36]

A Baltimore to Bay Shore steamboat line was announced in May 1924. Leaving Pier 2 at Light Street, the *General Lincoln* transported beachgoers to Bay Shore and the nearby Sandy Beach park for the modest fee of 15 cents each way. The *General Lincoln,* formerly the steamer *Nahant,* was built in 1878 at Chelsea, Massachusetts. The Bay Shore-Brighton Excursion Company, headed by local attorney Charles Jackson, purchased the steamer from the Annapolis and Claiborne Ferry Company and contracted to have the 160-foot side-wheeler ready to carry passengers within a month's time.[37] The venture did not last more than a few seasons, however.

Several significant events were held over the years at Bay Shore, which was frequently advertised as "Baltimore's Atlantic City." The most significant was probably the Schneider Cup Race, held on October 28, 1925. Named for the famed French aviator Jacques Schneider, the annual seaplane race first conducted in 1913 showcased the cutting-edge aircraft and flying skills of top aviators from around the globe. The 1925 contest pitted England, Italy, and the United States against one another. About 5000 spectators, including Orville Wright and Glenn L. Martin, crowded the pier areas at Bay Shore Park to watch the spectacle. The triangular-shaped racecourse stretched from Bay Shore south to Gibson Island, then across the bay to Huntington Point before the last leg back across the bay to the park. The aviators would fly seven laps around the course, covering a total of 207 miles in total distance.

Three fliers competed for the U.S. One, a young army lieutenant, amazed the crowd from the start with speedy dives and extremely close approaches to the course pylons, at a height of just 50 feet above the bay. The young flier averaged 230 miles per hour in his small Curtiss racer and wound up breaking several world records for seaplane flight, capturing the cup for America. A boat towed the winning seaplane, with its flier sitting on the wing, past the appreciative crowd. The young aviator's name? Jimmy Doolittle, who would go on to even greater heroics in World War II. The Schneider Cup Race was held continuously until 1931, when the depression years afforded too little financial support for many nations to compete.[38] Also, in that same year, noted expert swimmer Lillian Cannon completed a difficult swim across the bay. Cannon gave regular swimming and diving exhibitions at Bay Shore and other East Coast locations, as well as providing swim lessons for the willing.[39] Douglas C. Turnbull was manager of the park during the 1920s up through the 1932 season. He transferred over to

Gwynn Oak Park for the 1933 season, with C.E. Graham assuming his position as park manager at Bay Shore.[40]

August of 1926 marked the fourth annual swim meet to be hosted by the Bay Shore Swimming Club. Twelve South Atlantic championship events and the National Junior championship were contested that weekend, with swim clubs representing Richmond, and the naval academy in Annapolis making the trip. Local clubs from Patterson Park, Clifton Park, Druid Hill, and the Baltimore Athletic Club competed as well.

Fire destroyed the steamer *Eastern Shore,* which was docked at a pier near Bay Shore Park, on January 4, 1928. The ship was owned by the Baltimore, Eastern Shore Ferry Line, Inc., which had been placed in receivership the previous summer. Originally built at a cost of $200,000, the ship, pier, and other company assets were slated to go to auction the following week.[41]

In time, Bay Shore Park became known as a popular Mid-Atlantic region venue capable of supporting a multitude of special events. In June 1928, the park hosted the eighth annual regatta for Chesapeake Bay workboats. The workboat races, as they were known, originated in Baltimore. The idea was to have men who made their livings plying the Chesapeake in their various watercraft hold a competition to see who owned the fastest workboat. The annual event had previously been held just offshore of various boating towns further down the Chesapeake, including Claiborne, Crisfield, Cambridge, and the Solomons. Several classes of boats competed for cash prizes and the coveted silver cup, including schooners, skipjacks, crabbing skiffs from Smith's Island, and "bugeyes." Captain William C. Todd steered his Deal Island schooner to victory in that race. A host of city and state politicians were on hand to view the spirited matches.

In spite of the difficult times during the depression years, Bay Shore continued to offer activities for Baltimoreans to forget about their troubles, if only for a day's time. Two new forms of entertainment were introduced to Bay Shore in 1930. Park guests could now enjoy a game of miniature golf or test their skill with the bow and arrow on the new archery range.[42] For Bay Shore's 1931 opening, "Baltimore's Claim to Salt Water Fame" offered something for everyone. Fishermen could take low-cost daily charter trips with all fishing equipment provided. Modern bathhouses were advertised, along with new bathing suits for rent. Farson's orchestra offered soothing sounds for moonlite dancing in the new ballroom. A brand new thrill—the Bike Boat—made its debut. Billed as a bicycle ride on the water, "last season's sensation in Europe" offered thrills, and quite a bit of exercise.[43] In August of that year, the Bay Shore Swimming Club won the AAU Junior Distance Swim Meet held at Bay Shore. Nine young ladies fought through a cold rain and choppy waters to navigate the course, which was trimmed from two and a half miles to a mile and a half due to the adverse conditions. This was the first national long-distance meet to be held in the Baltimore area.[44]

Unfortunately, a combination of the depression and a decrease in streetcar ridership due to the widespread use of the automobile was seriously hurting United Railways. Although they were attracting good numbers of people to Gwynn Oak and Bay Shore, both parks were operating at a loss from the late 1920s to early 1930s. A decision was made to lease both parks out. Bay Shore was leased to the park's former assistant manager. For the 1931 season, Bay Shore added the Pretzel dark ride. This ride from Leon Cassidy's Pretzel Amusement Ride Company received its name from the ride's twisted curving track layout that guests navigated in the dark. Various tricks and stunts were triggered throughout the mysterious course to scare unsuspecting riders. A 40-pound metal pretzel-shaped figure, acting as a weight on the car's front wheels, adorned both sides of the ride vehicle. Cassidy unveiled the popular ride in 1928.

In late April 1933, receivers of the United Railways (receivership having been in effect since January of that year) disclosed in a report to the United States District Court that United had cut their expenses by over 32 percent since 1929, amounting to over $2.7 million in cuts. Essentially, a 10 percent wage reduction in April of 1932 had placed wages at the same level as they stood in 1924. A table within the report noted that expenditures for materials and supplies, as well as payments to accident victims had significantly been reduced. The receivers had also been tasked with finding additional economies that could lighten the burdens of the traction company. Revising the existing contract between United and the local power company—Consolidated Gas Company—was considered, the contract having taken effect back in 1921. It was thought that additional cost savings could be realized through the rescheduling and merging of certain streetcar lines. The receivers also worked on a plan to consolidate the company's various office locations into buildings actually owned by the traction company. It was hoped that this would create a benefit of approximately $12,000 annually.[45]

In the report from United's receivers, it was also noted that the company would benefit from the park-tax ordinance that was passed in 1932. Under this agreement, instead of paying the flat 9 percent park tax that was assessed annually, the tax on gross receipts would be reduced by 1 percent a year until it reached 3 percent. So by 1937 the tax would be 3 percent. Interestingly enough, the feedback generated from the filing of this report noted that even with the severe cuts taking place, the actual service afforded to the streetcar-riding public had not suffered much. One change to the URC's normal operations that did cause some initial heartache was the introduction of the one-man streetcars. The company had ordered 150 "Baltimore-type" streetcars, which required only one man to operate. The total cost was $2.6 million. But, this new lightweight model offered greater speed and less wear and tear, and it was estimated that the company would save $400,000 a year in operating costs.[46] Bay Shore Park would continue to operate under various operators who were leasing from the traction company.

In recovering from an early spring storm in 1937, the park rebuilt many of the wooden structures on the bay, including a pier, the bathhouse, and diving boards. The children's playground was renovated as well.[47] In 1939, millionaire George P. Mahoney, a former chairman of the Maryland Racing Commission, leased the park from the transit company. It was announced in late May that the new Crystal Spray Pier would open. New lighting effects were installed to enhance the night amusements and bathing. The revamped beach was named the Silver Strand Beach, and the updated bathhouse boasted 12,000 new lockers. The "New Bay Shore Park" also claimed to have 50 amusements, and also unveiled the new Beach Hotel offering fine Maryland foods.

One of Bay Shore's noted attractions, the Speedway roller coaster—also referred to as the Racer Dips—debuted in May of 1940. Believed to have been built by Oscar Bitler, this exciting ride replaced the relatively tame coaster that had operated for years[48] and was claimed to be one of the nation's longest and fastest.[49] (Surprisingly, at least one of Bitler's roller coasters still stands today, the Cyclone at the now-shuttered Williams Grove Amusement Park in Mechanicsburg, Pennsylvania.) Additional rides and games were added that summer, as well as a complete animal circus. Other exciting rides in operation at that time included the Ferris wheel, Loop-O-Plane, and the Chair-O-Plane.

A large opening day crowd on May 24, 1941, witnessed an unplanned park event, as fire destroyed Bay Shore's midway. It was believed that a discarded cigarette in the Skooter building may have been the cause. At least nine concession stands burned to the ground, and as the fire reached the shooting gallery many cartridges from the rifles were heard exploding. Park employees and firemen from three local fire departments joined forces to bring the blaze under control. Three employees were overcome by smoke and received treatment at the park's first aid office. Mahoney estimated the uninsured loss at $150,000. Despite the damage, work was begun immediately to clear away the debris, and the park was open for business the following day.[50]

Long-time Baltimore resident Harry Young recalls working at the park's bowling alley as a young man in the mid–1940s: "I made 5 cents a game as a pinsetter; we'd sometimes receive tips also. For some reason, the men that didn't tip us just couldn't roll many strikes at all." The Skee-Ball concession was very popular also, and was located in the same building." In July 1941, weekly boxing programs were started, with participants from the armed services entering the ring for five-round bouts. Soldiers from the army's Aberdeen base constituted the entire card for the opening week, which drew over 3000 spectators.[51] In 1943, Bay Shore would enjoy its best season in 35 years, with the announced season attendance of 850,000. Daredevil "Speedy" Merrill was booked to ride the "Wall of Death" for the season. Thrilling rides to be enjoyed that summer included the Octopus and Tilt-A-Whirl. Mahoney formally purchased Bay Shore Park in 1944. A beautiful spring Sunday in May saw over 7000 guests attend the park's preview weekend. A partial list of attractions for 1944 included the miniature railroad, Whip, Skooter, kiddie rides, roller skating, shooting gallery, and 12 game concessions. Food and snack stands sold peanuts, popcorn, frozen custard, snowballs and candy floss.[52]

Mahoney provided some thoughts in the National Amusement Park, Pool and Beach's (NAAPPB) 1945 Manual and Guide in the "Opinions and Forecasts by Leading Operators" section. This was a forum for park operators to pass along their perspectives and prospects for the upcoming park season"

The outstanding feature at our place is a magnificent white sand beach which affords the only salt water bathing in metropolitan Baltimore. The size of this beach will be enlarged 50 percent and the bathhouse facilities, which now care for 15,000 with individual lockers, will be increased correspondingly. We have been fortunate in securing 50 large rafts which will accommodate parties of 25 each and will be anchored a short distance from the shore and fitted with deck seats and beach umbrellas. This fleet of pleasure floats will be decorated in the gayest holiday colors and among them will glide small launches to vend food and drinks. A larger raft, stationed in the center of this flotilla of peace, will carry a band of Hawaiian artists whose music will be broadcast over the waters of the bay.[53]

New horseshoe courts and the baseball diamond provided fun and a bit of competition for those who preferred to stay on dry land.

One of the largest turn-outs for the 1945 season was American Legion Day held on August 10. A crowd estimated at 10,000 flooded the park and witnessed many activities, including a parachute jump into the bay followed by a PT boat rescue, drum and bugle corps demonstrations, and a beauty contest. Miss Ruth Beasley was crowned Miss American Legion Day by an enthusiastic crowd. The 18-year-old was part of a field of 30 young women competing for the title. Governor O'Connor and William Preston Lane, Jr., were part of a small group that decided to travel from Baltimore to the park via a speeding PT boat. The Army Ground Forces Band met the dignitaries at the end of the pier and led them to the dance hall to take their place on stage for speeches.[54]

The Jolley Trolley, an authentic trolley car retired from service, is seen here in a July 1922 photograph. It was a popular addition to the kids' playground (courtesy Hearst Newspapers LLC/*Baltimore News-American*).

Friends sharing a sled on the thrilling Toboggan Slide (courtesy Hearst Newspapers LLC/*Baltimore News-American***).**

Mahoney's concern for the satisfaction of his customers was always evident. However, a difficult decision to sell Bay Shore Park was made in May of 1946—to O.L. Bonifay's Town Real Estate Corporation. Bonifay in turn sold Bay Shore's 35 acres to a holding company on November 25, 1946, but with a provision to continue operation of the amusement park for the next two years. The price was reported to be $410,000. Over the next few months, rumors were rampant on the anticipated industrialization of the Bay Shore area. Several land deals involving various holding companies fueled speculation that Bethlehem Steel was behind the acquirers of the 35 acres and was looking to expand on its immense Sparrow's Point holdings. Still other rumors had industry rival U.S. Steel looking to build a steel plant across the water from Bethlehem Steel.

Hopes remained high for the 1947 season, however. Just prior to its May opening under new ownership, a *News-American* article detailed what was expected to be Bay Shore's best season ever. A record number of nearly 120 school and church picnics were booked for the summer, as well as a few large corporate outings, including the Glenn L. Martin Co. and the ever-popular Baltimore Transit Company picnic. Several dozen tons of white sand were brought in to help revamp the beach, and a new funhouse, the Zombie, was purchased for young park-goers to navigate. Hoping to capture some of the excitement that Cypress Gardens, Florida, was enjoying with its famous water skiing

Plenty of cars are evident in Bay Shore's parking lot in this aerial view. The figure–8 roller coaster can be seen to the upper left of this photograph (from the Maryland Rail Heritage Library, courtesy of Baltimore Streetcar Museum).

show, a club called the Bay Shore Park Ski Club was put together to perform similar aquatic spectacles. The thrilling Moon Rocket ride spun riders to dizzying speeds.

Meanwhile, George Mahoney was making headlines again in April of 1947, when he announced the purchase of three islands in the Chesapeake Bay, just north of the Bay Shore site, from the Pleasure Island Development Company. Mahoney's initial plans were to develop houses and recreational areas on Pleasure, Hart, and Miller islands. At that time, a bridge was already in place on Miller's Island Road which connected the mainland to Pleasure Island Beach. Pleasure Island had operated as a bathing beach and also a dance venue for several years. Mahoney's long-range plans included the addition of a new clubhouse, a boat club, and a new hotel which would cost $1 million. The boat club would cover 50 acres on Miller's Island, with a limited number of memberships available. Nearly three dozen duck blinds were to be constructed to take advantage of the large duck population that was attracted to the islands' abundance of wild celery, which grew in the flats creating a popular feeding ground near the shore.[55]

With rumors still flying, Bay Shore's inevitable fate was finalized on August 19,

The trolley tracks sliced through the structure of the Speedway roller coaster (from the Maryland Rail Heritage Library, courtesy of Baltimore Streetcar Museum).

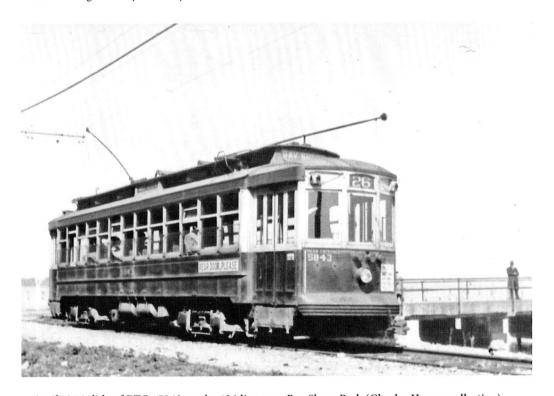

April 1946 slide of BTC #5843 on the #26 line near Bay Shore Park (Charles Houser collection).

The roller coaster was just one of several rides in Kiddieland (courtesy Dundalk-Patapsco Neck Historical Society).

BTC #5193 (nicknamed the Red Rocket) crosses Bear Creek on the way to Sparrows Point. Both bridges have long since been removed.

1947, as Bethlehem Steel was confirmed as the owner of the Bay Shore property. The company then proceeded to announce its plans for the Bay Shore grounds. Bethlehem Steel originally planned to use some of the beachfront to dock freighters that carried ore for use in the plant's tall blast furnaces. Also, the trolley station was to be kept intact, to be used as construction offices. Early November saw work crews begin demol-

Rare advertising card from the New Bay Shore Park from the 1955 season. The park hosted outings and crab feasts for groups of up to 5000 people.

ishing the park, and Baltimoreans were saddened at the prospect of losing a favorite family playground.[56]

However, it didn't take long for another amusement park to attempt to replace Bay Shore Park. George Mahoney must have missed his park, and plans were announced in late 1947 for a new amusement resort, Bay Island Beach to be opened on Mahoney's Pleasure Island. On May 30, 1948, this "New Bay Shore Park" resort opened to the public. Developers Mahoney and Col A.T. Miller had ambitious plans for Pleasure Island, which was only one of the three islands targeted for resort development. Improvements on nearby Hart Island and Miller's Island also figured into their grand vision.

Much work was completed in time for the Memorial Day opening. Several thousand tons of sand were dredged from the bay and added to Pleasure Island's beach, which, in a bit of a stretch, was claimed to be the largest in Maryland. A casino for dining and dancing was a feature attraction, and the large bathhouse could handle thousands of swimmers. A five-acre midway offered nine amusement rides, including a Ferris wheel and a small roller coaster. A giant paved parking lot that could hold up to 6000 cars was built to handle the expected large crowds; one pavilion would handle at least 2500 guests.[57] Thousands of picnic tables and an ample supply of cabanas and umbrellas were on hand for pleasure-seekers. Athletic fields were available for organized sports and games.[58]

Detailed plans for Hart Island were soon unveiled. A causeway was planned to connect it with Pleasure Island. The two islands were actually close enough for swimmers to wade between the two. A large 350-room hotel and many guest cottages were

This airplane view from May 1948 shows the New Bay Shore Park beach that was built up by pumping in sand from the Bay. The bridge connecting the park to the mainland can be seen to the left and middle of this photograph (courtesy Hearst Newspapers LLC/*Baltimore News-American*).

expected to draw vacationers for extended stays. Resort offerings were to include tennis courts, miniature golf, and horseback riding. Mahoney also had plans to relocate the old Bay Shore Park miniature railroad line here. The track layout was to run from Pleasure Island's parking lot to Hart Island's hotel. The last phase of the project to be developed would be Miller's Island. Located about ¼ mile from Hart Island, its 90 acres were to be accessible only by boat or seaplane. The island resort would cater mostly to boaters by offering docks, the originally proposed boat club, supply stores, and a service station.

This was not the first time that a proposal to develop Hart and Miller's Islands was revealed to the public. In August of 1933, New York financier George S. Groves, president of Personal and Industrial Banking of New York, announced plans to purchase Hart and Miller's Islands and convert them into a private estate that would include space for yachting as well as a game preserve. What really grabbed the attention of Baltimoreans was the resurrection of the legend that the former owner of these islands, Joseph Hart, who acquired the land that extended from Bay Shore to Hart Island in 1821, had buried his entire fortune in gold on Miller's Island. Hart had become a wealthy man over the years but did not have much trust in banks, and his family believed that he buried his gold, telling only his wife of its location. She died suddenly several years later and never disclosed the location of the buried treasure. As of 1947, the last documented search for his fortune was reported to have been held in 1913.[59]

Mahoney hired Charley Swan to direct the Recreations and Special Events area of the park for the New Bay Shore Park's inaugural season. Swan was best known as the manager of the local Bombers sandlot baseball club and as the secretary of the All American Amatuer Association.[60] Swan would later move on to manage Baltimore's Kiddyland Park for several seasons, starting in 1950. Attractions unveiled for the New Bay Shore Park's season opening in 1949 included Star Baby, the world's smartest horse. The horse was capable of counting, discerning colors, and see-sawing, among other feats.[61] In May of that year, a new bus line was unveiled to carry patrons to the New Bay Shore Park via city hall, Fayette, and Eastern Avenue. The new Bay Shore Park on Pleasure Island did attract sizable crowds in those early years; attendance for the 1949 season was reported to be around one million.

Mahoney didn't see his multi-island resort plans come to fruition, however, as he decided to get out of the resort business shortly after the 1949 season. The $3 million overall concept never materialized past the Pleasure Island stage. Mahoney sold the New Bay Shore Park to Baltimore realtor William F. Chew just prior to the park's 1950 season. His reason for selling was based mostly on his decision to run for the Democratic nomination for the office of governor of Maryland. But he sold under assurances that the New Bay Shore Park would continue to operate as a seaside family resort. He was greatly concerned that if the New Bay Shore was closed Baltimore residents would not have a bayside summer facility to enjoy. He cited the delays in the state's opening of the new Sandy Point Beach Park on the Chesapeake as a major influence on his decision.

Tragedy struck the New Bay resort in July of 1951, when three boys drowned, a $150,000 lawsuit was filed later in the year against William Chew by the victims' parents. Miscellaneous improvements were made to the park throughout the early to mid–1950s, under general manager Bernard Seaman's guidance. Changes announced for the 1954 season detailed a dredging operation that would extend the park's beach to nearly a mile in length. Additional picnic areas and parking spaces were added as well.[62] Rides for both adults and kids were added, and the entrance bridge to the island was rebuilt.[63] Disaster was narrowly avoided on July 6, 1954, when nine people were struck by lightning. The group was taking shelter from a thunderstorm in a picnic pavilion when the bolt struck close by. All were treated at local hospitals, but sustained no serious injuries. Another severe storm hit the park just over a year later, on August 3. Strong winds leveled four picnic pavilions and generated a panic as visitors scrambled for cover. Twenty people suffered injuries during the height of the storm, which scattered debris over much of the park. Several autos in the parking lot were damaged by objects driven by the violent winds. Witnesses described the storm as "worse than Hurricane Hazel."[64]

Bay Shore hosted several beauty and fitness competitions over the years. In 1959 Edward Lanehart of Pikesville was crowned as Mr. Baltimore, and Judith Simpson was selected as Miss Chesapeake Bay. Judges were asked to "ignore" the swimsuit-clad young women until they reached their perch on the posing platform at that event. Each contestant had to deal with a stiff breeze as she navigated in high heels through the sand and then scaled two milk crates to reach the podium. Organizers feared that the girls' poise would be difficult to judge given the laborious approach to the platform.[65]

On June 15, 1964, it was announced that the New Bay Shore Park was closing for good. In December of that year, Bethlehem Steel undertook the razing of the park; most structures were burned to the ground, with the restaurant being the first to succumb.[66] Today, the island is almost entirely cleared of any traces of the New Bay Shore Park, and the connecting bridge from the mainland has long since been dismantled. The site of the original Bay Shore Park was used as a hunting retreat for some of the Bethlehem Steel executives for a time and was also utilized as a training ground for the Baltimore County firemen.

And what ever happened to George P. Mahoney? He was credited for helping clean up the State [horse] Racing Commission. He would be unsuccessful, though in his attempts at winning the nomination for the Maryland governorship in 1950, as well as in subsequent bids, in 1954 and 1962. He would also throw his hat into the ring for attempts at the U.S. Senate in 1952, 1956, and 1958; but he was met with defeat each time. Mahoney was tapped as the Democratic Party's nominee for governor in 1966. His controversial campaign slogan—"Your home is your castle; protect it"—raised a few eyebrows, and he lost the election to Spiro Agnew. He launched one last campaign for the Senate in 1970 (nearing the age of 70) with plenty of energy and enthusiasm but was again denied. Mahoney was appointed the head of the State Lottery Commission in 1973 and served several successful terms. He would not be reappointed for a final term in January of 1981.[67] He died at the age of 87 in Baltimore on March 18, 1989, after a long life of service to the public.

The land on which the original Bay Shore Park operated was eventually purchased from Bethlehem Steel by the Department of Natural Resources in conjunction with the Nature Conservancy and Baltimore County. This would form the new North Point State Park. A visit to North Point today provides some intriguing evidence of the original Bay Shore Park's nearly forgotten history. Remnants of the concrete pier still extend far into the bay. A hike to the end of the pier offers a stunning panoramic view of the bay. The trolley station is in use today as a picnic pavilion. Its $150,000 renovation began in 1993, a key component of the development of the North Point State Park, which resides next to the Black Marsh Wildlife Refuge. The overall $6 million development project also included the construction of a modern multipurpose building which serves as the park office. The 1000-foot-long pier was shored up to allow safer access for fishermen.[68] Several of Bay Shore's old paths are still evident, particularly the one leading from the trolley station to the ornate fountain, which has been restored under the guidance of park ranger Steve Takos. Baltimoreans should be proud that the remaining heritage of the sorely missed Bay Shore Park is being preserved.

3

Betterton Beach

Betterton Beach is situated on the Eastern Shore of the Chesapeake Bay in Kent County, near the mouth of the Sassafras River. The town of Betterton's origins can be traced back to the year 1698, with a land grant awarded from Lord Baltimore to Edward Crew. Crew's Landing, as the town was initially known, soon saw the first home erected, Fish Hall. Portions of the house were reportedly built with the wainscoting from the first settlers' ships that originally landed at the site. The Tochwogh Indians were believed to have inhabited the area prior to the arrival of the settler. "Large amounts of oyster shells can be seen at nearby Kitchen Middens, where the Indians reportedly held their councils. Various relics including arrows and even an Indian skull have been unearthed."[1] In addition, "local tradition has it that a band of 17th century pirates buried their dead on a bluff here. Centuries later, as Betterton grew from a remote fishing village to a rural resort town, children digging in a ravine called Dead Man's Gulch on occasion uncovered bleached bone fragments, somewhat adding to the site's legend."[2]

The Betterton area was also known as Fishing Valley in the early years and its history is somewhat sketchy until the 1840–1850s period, when the Turner family settled there. Richard Turner, a hardware man and a partner of Enoch Pratt,[3] erected a steamboat wharf on his plantation to attract business. When he married Elizabeth Betterton in 1843, he decided to change the village's name to Betterton, in honor of his new bride. In March of 1850, the state legislature approved a House bill to construct a wharf at nearby Turner's Creek. By 1855, Turner had a new wharf erected at Betterton, which was now on the regular Sassafras route plied by the steamer *Cecil,* under the watch of Captain F.A. Sturgeon. The Sassafras route carried passengers and freight from the Light Street wharf to Wilmer's Point, with several additional stops on the Sassafras River including Fredericktown and Georgetown. Picnic excursions to Betterton Landing were underway by 1857, with the steamer *Wilson Small* transporting church groups from the Light Street wharf. In 1887, the amusement pier was erected by Richard Turner, Jr., and his son Howard Jr.

Things would begin to heat up between competing steamer lines in June of 1899, when the Sassafras River Steamboat Company and the Baltimore Port Deposit Steamboat Company merged with the Tolchester Steamboat Company. That same year, the Turners sold the pier to the Tolchester Beach Improvement Company. The Tolchester Line planned to add Betterton as another desirable beach resort for their steamers to transport guests to and began operating excursions that summer to Betterton at 50 cents per round-trip. In August of 1899, the Ericsson Line announced its plans to begin running freight steamers into the Sassafras River, which prompted reports of an impending war between the Ericsson Line and the Tolchester Steamboat Company, which already operated steamers on that river. The Ericsson Line quickly completed a new wharf at Betterton, and undercut the Tolchester Line by selling round-trip excursions to the beach for just a quarter. Speculation in the local steamboat industry pointed to the Tolchester Line's intention of capturing a large portion of the Betterton trade business as the factoring reason behind the Ericsson's encroachment into the Sassafras River area.[4]

The number of excursionists greatly increased with two piers handling incoming steamers. Several hotels were erected in the early 1900s to increase the length of stay for beachgoers. The Rigbie Hotel, perhaps the largest of the Betterton accommodations, was opened in 1900 by the Turners. It could house up to 200 guests and boasted unparalleled views of the bay, there was also hot and cold running water. The 14-room Lantern Inn was built in 1904 and is still in operation today. The large Chesapeake House hotel was a popular place to stay around this time as well. Other accommodations like the Royal Swan, Chesapeake, Emerson, Betterton, and Bayside Inn offered first-class amenities to guests. Room and board for a full week's stay was only about twelve dollars at that time. Popular dwellings like the Owens Cottage and the Maryland Cottage could house families for a week's stay at the beach. Daytime activities included swimming and boating, and Betterton was well known as a sportsmen's paradise. The prospect of excellent duck hunting and fishing attracted many enthusiasts over the years. The most popular nighttime activity was the dances held at the beach in Turner's Dancing Pavilion. Dances at the spacious hall at the Chesapeake House were very popular at this time as well.

The Betterton Bayside Land Company was formed in March of 1907. This group included Howard Turner, Capt. W.C. Eliason of the Tolchester Steamboat Company, and E.W. Giles. The group purchased the 250-acre Canby farm, which was located just north of the Hotel Rigbie.[5] Just over 140 acres of farmland were set aside for private lots and streets, paving the way for additional places to stay at Betterton. The new steamer *Susquehanna* was providing excursions to Betterton for just fifty cents at that time. Howard Turner, Jr.'s home was built in 1910 on a spread of 20 acres, and he resided there until his death in 1936.

For decades, the preferred mode of transportation to Betterton was the steamer *Bay Belle*. It was completed in the Wilmington, Delaware, shipyards in 1910 and could carry up to 2500 passengers. Reconditioned some 30 years later, it continued to ferry guests on the bay for several more decades. Long-time Baltimore residents can still recall dancing on the *Bay Belle,* returning home after a hot summer day at Betterton. Two main piers were in competition to handle the incoming steamship traffic during the resort's hey-day. One pier was the berth for the Tolchester Line and the other for the Ericsson Line. The Ericsson Line was named after John Ericsson, the inventor of the screw propeller, which allowed for steamships to safely pass through the Chesapeake and Delaware Canal, too narrow for typical paddlewheel steamers of that period.[6]

Improvements to Betterton Beach for the 1913 season included a large dance floor on the pier, and a new boating and bathing pier. Resort owners worked with a new concern, the Delmarva Advancement Company, to outline future attractions and improvements for the popular bay resort. Large crowds encountered during the 1913 season at Betterton caught resort management off guard. An overflow crowd on the 4th of July prevented the steamboat company from being able to transport nearly 500 guests back home from the resort. This prompted the company to plan ahead for large crowds over Labor Day weekend. The successful summer season was extended past Labor Day, after which hotels and cottages normally closed, keeping the resort open until September 15.[7]

A strong storm in early August of 1915 flooded the beach and lower floor of the Chesapeake House. The boardwalk, bowling alley, and bathhouses were also damaged by the rising water. A large load of Howard Turner's lumber was washed off the shore and floated down the Sassafras River.[8] Some $10,000 in improvements were made to the beach resort in 1916, including work on sidewalks, streets, and storm drainage. The town would have a new sewer system in place the following year.[9]

Betterton's simple amusements helped to draw in the crowds. Turner and Son's two-level pier—the Betterton Casino and Pleasure Pier (which at one time was referred to as Sea-Scape Pier)—was in operation during the 1920s and offered a casino. It also contained a dance pavilion over the bowling alley, and popular motion pictures were presented in the pavilion. An ice cream parlor and a billiards room were popular draws in a separate building on the pier. Advertisements from this period welcomed Moxie Cunningham's All-Star Orchestra, which presided over dances twice a day on occasion. Fondly recalled are Betterton's "Eastern Shore Dinners," Maryland fried chicken, crab cakes, steaks, and chops being served up in the dining rooms. In the early 1920s, Baltimoreans could take a Sunday cruise to Betterton aboard the *Susquehanna* or the *Lord Baltimore* for the round-trip fare of $1.

Auto traffic to Betterton would pick up in the 1920s as Kent County passed a resolution in January 1922 to overhaul the county road construction system. Looking to abolish the practice of scraping the substandard clay roads once a year, the goal was set to instead construct permanent gravel roads throughout the county which would be passable every day of the year.[10] With the influx of tourists, Betterton experienced a surge in the building of cottages and boardinghouses as surrounding farmland was purchased and utilized for the expanding beach resort. The park hosted an annual trap-shooting tournament that attracted the state's most skilled marksmen. The Oriole Gun Club helped organize the event in July of 1924. Hundreds of shooters competed, aiming for the clay pigeon targets at a distance of 16 yards.[11]

The late 1920s brought many improvements and an increase in group patronage. Surrounding farmland was purchased and boarding homes and summer cottages erected. Prior to the 1927 season, several of the hotels were renovated, including the Rigbie, Betterton, and Chesapeake. The dance hall was redecorated with a Spanish garden theme. Several additional concessions were added to the Turner Pier's main deck, and the theater was upgraded with modern equipment to present vaudeville and movie films. With the continued improvement of the highway system on the Eastern Shore, an increase in auto traffic was noted. Steamer traffic did not seem to suffer, though. Over three dozen organizations booked excursions from Baltimore and Philadelphia through the Ericsson Line. The steamer *John Cadwalader,* manned by Captain Albert

Willis, ferried many groups to Betterton that summer.[12] A forecast for a successful summer was also given prior to the 1928 season, when several swim meets and regattas were planned. The Royal Swan Club built a golf course for use by hotel guests. In addition, a dozen tennis courts were constructed, and horseshoe pits and baseball diamonds were erected. Several amusements for children were added, and additional bathhouses placed on the beach.[13]

The end of the prohibition era in the early 1930s signaled some changes in Betterton's character. Drinking at the beer halls replaced the long-standing nightly dances. At Betterton's peak in the 1930s and 1940s, up to 2500 people a day arrived at the beach via steamer, especially with the Ericsson Line and pier in operation.[14] Additional waterfront property was acquired in 1938, allowing Betterton's beach area to be expanded by approximately four times its previous size, stretching from the casino to the old Ericsson pier. An elevated boardwalk about 16 feet wide was constructed at this time,[15] as well as new concessions and a bowling alley above the boardwalk. Picnic grounds open to the public were placed on top of the hill overlooking the beach. A new dock and pier were erected for the summer of 1940.[16] The amusement pier was renovated for the 1941 season, with new diversions added.

The Wilson Line's all-new steel SS *Bay Belle* took its first cruise in May of 1941, leaving Pier 8 for a sail down to Cambridge. Joe Dowling's orchestra provided the dance music, and free movies were offered as well. A modern sewage system was constructed prior to the 1950 season opening. Around this time, a new bridge erected in Chesapeake

Well-dressed crowds are lining up for an evening at the moving picture parlor on Turner's Pier in this 1913 postcard view (courtesy Cindy Blevins).

An early family souvenir photograph from Betterton Beach.

View of the pier and beach at Betterton.

An early view of the boardwalk and pier at Betterton. Space on Betterton's beach was at a premium with the addition of the boardwalk and other structures.

City, which spanned the Chesapeake and Delaware Canal, allowed for increased auto traffic to the park. Many of Betterton's hotels and cottages listed hot and cold running water in their rooms when advertising a stay in the mid–1950s. A room at the comfortable Royal Swan hotel was only $5 a day at that time.

The large Amusea building on the water at Betterton.

c. 1920s view of two young ladies out for a stroll on the deserted Betterton pier.

In February of 1956, it was announced that the city of Baltimore would soon have just one excursion boat plying the Chesapeake. The Tolchester and Wilson lines merged, forming the Excursion Boat Line, which would operate just the *Bay Belle* to Betterton and Tolchester. The SS *Tolchester* would be kept in reserve as a backup. The *Bay Belle*

EVERGREEN KNOLL – BETTERTON, MARYLAND

A view of the beach playground from the Evergreen Knoll cottages at Betterton Beach.

would also continue to sail on its popular nighttime excursions. Since the mid–1940s, the *Bay Belle* had offered three-hour moonlight cruises. Departing every night at 8:30 from Pier 8 on Light Street, the ship would sail down the bay, turning around at approximately 10:00 in the vicinity of the Seven-Foot Knoll lighthouse. Students, GIs, and couples would dance on the ballroom deck, and many liked to do the jitterbug.[17] Victor Cook, the Excursion Boat Line's district manager, announced that the new sailing arrangement would provide an improved service to the public, as a single boat would make daily stops at both Betterton and Tolchester. Old customers from each line would be granted their date preferences as nearly as possible.[18]

Beatty's Amusement Pier and Earl Becker's Beach Club were popular beach spots in the postwar years. In the late 1950s, the Wilson Line (having acquired the Tolchester Line) heavily advertised its three-hour cruises to Betterton aboard the *Bay Belle*, which departed Baltimore Harbor daily during the summer season.

Several rides that operated at Tolchester Beach were relocated to Betterton, after Tolchester's demise in 1962. However, there was a downside to Betterton's upgrades, as the addition of amusements and concession stands reduced the size of the bathing beach considerably. With the arrival of the Bay Bridge, and the public's willingness to drive their automobiles to Ocean City's plentiful beaches, the resort began a slow decline. In the summer of 1964, two men from Chestertown—Thomas Hyland, and Steve Hickman—purchased some of the old Betterton buildings and started making renovations in an attempt to revitalize the aging resort. They constructed a cocktail lounge and a restaurant on the pier, and installed additional boat slips.[19]

During the summer of 1966, the *Port Welcome* sailed from Baltimore to Betterton

Nice view of the Hotel Chesapeake and a portion of the boardwalk at Betterton Beach from a 1940 postcard.

twice a week, allowing excursionists to enjoy the beach for three hours. The round-trip fare for the cruise was just $3.25 for adults and $1.85 for children. Betterton would continue to offer affordable family stays at the beach. In the late 1960s, accommodations could still be had for $3 to $10 a day.[20] An advertising mailer from the Hotel Rigbie for the 1973 season shows that room rates were still well within a typical family's budget. Daily rates were below $20 a day, and a week's stay could be arranged in the $80–$100 range. The *Port Welcome* continued to sail from Baltimore to Betterton on Tuesdays and Saturdays that summer. Attractions at the beach at that time included teen dances, bingo, an arcade, and a few amusement attractions including bumper cars, a crazy house (funhouse), and the Whip.

The 1970s would not be kind to Betterton, though. It was one of many of Maryland's bay beaches that experienced a steady drop in attendance. It became difficult for the small bay resorts to compete with Ocean City for the summer tourist dollars. One by one, the old hotels continued to deteriorate, and were shut down. Fire destroyed the old Betterton Hotel in January of 1972, owned by George Chladek at the time.[21] The Chesapeake Hotel, which had stood for over

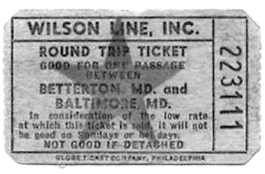

A Wilson Line ticket for the steamer trip from Baltimore to Betterton.

SKATING RINK AT BETTERTON, MD.

Kids enjoying a long-time favorite at Betterton Beach—the roller-skating rink.

100 years, closed in 1973 and was leveled in 1980. Still, the *Port Welcome* cruised to Betterton twice weekly during the summer season over the decade. The round-trip fare of $4.75 for adults and $2.85 for kids was in place for the 1973 season.[22]

The resort experienced a brief resurgence in interest and attendance in 1978. The *Port Welcome* ship sailed to Betterton on Tuesdays and Saturdays. However, other than the beach, only a bingo hall on the deteriorating pier awaited passengers. A solitary public restroom offered the only means for guests to change into their swimsuits. By this point, Betterton was no longer a commercial beach resort, but rather a small beach community.[23] Later that summer, it was soon realized that this would be the last season that the *Port Welcome* would stop here. The Hotel Rigbie was soon torn down, having sat vacant since 1975. The pier and Becker's Beach Club were removed by 1980.

Betterton Beach has managed to survive to this day, but on a somewhat lesser scale. Kent County purchased the property in the early 1980s and erected a bathhouse, fishing jetty pier, and a picnic area.[24] Betterton still draws hot visitors to its Chesapeake Bay beach today. While just five acres in size, it offers a sandy beach, concession stand, and volleyball courts. An expansion in April 2001 saw the addition of a 500-foot boardwalk. Betterton is recognized as the largest public beach on Chesapeake's Eastern Shore today.

4

Carlin's Amusement Park

"Baltimore's Million-Dollar Playground Opens Tonight" blared the *Baltimore Sun* headline on August 13, 1919. In a well-publicized statement from John J. Carlin, local real estate man and builder, Liberty Heights Park's opening was announced to the public. "Our intention and desire is to make Liberty Heights Park the sort of place you have always wished for, a park of which you and every other Baltimorean could rightly be proud, a park which would abundantly justify your patronage because it deserves it."[1] In this statement from the management, Carlin reflects on the need for a top-flight amusement resort to serve a growing Baltimore population. Plans for the $500,000 project were originally unveiled in April of 1919 when Carlin announced tentative plans for a new park, contingent upon the outcome of proposed housing plans for the 45-acre tract. He had recently purchased this land, part of the old Ashburton estate, from John S. Gittings, for approximately $91,000. He had also purchased the adjoining 10-acre Iverson estate. Carlin declared he had 500 men ready to begin work on the big amusement park.[2]

John Carlin was born at Boyd Station, near Frederick, Maryland, on October 20, 1880. One of six children of John Thomas and Frances (Himmel) Carlin, he helped out on his family's farm, and also worked at a local country store as a young man. When he made the decision to join the army, he had to consume enormous quantities of milk, butter, and other fattening foods to meet the military's stringent physical requirements. He was accepted but had to endure a 49-day sea voyage with unrelenting seasickness aboard a troop transport to the Philippines, during which his weight dropped to 110 pounds. He would serve in the Philippines and Japan, transferring back to the States after the Boxer Rebellion, receiving his discharge in 1902. He attended Maryland Agricultural College (now the University of Maryland), and later earned a bachelor of law degree at the Baltimore Law School (now the University of Baltimore).[3]

Oddly enough, the Great Baltimore Fire of 1904 provided Carlin with his first job opportunities. He realized the potential for construction in the devastation following the fire, and he formed his own construction company. The company would help rebuild office buildings in downtown Baltimore before proceeding to construct new private homes. Carlin was credited with building the first moderately priced row houses that were equipped with electricity in Baltimore. With the 45-acre park site sitting vacant for quite some time, he realized that the underutilized property was costing him money, so he decided to erect a dance hall. His business plan included a practical alternative for the use of the property and lumber; if the dance hall did not pan out, he would simply pull it down and use the lumber to construct twenty houses.[4]

Attendance at the new dance hall exceeded expectations, and Carlin soon erected a hall three times larger than the original, which opened in June of 1917. Touted as the largest dance pavilion in the state, it measured 186 feet by 64 feet, and was capable of accommodating nearly 800 couples. Thomas L. Keating was hired to manage the dancing, and plans for both an orchestra and jazz band to perform were made.[5] When Carlin caught wind of Gwynn Oak's Professor Farson's plans to erect a competing hall on Harford Road, he decided to develop a first-class amusement park on his own property.[6] Located just north of Druid Park Drive, between Park Circle and Liberty Heights Avenue, Carlin's Park is sorely missed today. The #5 streetcar line brought Baltimoreans to the park. They entered under the famous Japanese pagoda towers, several of the park's structures featuring a Japanese-influenced design.

Carlin had initially planned to hold a spectacular grand opening, but construction at the park was not fully complete by opening night. So, he decided to go ahead and offer sneak peaks of the park through the end of the inaugural season. Operating attractions to be enjoyed included the Dip-the-Dips roller coaster, the carrousel, the Old Mill and Chutes ride, and the Kentucky Derby. Carlin's opening day statement also included his immediate plans for the park:

> We are busy now erecting an immense and imposing Coliseum, to which we propose bringing such world-renowned directors as Sousa, Pryor, Creatore, Victor Herbert and their celebrated bands. There will be a massive Natatorium, a concrete swimming pool one thousand feet long, fashioned after the baths of ancient Rome, and encircled with a wide beach of velvety sand in which bathers can frolic to their heart's delight! There will be a series of extravagantly beautiful Sunken Gardens, where outdoor dancing will be staged. Fantastic Pagodas and Japanese Tea Rooms will impart a quaint touch of the Orient. The popular "Ginger Snap" will also be here. A tremendous Casino, dazzling Electrical Bridge, and pretentious Moving-Picture Theatre will also offer diversion and recreation. The vast shady groves, with plenty of benches and tables, make an ideal picnic ground for the family outing. We have various other elaborate features in mind, which will be announced in the order of their completion.[7]

The 1919 season at Liberty Heights Park, soon to be known as Carlin's Park, were a busy time, as continuous park improvements were underway. A spring visit to the park by the Philadelphia Toboggan Company's (PTC) Henry B. Auchy at Carlin's invitation initiated the park's whirlwind development. A contract was drawn up to purchase three large PTC rides for the first season.[8] PTC was a major supplier of amusement park attractions at that time. The park ordered an elaborate carousel from PTC and PTC model #47 amused the crowds until it was moved to another park in Auburn, New York, in 1930. This impressive ride was later relocated to Hershey Park in 1944, where it still spins today near the park's entrance. This ornate ride featured 42 jumpers and 24 stationary figures, along with a German band organ.[9] PTC also erected the Dips Coaster and the Mill Chute rides. The Dips offered a thrilling ride for its time, and included a dark, winding tunnel encountered prior to the lift hill. The Mill Chute combined the classic tunnel of love boat experience with a long drop ending with a wet splashdown. Carlin's intent was to install high-quality, state of the art rides on a scale that rivaled the country's best amusement parks. In March of 1920, construction was started on perhaps the most-remembered park attraction—the intimidating Mountain Speedway roller coaster. Designed by master coaster designer and builder John Miller, with construction directed by A. Carl Hulsey, it boasted a height of 82 feet, as well as the claim "World's Greatest Tunnel Route." Hulsey relates some specifics, during a *Sun Magazine* interview in 1978:

> Building costs were low, even for those days of low prices. The end of the war had caught the Army with a lot of surplus lumber piled up at Canton (a neighborhood in Baltimore's "outer" harbor), and we were able to buy it at a ridiculous price. Our lumber was hauled from Canton, however, by long wagons, each drawn by several teams of horses. We hired up to 35 carpenters at a time, We used no cranes or other such machinery in use today. We painted the upright beams, cross-timbers, and bracing studs on the ground, to save ourselves what would have been an expense. We put together huge sections of the framework flat on the ground ... and we'd pull it into an upright position with long ropes, nudge the uprights into their foundation holes, and hold the framework section into place while the men scampered up the structure to bolt in the cross timbers and nail on the reinforcing bracing.[10]

Just 20 cents got you a trip on the 4,500 foot-long track, which opened in June for those who were brave enough to ride. (Hulsey later became park superintendent and held that position until 1945, when he accepted a similar post at Gwynn Oak Park). Park managers from across the country traveled to Baltimore that year to take a look at the popular thriller. The Speedway operated until the park's closing in the 1950s and never lost its popularity.

Another of the more popular attractions to appear during the 1920 season was the Coliseum Funhouse. This ultimate indoor playground featured the human roulette wheel, a spinning bowl that flung its riders from the center to the sides of the bowl as the speed increased. The rotating barrel, a two-story slide, and the hall of mirrors each

A pre–1920s postcard view of Carlin's elaborate Liberty Heights Park Dance Pavilion.

A view of Carlin's original carousel. Manufactured by the Philadelphia Toboggan Company (PTC#47), it debuted at the park in 1919. It still spins riders today near the entrance to Hersheypark in Hershey, PA (from Philadelphia Toboggan Coasters, Inc./Tom Rebbie, president/CEO).

The entrance to the Dips roller coaster. This was the Philadelphia Toboggan Company's 29th coaster. Erected in 1919, it was designed by coaster mastermind John Miller (from Philadelphia Toboggan Coasters, Inc./Tom Rebbie, president/CEO).

Opposite: Looking back down the lift hill of the Dips. A coaster train emerges from the approach tunnel for a test run (from Philadelphia Toboggan Coasters, Inc./Tom Rebbie, president/CEO).

Much construction is underway on the Liberty Heights Park midway in this June 1919 scene. PTC provided the coaster, carousel, and Old Mill attractions for the park's first season (from Philadelphia Toboggan Coasters, Inc./Tom Rebbie, president/CEO).

provided plenty of laughs. The ad for the opening weekend described the coliseum as "a smile every step, a laugh every turn. A sure cure for the blues. Roulette Wheel, Social Mixer, Squeezer, Barrel of Fun, Ocean Wave, and many other laugh-producing attractions. A Pony ride for the children. A Thoroughbred ride for the grown-ups. 'Denver Joe's' original Texas Pony Track."[11]

June 1920 ads described Carlin's as "Baltimore's Refined Park—the Willow Grove Park of Maryland." Willow Grove was a spectacularly large amusement park serving the masses in Philadelphia. The Noah's Ark funhouse was another popular attraction that appeared during this time. One of several similar attractions to appear at amusement parks during this period, Noah's Ark was developed by LeRoy Raymond of Venice, California. He sold the Noah's Ark rights soon afterward to carousel builder William H. Dentzel, who erected the Carlin's ride. The wooden ark certainly looked like the real thing, and it rocked back and forth to provide park patrons an unstable "voyage." It contained airjets, moving floors, dark passageways, and other surprises. Today, only one Noah's Ark funhouse still remains operational in the U.S., at Pittsburgh's Kennywood Park. Other rides in Carlin Park's early years included the Bicycle Race (a circular chain of bicycles that operated in the funhouse building), Whirlpool, Teacups, Haunted Castle walk-through, Just for Fun, and the Caterpillar.

In late June of the 1920 season, Carlin purchased a full-page ad in the *Baltimore Sun* touting the upcoming mammoth fireworks spectacular to celebrate Independence Day. Promising to present daytime and nighttime displays "never before attempted by any other park in Baltimore," Carlin boasted that it would the most expensive and elab-

Owner John J. Carlin hands out "gold watches" to Mary Brown and Leon Friedlander, winners of Carlin's "Freckles Contest" in this c. 1920 photograph (courtesy Jim Abbate collection).

This rare photograph shows kids lining up at the entrance to Carlin's on Kiddie's Day 1919 (from Mangels Museum/Jim Abbate collection).

orate pyrotechnic display Baltimore had ever seen. Daylight displays would include fireworks with animal shapes for the children as well as various flags of America and Uncle Sam. The extraordinary nighttime display included the Statue of Liberty, the Whirling Wheel of Fire, and a reproduction of the Bombardment of Verdun."[12]

Carlin's flourished in the Roaring Twenties with its stunning array of events and attractions. Boxing and wrestling matches were presented in the Green House. Baltimore's hockey team at that time, the Orioles, played in the park's Ice Palace. Like many other amusement parks, Carlin's offered titillating daredevil shows, including the human cannonball and a flagpole sitter, the famous "Shipwreck" Kelly being one of them. Kelly sat on a flagpole at Carlin's for an entire month, and the park paid quite a sum for advertising to promote the day that Kelly would descend. The resulting crowd, estimated at 40,000, was believed to have been the largest in park history to that date.[13] Open-air operas were presented at Carlin's, with DeWolfe Hopper directing many of the productions. The open air arena debuted in June of 1921, with a vaudeville and circus program being presented.

September 1921 saw the opening of the Fall Automobile Show at Carlin's Park. The notion of an auto show was originally introduced by Carlin at a meeting of the Automobile Dealer's Association. The show was organized to discuss additional methods with which to inform the general public of the new automobile models that were rolling off assembly lines on a daily basis. Twenty-two dealers set up booths to display the latest models, including new vehicles debuting for 1922. Dozens of other merchants offering auto accessories were on-site as well. Opening the show was a special guest of honor, Eddie Rickenbacker, president of the Rickenbacker Motor Company of Detroit. Local sports celebrities were also recruited to appear and present facts and details on models like the Aero-Eight, the Auburn-Six, and the Durant car.[14]

Just one month later, Carlin found himself on a train with the De Feo Grand Opera Company bound from New York to Houston, Texas. Not a man given to taking things easy, Carlin wanted to see firsthand the reaction of Houston crowds to the opera stars and production steps. With the 1922 season fast approaching, his intentions were to provide Carlin's patrons with at least three weeks of summer opera. Performers from the current season would almost certainly be booked again for the new season, but Carlin was also looking for new talent and operas to present.[15] Carlin's Park would host the crew of the new battleship *Maryland* for a day in October of 1921. The new dreadnought was anchored off Sandy Point on the Chesapeake, and was met by a monitor

In operation from 1920 to 1956, the Mountain Speedway was probably the most exciting roller coaster to operate in Baltimore over the years (courtesy Hearst Newspapers LLC/*Baltimore News-American*).

ship, the *Wyoming*, which carried Mayor Broening and a host of city and state officials out to greet the crew.[16]

A new $5,000 dance floor was one of the improvements for the 1922 season. Also, some $20,000 was spent to erect roofing over the open air arena in an effort to provide shelter for the upcoming second summer opera season.[17] Additional park acts that were

The Mountain Speedway very well may have had the "World's Greatest Tunnel Route"; at a pitch-dark 800 feet long, it was the ideal start to a thrilling coaster ride (courtesy Hearst Newspapers LLC/*Baltimore News-American*).

announced included Klatawa the diving horse. Accompanied by the brave "Girl in Red," Klatawa leapt into a pool of water from a 40-foot tower. Jack King's Wild West Circus appeared in Carlin's new stadium that summer as well, and Robinson's Military Elephants performed twice daily. A May evening in 1923 was the scene of more than 5000 women screaming in anticipation of the arrival of the legendary Rudolph Valentino. Valentino's appearance as a beauty contest judge caused a huge commotion, requiring a large security force to be on hand. Some women cried, others fainted, while a few chose to throw notes as Valentino danced with his lady partner.[18] Quite the innovator in the park's early years, Carlin realized the potential for inflated gate receipts with the appearance of a popular movie star.

The highly anticipated opera season returned to Carlin's two months later. A *Sun* writer commented at that time,[19] "It is sincerely to be hoped that the summer light opera season at Carlin's will be successful again this year. It is not only a unique distinction which Baltimore enjoys, but is also rather a paradox to possess a general amusement park which can provide summer entertainment for every type and frame of the public mind and to find the subtle wit and satires of Gilbert projected to the strains of Sullivan's melodies within a stone's throw of the more obvious 'low comedy' methods offered to delight the patrons of the Coliseum."

June 1924 marked the opening of Carlin's Fight Arena, which hosted boxing and wrestling matches. Promoter Les Sponsler oversaw the development of the fight arena and arranged the opening night card, headlined by a bout pitting a promising young fighter named Joe Dundee against a veteran boxer from Chicago, Sailor Friedman.[20] Carlin's knowledge of the amusement industry was quite extensive, as he was also the owner of the Buckeye Lake Amusement Park in Ohio and was a part owner of the State Fair Park amusement grounds in Wheeling, West Virginia.

A children's play park, which included slides, games, and sand boxes, was added for the 1925 season. Also, new devices were added inside the expanding coliseum building.[21] Over 25,000 boys were in attendance on Carnival Day, the last day of the Boys' Week program held in May that year. George Morris, a student at Calvert Hall High School, was crowned the "King of Boys' Week" and dubbed King Toots I by local officials. He was presented with a key to the park, and all were treated to a fireworks display at the end of the evening.[22]

An annual late season promotion that never failed to attract crowds was Carlin's Mardi Gras event. Starting on Labor Day, the lengthy celebration featured special events spread out over several weeks until the park's seasonal closing. A grand masque ball, a nightly mummers parade and special contests offering prizes were part of the fanfare. During the 1925 Mardi Gras festival, Baltimoreans who showed up in mask or costume received a free book of park tickets, with additional prizes being awarded to the best costume. One feature of the carnival was the "Mysterious Locked Box." Each guest that braved a ride on the Mountain Speedway received a key. The guest would then make their way to the Mystery Box, and, if they could unlock the box with their key, would win the valuable prize inside the box. A special Movie Queen contest was also held that year. The Famous Players-Lasky Movie company, in conjunction with Carlin's, awarded the talented finalist a film test at their Long Island, New York, studio. Scores of local girls were prompted to storm the registration booths in advance of this contest, billed as one of the greatest features staged to date in the city.[23]

Many Baltimore natives reminisce about the big band shows held at the Green Palace ballroom. Many of the nation's most popular acts performed here, including Tex Beneke, Gene Krupa, Rudy Vallee, and Duke Ellington. The dance hall was the park's biggest revenue producer in the early years, turning in grosses nearing the six-figure mark. A number of changes were made to the dance hall prior to the 1926 opening. A steam-heating plant was added to keep patrons warm in chilly weather, and the building was overhauled, with additional soft lighting installed.[24] Overlooking the dance hall was the "class" of the park, Mario's Restaurant, which offered fine Italian dining.[25] Other improvements for the 1926 season included a renovation of the huge Arena Theater. All seats were removed, and a 17,000 square foot floor was installed to transform into a roller skating venue. A new miniature railroad was also installed, by the picnic manager of the park, James Trimble.[26]

Fires at Carlin's were a constant threat to the park's wooden structures. A repair shop near the Whirlpool ride caught fire in July of 1926; machine oil that had ignited was the culprit. Luckily the blaze did not spread to the adjacent structures. A late night fire in September of 1927 destroyed three concessions across from the coliseum building. The Orange Shell, a photograph gallery, and a hot dog stand were lost when the large concessions building caught fire shortly after the park had closed for the evening. Park business manager Sam McCallister did not offer an estimate on the damages, but noted the loss was covered by insurance.[27] A costly fire in February of 1928 destroyed the dance hall, attracting thousands of nighttime gawkers. The blaze appeared to start in a storeroom in a corner of the large dance pavilion, just after hundreds of spectators had witnessed a basketball game. The light from the tremendous fire could be seen in many parts of Baltimore, drawing thousands of people whose cars interfered with the firefighters' efforts to control the blaze. Fortunately, there was only one injury. A woman who had run back inside the hall to save some concession equipment was overcome by the smoke and had to be rescued by a policeman. The collapse of the pavilion's two large towers prompted residents on nearby streets to begin packing some of their valuable possessions, in the event they would be forced to flee. Carlin estimated the loss at approximately $100,000.[28]

Many upgrades were evident at the beginning of the park's 1929 season. A fresh coat of paint had been applied to many of the structures. One unusual new attraction was billed as the "The Big Show," somewhat of a replica of a traveling circus, but instead with animated animals that were very realistic-looking, accompanied by animated trainers. One newspaper article noted that a "blood-sweating behemoth" was part of the new menagerie.[29] A kids' playland and a funhouse were ready for action as well. One of the most popular amusement rides of its time, the Circle Swing, was re-themed and made its debut as the Lindy Planes, in honor of the famed aviator Charles Lindbergh; gondolas holding several people slung from cables soared through the air around a central mast. Additional new attractions included the looping Tailspin ride, the Whoopee Palace funhouse, and the Bug (or Tumble Bug) from the Traver Engineering Company of Beaver Falls, Pennsylvania.[30] The Traver Company was run by amusement device inventor Harry Traver, the man responsible for some of the most frightening roller coasters ever built.[31] Other improvements for the 1929 season included an expanded parking area and a new entrance gate. Also, Fred Robbins was on hand to conduct the Modernistic Melodies Orchestra in the renovated Green Palace ballroom.[32]

On opening day in April of 1930, a small fire broke out in the circus menagerie. The menagerie's "keeper," Harry Goldman, reported that it appeared a short circuit in Rollo the elephant was the culprit. The fire was quickly contained and did not harm any of the actual menagerie animals, which Goldman controlled via levers. The Giant Bug ride reportedly made its debut that summer.[33] During this season, Carlin took advantage of the dance marathon craze that was sweeping the country, staging a well-promoted marathon that ultimately lasted four months. One of the couples actually got married on the dance floor. A later dance was carried out (literally) on large flatbed trucks, in a procession leaving from the park and traveling to the local airfield. Joe Kayser and his Chicagoans provided the music for the flight.[34]

Carlin's unique use of the park's new ballroom was detailed by long-time park employee Harry A. Ackley in the August 1932 issue of the trade journal *Amusement Park Management*. In an attempt to generate additional revenues during the winter season, Carlin decided to convert the ballroom to an ice skating rink. The ballroom offered a 120-foot × 150-foot main floor space with an ice surface approximately 85 feet × 120 feet. Bleacher capacity for spectators was estimated at approximately 1200 people. Carlin's Iceland, as it came to be known, proved to be a huge success, as ice skating and hockey games drew large crowds. Carlin was proud of this new venture and presented the detailed methods used in installing the ice-making machinery to the assembly at the 14th Annual Convention of the National Association of Amusement Parks.

Carlin and Sam McCallister requested help in forming a six- or eight-club amateur hockey league, with potential college teams forming at Johns Hopkins, Western Maryland, Walbrook, the University of Maryland, and the naval academy. The first Iceland season ran from around Thanksgiving of 1931 through April 1, 1932. The hockey matches drew large enthusiastic crowds during the inaugural season. An expanded Iceland would host the Baltimore Orioles, of the four-team Tri-State Hockey League, during the winter of 1932–33. Other league clubs included Hershey, Philadelphia, and Atlantic City. The local hockey league would play their matches at the new Sports Centre rink, which would open that winter with manager C. Starr Matthews in charge.[35]

The versatile Iceland underwent yet another transformation in May of 1936, when the interior was remodeled into a streamlined ocean vessel, including a promenade deck. This dancing and dining venue was dubbed the "S.S. Showboat and Merry Time Salon." It offered musical comedies and vaudeville acts as well. A small fire in January of 1932 burned a concession building at the park, causing $500 in damages. The 1933 season would be a busy one for Carlin's, as over fifty group outings were booked. One of the many free attractions on display to the public that summer was a new baby monkey.[36]

The park received bad news in April 1934, when the city ordered that the Green Palace be banned from holding any amusements or entertainments because it held

A September 1925 ad for the wildly popular Mardi Gras celebration at Carlin's. Many events could be attended at this fall carnival, including the Grand Masque Ball and the Mummers Parade. The ad is from the *Times*, Baltimore's sport and amusement weekly.

"serious menace to life due to fire hazards existing in the building." This was a serious blow to Baltimoreans, as the only other major sports venue in the city, the Regiment Armory, had been ordered to shut its doors just a week earlier due to a fire. The Green Palace had offered basketball games, tennis matches, and boxing and wrestling programs up to that point. William Parr, buildings engineer of the city, showed great concern in renovations made to expand the arena over the last several years: "This building originated from a permit to erect and construct a roof over the arena at Carlin's Park—in other words, an open-air pavilion. Since that time, little by little, this building has been enclosed with inflammable walls, partitions have

Top: The impressive Carlin's Arena, which presented many events over the years, including top-notch boxing and wrestling cards (courtesy Hearst Newspapers LLC/*Baltimore News-American*). *Above:* Goat cart rides were a very popular—and tame—kids' attraction at many amusement parks over the years (courtesy Hearst Newspapers LLC/*Baltimore News-American*).

A rare view from the top of the Mill Chute drop provides a good view of the surrounding park attractions (from Philadelphia Toboggan Coasters, Inc./Tom Rebbie, president/CEO).

been erected, a balcony erected or extended and other changes made until now this building has been converted into a building for public amusement."[37] Essentially, the Green Palace had evolved into a structure that fell under the classification of a theater, and much of its construction was now in violation of the city's theater fire code. City authorities did manage to work out a deal with Carlin's; temporary permits were issued that allowed the park to present their weekly wrestling shows until all improvements were completed to the arena. Ten firemen staffed each event until the hazards were addressed.

Improvements for the 1935 season included a Pretzel dark ride, a new Whip, and the refurbishing of the Old Mill. Other new rides announced included the Whirl-O-Whip, the Upsie-Daisie, and two additional flat rides. Carlin's also decided to upgrade the park's lighting that season. Effects that were modeled after the recent Century of Progress Fair were unveiled, providing the park with a vibrant appearance.[38]

As popular as Carlin's Park was during the 1930s and postwar 1940s, they also proved to be difficult times for Carlin. Funds were limited and it was difficult for the park to continually add new attractions on a consistent basis. The park suffered several fires during this period. A fire in January of 1932 leveled a concession building. During an April 1933 General Motors exhibit, the new dance hall was severely damaged by a blaze.

In 1935, nightly dancing in the new ballroom cost a total of 15 cents, of which 5 cents was collected for a hat check. Carlin would upgrade the park's funhouse for the 1936 season, adding several new devices for patrons to enjoy. Also, he arranged for several Maryland county outings that summer. Each Maryland county had the opportunity to host a special outing at the park and also receive part of the day's gate receipts to be used for community projects within their county.[39] Open-air movies and 5-cent Kooler Keg beer were advertised for the 1936 season. Offseason maintenance prior to the 1937 season included repainting of all the carousel horses. By that time, the trend had moved towards creating carousel figures from aluminum, but Carlin thought the aluminum horses were "stiff and lifeless mounts" when compared to his hand-carved wooden horses.[40]

Carlin Park's most devastating fire was a 10-alarm blaze on September 30, 1937, referred to as one of the most spectacular blazes since the great Baltimore Fire of 1904. Over 300 firemen fought the inferno, with three requiring treatment for injuries. An estimated 15,000 people witnessed the spectacle, and 100 officers were called to keep spectators at a safe distance.[41] The total losses were estimated at $300,000, none of which were covered by insurance. Many of the park's buildings were destroyed, including at least a dozen concession stands. The Green House arena, funhouse, bowling

A view of the interior from Carlin's Dance Hall—a Fulton Studio photograph (courtesy Hearst Newspapers LLC/*Baltimore News-American*).

The kids sat still just long enough for a quick snapshot on the Teacups ride. This was taken during the "Poor Children's Outing" held in August of 1930 (courtesy Hearst Newspapers LLC/*Baltimore News-American*).

alley, and rifle range were also burned to the ground. The skating rink and almost 2000 pairs of roller skates were lost. Recovering from this setback was tricky, as city councilman Meyer Reamer stated that he would prevent the erection of any wooden structures that were planned to replace those lost in the fire. Reamer lived within 500 feet of the park and was concerned about protecting the nearby houses from future flare-ups at Carlin's.[42]

John Carlin managed to find the positive in any situation, though. The park's 20th anniversary was recognized in a weeklong celebration in June of 1938. Carlin wanted to show his appreciation, and over 100,000 complimentary tickets were handed out to Baltimore residents. Carlin stated, "Baltimore folks have been mighty good to me these last twenty years, and I hope I'm around to serve them another twenty or forty years."[43] The large Olympic pool was opened in July of 1938. At approximately 200 feet long and 100 feet wide, the pool could handle thousands of guests seeking relief from Baltimore's hot summers. The pool area offered a separate high-dive area, a sandy beach, and a modern locker room.[44] The pool played a key role in Baltimore's social scene as well, hosting many a blind date over the years, some that eventually led to marriage.

A major boxing card highlighted by a bout between Lou Transperanti and Sammy

LaPorte would take place in the debut of Carlin's new arena in November of 1938.[45] Local officials were a bit concerned when it came time to formally open the newly rebuilt sports arena a few months later, however. Even though a few wrestling and boxing matches had been held in the new 4000-seat facility in late 1938, a complaint was issued in January of 1939 stating that the arena was unsafe and that some of the construction had been completed without the proper permits. The city fire department considered the building a fire hazard and compiled a list of objections. Mayor Jackson was called before a grand jury on the matter, as it was revealed that the city council had not passed an ordinance for the construction of the sports arena. Just a few weeks later, though, approval was given to hold further events, pending the installation of a sprinkler system.

Carlin's hosted a circus early in the summer of 1939. Among the performers were a 13-year old daredevil, an aerialist, and Jumbo, the 500-pound clown. Attractions in place for 1941, Carlin's 22nd season of operation, included a new Whip ride and Selderi, the Stratosphere Man, whose thrilling act was performed atop a 138-foot pole.[46] Both ice and roller skating were featured during the spring opening in 1942. Carlin's was the site of the Baltimore Miniature Race Car Association's meet in September of 1942. Quarter-mile races were held with speeds kept lower than normal due to poor track conditions. A Western village was erected inside of the Iceland structure for the 1943 season. Yet another blaze at the park leveled the open-air theater, used for plays and motion pictures, in April of 1944. The damage, estimated at $5,000, was believed to have been caused by a small fire nearby built by youths to keep warm.[47] Tragedy would strike the park in May of 1944 when a 28-year-old woman stood up on the second dip

Rare view of Carlin's Coliseum funhouse. Many challenging attractions could be found inside, including the spinning barrel, moving stairs, slide, and roulette wheel. Guests could rent overalls to wear inside the funhouse to try to keep their clothes clean (courtesy Dr. and Mrs. Edward Heir).

of the Mountain Speedway and was hurled out of the train, falling to her death. Another mishap on the Mountain Speedway in June 1945 sent fourteen riders to the hospital when one coaster train rear-ended a stalled train about sixty feet above the ground. Fortunately, no serious injuries resulted from the collision, and park employees helped riders descend from the wooden framework.[48]

A perennial favorite of the traditional amusement parks was the popular game concessions, and Carlin's had many of those in place over the years. People wishing to test their skills could drop a few coins at the following game stands during the 1944 and 1945 seasons: Cat Game, Penny Pitch, Coca Cola Fish Game, Dump the Lady, Spill the Milk, Mule Game, Guess Your Weight & Age, Pitch 'til You Win; there were also the Tommy Guns. Certain games unveiled during the wartime years tended to lean towards the patriotic themes; what true-blue American could resist Carlin's "Kill the Axis" game?[49]

Robert Paul Iula, conductor of the 50-piece orchestra that performed weekly pop symphony concerts during the 1946 season at Carlin's lamented the abrupt discontinuation of the music series (evidently a shortage of beer had taken a toll on attendance): "There are hundreds of Baltimoreans who think that a Strauss waltz without beer is like terrapin without sherry. Pop concerts without beer don't pop."[50] Ever willing to help out with charitable causes, Carlin's hosted a fundraiser to help combat rheumatic

Carlin's Coliseum funhouse included the challenging Human Roulette Wheel, among two dozen other attractions (courtesy Hearst Newspapers LLC/*Baltimore News-American*).

The Bicycle Race was yet another exciting diversion inside Carlin's fun house. Note a portion of the wooden slide in the upper left portion of the photograph (courtesy Hearst Newspapers LLC/*Baltimore News-American*).

Carlin's was just one of several amusement parks to offer the fun-filled Noah's Ark. Sadly, just one of these funhouse attractions remains in operation in the U.S. today (courtesy Hearst Newspapers LLC/*Baltimore News-American*).

A view of Carlin's Summer Theater, which offered first-rate operas and plays for park guests' enjoyment (courtesy Hearst Newspapers LLC/*Baltimore News-American*).

fever during the summer of 1947. A swim and beach party was held by the Ladies Trenton Club, which included dancing and card games as well.[51]

The early postwar years were prosperous for Carlin's. The park invested quite a bit of money in the spring of 1948 to add several exciting amusements. Joining the new, large merry-go-round were a funhouse and the Octopus and Spit-fire thrill rides.[52] A *Sun* article from August of 1949 featured 65-year-old John Cypulski, the lucky man who operated the air jets in the funhouse. With the press of a button, he would trigger a cold air blast to raise the ladies' skirts, to the embarrassment of the victims, and the amusement of the surrounding crowd. Cypulski would go on to relate that "pressing this button is an art—just like the art of candid photography. It's a matter of timing. Some women expect it; others don't care at all. Whatever they try though, I get them all, coming or going."[53]

Carlin's offered dozens of rides during the 1940s, including the Lindy Planes, Heyday (a spinning flat ride built by the Spillman Company, which also manufactured carousels), the Dangler, the Waltzer, Skooter Cars, the Bug, Submarine, Holland Fling, Sky Rider, and the Old Mill. Carlin's Penny Arcade could provide a kid with hours of entertainment. Hand-cranked "moving pictures" were a popular draw, as well as fortune cards, cowboy cards depicting western heroes of the time, and various games, including the early claw machines, the fortune teller, and the test-your-strength. The venerable Skee-Ball game could be found here. This popular game still attracts kids of all ages today. Other popular attractions in the early 1950s included Honeymoon Lane, the

International skating legend Sonja Henie appeared at Carlin's Iceland for an exhibition in March of 1934.

This Carlin's publicity photograph shows a young beauty on the Lindy Planes.

Bombers, Chair-o-Plane, Whip, Tumble Bug, Octopus, Looper (a hamster cage-type ride), Strato-Ship, Skeeter Boats, Ferris wheel, merry-go-round, Rocket, and the canoe lake.

Longtime Baltimore resident Stan Rosenstein recalls his time spent at Carlin's as a young boy in the 1950s: "We lived in Park Circle, about 4–5 blocks away from the park. We'd walk to the park under the pagoda entrance and spend the day there. My older brother and his friends would drag me on the Mountain Speedway (quite a ride for a 7 year old), but they made sure I was sitting next to one of the larger guys, to wedge me in and keep me from flying out." Mr. Rosenstein fondly remembers the immense Olympic pool, complete with slides and diving boards: "There was a pavilion at the pool with a great food stand. They served some of Baltimore's best pizza by the slice. There was also a juke-

You Are Invited To
...OPENING...
COLLEGIATE SKATING PARTY
FRIDAY, OCTOBER 30th, 1936
CARLIN'S NEW ROLLER SKATING RINK

This Invitation & **20¢** Entitles You To Admission Ticket, Skates, & Skating Privileges Between 8 & 11 p. m.

The Management Reserves The Right To Refund Money To Anyone Not Abiding By Rink Rules.

RINK OPEN EVERY DAY EXCEPT MONDAY and TUESDAYS.

Above and Opposite: Miscellaneous Carlin's tickets.

box that played the popular songs at that time, Elvis Presley, Ricky Nelson, the kids would get up and dance to the music." Another favorite activity was watching the Clippers ice hockey team skate against some of their Eastern Hockey League rivals, like Charlotte and Richmond.

The 1950s would present new challenges to Carlin's Park. Much of the park's infrastructure was showing its age, and the park was also targeted for theft several times during July of 1951. One bold robber wielding two handguns made off with over $2,000 during one incident which occurred one evening after closing.[54]

In April of 1953, Carlin's experimented with a "throwback" type of promotion as the park announced the opening of a Nickelodeon, which was probably the first to operate in several decades. Films from the collection of exhibitor Robert T. Marhenke were shown, featuring stars of the silent film years.[55] With other forms of summer entertainment emerging during the 1950s and the park showing increasing wear and tear, attendance began to drop off. A new funhouse was added for the 1953 season, though. Carlin's "thrill" rides at that time cost 14 cents each.

Sadly, John Carlin passed away on May 21, 1954, and the amusement industry lost one of its true leaders. Carlin was a long-time and respected member of the National Association of Amusement Parks, Pools, and Beaches (NAAPPB) organization. In his obituary, it was noted that he "was lawyer, architect, artist and musical impresario in his own right. He pioneered many 'firsts' in Baltimore during the last 45 years, that his fame and reputation were actually greater at the national level, than the local. Nor did he just excel in these particular fields. He was an ardent figure in the field of sports, boxing, wrestling, and ice hockey. During the last 30 years he either developed or brought to Baltimore some of the country's biggest 'name' celebrities."[56] Heirs of John Carlin reached an agreement to pass ownership of the park to Mrs. William J. Fischer, one of Carlin's daughters, and Mrs. Thomas Beers. William Fischer had managed the park the last few seasons and was to continue in that role. However, the amusement park closed for good in 1955. Carlin's Park

KEEP THIS COUPON YOU MAY BE ONE
OF THE LUCKY WINNERS
MANY VALUABLE PRIZES GIVEN AWAY FRE

N.º 2072

FREE PRIZE DRAWINGS, 2 AND 5 P. M.

**MARYLAND STATE
GUARD DAY**

Picnic & Prize Carnival

SAT. JUNE 30th

1945

CARLIN'S PARK

PRESENT THIS TICKET
To Cashier in Park and upon payment
of 10c it will be redeemed and you can
enjoy the FIRST 6 AMUSEMENTS
printed thereon. 28

GOOD FOR ONE RIDE (Plus 1c Fed. Tax)
10 A. M. **PRETZEL** 2 P. M.
MD. STATE GUARD DAY

GOOD FOR ONE RIDE (Plus 1c Fed. Tax)
11 A. M. **SKY RIDER** 6 P. M.
MD. STATE GUARD DAY

ADMIT ONE (Plus 1c Fed. Tax)
10 A. M. **FUN HOUSE** 6 P. M.
MD. STATE GUARD DAY

GOOD FOR ONE RIDE (Plus 1c Fed. Tax)
10 A. M. **CHAIR-O-PLANE** 6 P. M
MD. STATE GUARD DAY

GOOD FOR ONE RIDE (Plus 1c Fed. Tax)
10 A. M. **TUMBLE BUG** 2 P. M.
MD. STATE GUARD DAY

GOOD FOR ONE RIDE (Plus 1c Fed. Tax)
10 A.M. **Mount. Speedway** 2 P.M
MD. STATE GUARD DAY

7c Plus 1c Fed. Tax....Total 8c
10 A. M. **CATERPILLAR** 6 P. M.
MD. STATE GUARD DAY

30c—THIRTY CENTS—30c
9 A M. **ROLLER RINK** 5 P. M.

CHILDREN 35c—ADULTS 60c
10 A. M. **OLYMPIC POOL** 8 P. M.
MD. STATE GUARD DAY

FREE ADMISSION TO PARK, FREE PRIZES
FREE SHOWS, FREE PICNIC GROVES
WIN WAR BOND, SPORTING GOODS,
GROCERIES, GAMES
AND OTHER VALUABLE PRIZES
DROP THIS STUB IN LUCKY BARREL

N.º 2072

was hit again by its long-time nemesis, damaging fire, when a portion of the midway was razed in November of 1955.

The final blow came in January of 1956 when an eight-alarm fire decimated the Iceland rink. Damage was estimated at $175,000. At the time, it was the largest skating rink in Baltimore and was the home of the Baltimore Clippers hockey team. Leaking ammonia from the refrigeration system compounded the blaze's intensity, which required nearly 40 pieces of fire apparatus to bring under control. Despite the closing of the park, Carlin's still managed to draw much attention. In 1957, it was one of several Baltimore sites being considered for the development of a new exhibition hall and sports arena. In

Roller Rink ad/label.

Rosalie Elbon, Evonne Fear, and Nancy Earnhartt enjoy a spin on the Whip during a June 1948 schoolchildren's outing (courtesy Hearst Newspapers LLC/*Baltimore News-American*).

A trackside view of the fearsome Mountain Speedway roller coaster, which would operate up until the park's closing in 1955—a Fulton Studio photograph (courtesy Hearst Newspapers LLC/*Baltimore News-American*).

addition to Carlin's Park, an area near Pratt and Light streets and one at Druid Hill Park were sites in contention for the $6,000,000 project, which eventually came to fruition as the Baltimore Civic Center.

William Fischer and members of Baltimore's Weinberg family announced plans for a large drive-in theater in June of 1958, and this new thrill soon took the place of the Mountain Speedway. The proposed plans for the Drive-in stoked claims for it to be considered as one of the largest in the nation. Plans included a dance terrace, a cafeteria-style concession stand, a large playground for kids, and even electric heaters for patrons' cars when colder weather set in. Construction of the project was marred in December of that year when Carlin's treasured carousel was mistakenly torn down, although it was to have been kept as part of the kids' playland being erected for the drive-in. In the ensuing court case, a verdict was returned against the Ridgely Construction Company and a subcontractor, and they were ordered to pay $5,174 in damages.[57]

Other commercial projects soon followed, with Carlin's gradually disappearing beneath new tenants, including United Clay, an Arlan's discount store, and an A&P food market. Reliable Stores National Headquarters transferred their operations from their Baltimore and Howard streets location as well, to what would become known as Carlin's Industrial Park.

5

Carr's Beach

Carr's Beach is recognized as one of the most popular beach resorts for African Americans of its time to operate in the Mid-Atlantic region. Perched on a stretch of land where the Severn River joins with the Chesapeake Bay, Carr's Beach's heyday was roughly the 1950s thru the early 1960s. The beach was introduced by Elizabeth Carr-Smith around 1929, who had received a parcel of bay front property from her father, Fred Carr. Previously, Mr. Carr had utilized the land for farming. This parcel was one of four that were created when he divided up the large property to share among his four daughters. One of the other daughters would use her land to open the neighboring Sparrow's Beach, another popular black amusement resort.

Elizabeth Carr-Smith hoped to offer a safe place for youngsters to swim, as some local youths were diving and swimming in dangerous waters around Annapolis at that time. In the late 1940s, weekly beach parties were held, offering games, swimming, and dancing. Carr's Beach was just one of several locations where the Red Cross offered swimming and lifesaving classes starting in the late 1940s. An annual Catholic Day at the resort drew several busloads of parishioners from Washington, D.C., churches during this period.

Rides like a Ferris wheel, carousel, Swings, and additional rides for children could be enjoyed here. While games, concessions, and swimming were all popular attractions, the biggest draw was the top-shelf entertainment that the park was consistently able to offer. "The Beach" was THE place for many to hang out on weekends. Popular singers like James Brown, Little Richard, the Drifters, Ray Charles, Marvin Gaye, Dinah Washington, Aretha Franklin, the Shirelles, Otis Redding, the Platters, the Four Tops, and a very young Stevie Wonder were just a few of many nationally acclaimed acts to pack the Beach's pavilion. Many came from as far as Philadelphia and New York City for the chance to dance there.

August of 1951 proved to be a busy time at the Beach, when boxing champ Joe Louis attracted huge enthusiastic crowds to his sparring sessions. A daily crowd estimated at 1000 watched the Brown Bomber's every move as the champ trained for his upcoming 10-round bout with Jimmy Bivins. Over 5000 people were in attendance at his last session, held just a few days before the fight at Baltimore's Memorial Stadium.[1] Louis would defeat Bivins in what would be the warm-up to the final match of his illustrious professional career, a loss to Rocky Marciano. Carr's Beach was a popular location for boxers training for upcoming fights. Heavyweight Clarence Henry trained at Carr's in June of 1952 in preparation for a bout against top contender Archie Moore

ALL ABOARD FOR ST. JOHN'S DAY!

BUS EXCURSION TO

CARR'S BEACH

Thursday, July 20, 1939

Buses leaving the Church, Carrollton Avenue near
Lanvale Street   8:00 a m

Adults ROUND TRIP **FARE $1.00** Rain or Shine

Children under 12 years $.50

J. R. Cossey, Chairman   Rev. H. R. Tomlin, Pastor & Assistant Chairman   Harry Biddle, Sec'y   Pearl Burley, Assistant Sec'y
Sarah Bailey   Geneva Taylor   Florence Bundick   Mildred Moore   Mattie B. Smith   Clarence Rice   Jerome Hall   Lelia Tomlin
Bertha Waters   Florence Lewis   Sidonia Harriday   Estella Hargrove   Arthur Cornish   Samuel Henson

W. HERBERT KNOX & SON, PRINTER, 816 N. FREMONT AVE

Poster for a St. John's Church excursion to Carr's Beach in July of 1939 (Russ Sears Collection).

that was also held at Memorial Stadium. Joe Louis was back in town to referee that fight.

Local radio station WANN—1190—catered to the African American audience and broadcast the popular *Bandstand on the Beach* program, featuring dee-jay "Hoppy" Adams. Order was kept by George Phelps and his group of officers. Mr. Phelps would later become the city's first African American deputy sheriff. Attractions to be enjoyed at Carr's Beach in the mid–1950s included four major rides, three kiddie rides, three "walk-thru's," a penny arcade, twenty game stands, sixteen refreshment stands, three restaurants, the Aquacade Pavilion, a cocktail lounge, a shooting gallery, and boat rides.[2] Carr's Beach fans reminisce quite a bit on the lengths people would go to reach the beach. Some would hitchhike, some resorted to floating down the Chesapeake on inner tubes from nearby beach.

The Beach's musical acts were so popular that a jazz concert on evening of July 12, 1956, resulted in what one county official referred to as "the worst traffic problem in the history of Annapolis." A huge crowd estimated at 50,000 descended on the Beach, leaving Route 665 nearly impossible to navigate. Traffic was backed up for five miles stretching to Route 2. Dozens of abandoned cars were towed from the highway to help break up the snarl, but normal traffic patterns didn't return until 3:30 a.m.[3] As Carr's amphitheater was believed to hold a capacity crowd of 6000 concertgoers, this was truly an overflow crowd. The beach's owners were warned shortly afterward that their operating license would be revoked if the problem arose again.[4] Additional complaints were received a year later, as local residents petitioned the Anne Arundel County Board to help reduce the noise levels at the Beach.

Group bus excursions to Carr's Beach were a very popular weekend trip for many church groups and social clubs. Groups from the Philadelphia area and the Petersburg area of Virginia organized several trips to the Beach.

The makeup of the resort began to change towards the mid–1960s. Carr's Beach experienced negative press following an all-day party in June 1964 that resulted in several arrests. A Homebuilders Jamboree party took place, attracting an estimated 2000 contractors for a day of drinking and gambling. Two plainclothes policemen witnessed what they considered an "indecent" strip show put on by two exotic dancers and arrested the ladies. An unruly crowd began to throw stones, prompting police backup to be summoned. Three contractors were arrested on charges of disorderly conduct and resisting arrest. Similar events had been held in previous years with no apparent trouble. A police spokesman noted that the incident was nonracial in character, as the event had drawn a predominantly white crowd.[5]

As Carr's entered the late 1960s and early 1970s, it was well past its prime, when the Beach's primary attraction was as a premier showplace for national R&B artists. This period saw a shift towards promoting rock and roll concerts. A three-day festival at Carr's (renamed Seaside Park) resulted in numerous complaints to the Annapolis city council and police and included marijuana use, illegal sale and drinking of alcohol, noise, and traffic congestion. Joseph W. Alton, Jr., Anne Arundel County executive, began to seek legislation to regulate the outdoor rock concerts. Essentially, permits would have to be granted for all forms of outdoor entertainment in the county. The promoter of the rock show in question, New Era Follies, then announced that the remainder of the summer shows at the beach would be cancelled, as the first two shows had lost money.[6]

In November of 1982, it was announced that a 52-acre tract of beach, including Carr's and Sparrow's beaches, would be sold for condominium development. Owned at that time by Baltimore businessmen William L. Adams and Henry G. Parks Jr. (former owner of Parks Sausage Company), the beach property was expected to fetch between $1 and 2 million.[7] Today, the condos of The Villages at Chesapeake Harbour occupy the land.

6

Chesapeake Beach/Seaside Park

While not patronized solely by Baltimoreans, Chesapeake Beach Amusement Park drew throngs of city residents for decades via steamers departing from the Baltimore harbor. The beachfront park's origins can be traced back to a group of Washington, D.C., and Maryland businessmen who formed the Washington and Chesapeake Railway Corporation in 1891. At that time, their intention was to build a beach resort on a grand scale, to be reached by a new railroad line stretching nearly 30 miles from the outskirts of Washington, D.C. (Seat Pleasant, Maryland) to the Chesapeake Bay. The resort was to be built a bit further south of the old Fair Haven resort on the bay that had operated several years earlier and was to include two hotels, a casino, and a racetrack. However, their ambitious plans were not realized, and the corporation was placed in receivership four years later.

A different group of interested parties from Denver soon formed a new company, the Chesapeake Bay Construction Company, with Otto Mears as the president and David Moffat as the chief financial backer. Realizing the potential for creating a link to the bay, Mears pressed on with the construction of the railroad. The rail project was completed by the summer of 1899; however, most of the attractions and concessions failed to materialize in time, resulting in a disappointing season. An October 1899 newspaper article cited the advent of the telegraph and the railroad finally reaching Calvert County. This article also reported on the status of the developing town. The large pavilion that was erected contained large eating rooms, a dance hall, and a bar, the only one in Calvert County at that time. The hotel was only partially constructed at that point, but contracts were in place to erect a dozen cottages for vacationers by the following summer.[1]

The Chesapeake Beach resort would formally open for business to much fanfare on June 9, 1900. The side-wheel steamer *J.S. Warden* embarked from the Light Street pier with a host of dignitaries for the inaugural trip down the bay. "The Atlantic City of Maryland," as the new resort was being touted, borrowed a few ideas from Atlantic City, New Jersey. The popular rolling sedan chairs that were a highlight of a visit to the famous oceanfront boardwalk were introduced at Chesapeake Beach. The German Village, bandstand, dance hall and other buildings were in place on the large pier for guests to enjoy. The Fourth Regiment Band was booked to play to crowds onboard the steamer, and a fireworks display was provided later that night.[2] Visitors could stroll along the mile-long boardwalk, take a dip in the bay, or listen to a band play. Two amusement rides were operating—a carousel crafted by Gustav Dentzel complete with a German band organ,[3] and a scenic railway, an early roller coaster built and patented by James A. Griffiths. Griffiths was a partner in the planning and construction of the very first Scenic Railway, with L.A. Thompson. He would later team up with designer George C. Crane and form the Griffiths and Crane Scenic and Gravity Railway Company. They would soon rival Thompson's company as the major players in the Scenic Railway market, and for several years afterward.[4]

The Chesapeake Beach Railway Company's officials and stockholders essentially owned the property and the town of Chesapeake Beach. The Mears management team was able to persuade the Maryland State Legislature to revise the town's original charter to allow for greater ease in establishing a multitude of new business opportunities. At the end of a successful first season of operation, Otto Mears announced plans for expansion by the Chesapeake Beach Improvement Company. A new resort at the beach, to be billed as the "Saratoga of the South," would be opened shortly. Prime features included yachting, bathing, aquatic features, and a new horserace track, accompanied by one of the finest clubhouses in the country. The clubhouse was by membership only, with only a high-class clientele in mind. The handsome three-story structure reportedly cost $80,000 and included a reception area, reading and smoking rooms, a café, a billiards room, and a room for a gambling saloon that would possibly offer roulette and other games of chance.

The Chesapeake Beach Railway Company was very cautious in protecting its own interests. In each deed registered for the lots and cottages that were sold to individuals, it was clearly stated that the sale of both liquor and gambling were prohibited on the property. However, the railway company reserved the right to lease the "privilege" of selling liquor or permitting gambling on those lots, so they essentially maintained control over all of these interests in the town.[5] In the fall of 1900, Mears offered his thoughts on the resort's expansion plans:

> Winter racing is to be the feature of Chesapeake Beach from December until June, and in the summer the attractions of the place will be those of a first-class seaside resort. The fact of the matter is, we have a wide-open charter from the Maryland Legislature, which permits of almost any enterprise we choose to carry on, but it will not be policy of us to go against public sentiment, and this we do not propose to do. Chesapeake Beach is incorporated as a city. We have a mayor and five commissioners. We own the town, and the mayor and commissioners are members of our company. Our charter lasts forever and is a very liberal one. To what extent we shall make use of its privileges is a question which we have not determined beyond the fact that in no way will we offend public sentiment. We are in this enterprise for the money, and no matter how liberal the laws are, it is the public which will pass judgment.[6]

In December 1900, the opening of "America's Monte Carlo" was postponed due to poor track conditions and pushed back one week. The impressive grandstand for the new racetrack was approximately 173 feet by 60 feet and enclosed in glass. It could hold up to 2000 spectators, and there was quite a bit of space reserved for the gambling windows. The track's infield was composed mostly of marsh, though, and would not support much in the way of new development. By this time, it was thought that millions had been already invested in this ambitious enterprise.[7] It was tough going in the early years. Suits were brought against the Chesapeake Beach Improvement Company fairly quickly to recover large dollar amounts owed from the completed construction and expansion work. James F. McCloskey of Philadelphia filed suit to recover nearly $39,000 owed to him for erecting the clubhouse. The architectural and engineering John D. Allen Company sued to recover close to $9,000 in fees owed.[8]

Lawmakers would not be swayed on the gambling issue, so the racetrack had to be removed and the casino was soon converted into a restaurant. It became evident that the projected profit levels would be difficult to reach without the anticipated gambling revenues. By the end of the 1902 season, with dim prospects, Mears resigned from the company. David Moffat, owning nearly all of the company's stock, tapped his friend Sylvester Smith to take over as president. Over the next few years, patronage was up slightly at the resort, but still no profit was realized. Several well-publicized railroad mishaps didn't help matters. Yet another hopeful, William Jones, took over the helm in 1905 and reigned as president until 1925. Under his control, the beach enjoyed several successful seasons.

With the amusement resort's popularity on the upswing, it was announced in May of 1909 that the rail service to Chesapeake Beach would soon be joined by an excursion steamer out of Baltimore's harbor. June 26, 1909, marked the first excursion of the steamer *Dreamland*. At the helm was Capt. A.D Guy, who ferried 500 guests on the *Dreamland*'s maiden voyage. A new pier was in place at the beach resort to greet the *Dreamland* and its happy cargo. This large 276-foot side-wheeler could hold up to 2500 passengers. Built around 1878, it was previously known as the *Republic* when it made

This is the first carousel to operate at Chesapeake Beach.

Early postcard view of Griffiths Scenic Railway at Chesapeake Beach (from the collection of the Chesapeake Beach Railway Museum).

A view of the covered dance pavilion on the Chesapeake Beach boardwalk.

the Philadelphia to Cape May run. After being sold to a New York interest, the vessel was renamed *Dreamland* and began to ply the excursion route between New York City and Coney Island.[9] In December of 1912, the Love Point Transportation and Development Company would formally sell the *Dreamland* to its own general manager, John

This c. 1910 view shows some of the various souvenir stands, games of chance, and shops that lined the boardwalk.

A c. 1915 postcard view of the casino at Chesapeake Beach.

C. Bosley. The dependable ship would regularly sail from Baltimore to Chesapeake Beach through the 1924 season, when it was then taken out of service by Bosley.[10] Probably the longest trip from the Baltimore harbor to any of the bay resorts, the voyage stretched close to 50 miles each way. Large groups of beachgoers crowded the decks, each paying the round-trip fare of 50 cents.

Couples and families alike enjoy a day at the beach. The thrilling Great Derby roller coaster situated on a pier over the Chesapeake is in the background; it began operation in 1916 (from the collection of the Chesapeake Beach Railway Museum).

This c. 1920s view shows swimmers in the netted portion of the beach. The steamer *Dreamland* can be seen docked at the pier in the background.

A souvenir booklet from 1912 best details Chesapeake Beach's early offerings. Billed at that time as "Washington's only Salt Water Resort," it attracted many from the nation's capital, most opting for the scenic ride on the Chesapeake Beach Railway. Trains made five round-trip excursions on weekdays and seven on the weekends. The following is an excerpt from the booklet describing Chesapeake Beach's many fine features:

> Here is to be found an abundance of shady ground provided with benches and tables for the accommodation of picnic parties large or small, the grounds being kept entirely free from all debris. In addition to the regular water supply there are a number of springs of cold, pure water, which have been made very attractive and acceptable. The purity of the water in these springs is indicated by the fact that not a single case of malaria or typhoid fever has occurred at this resort in the twelve years of its existence. Every boat and train to the Beach carries parties laden with baskets filled with good things to eat, and at no other place do things to eat taste quite so good as outside under the large shady trees where the cool breezes off the Bay fan the tired and hungry pleasure-seekers. The police force is a model of efficiency, thoroughly disciplined, and a terror to evildoers. A family camping here or visiting will be AMPLY PROTECTED.[11]

Among the pages in this souvenir book was an interesting Land Company ad touting "A Home at the Seashore." It offered choice bay-front lots in the nearby town of North Beach from $100 to $300, adding that North Beach is "a city where the living expenses are for the grocer and not for the doctor."

Perhaps the main attraction, the beach, was capably described as "being made up of fine white sand, and entirely free from objectionable features." With no undertows or strong currents, the bathing beach was safe for all ages. Popular activities there included camping, crabbing and fishing from the pier, and boating. Boardwalk attractions included the Photo Gallery, where visitors could purchase postcards, the dance pavilion, and the Souvenir Place, featuring Lowney's chocolate bon-bons. Also situated on the boardwalk was the post office/general store, as well as a barber shop. Several concessions and games of chance enticed visitors to part with their cash.

For beachgoers choosing to extend their stay, several hotels were located at the resort. The Belvedere, Calvert, High View, Maryland House, and Holliday House all offered clean rooms at a very reasonable rate (as low as 50 cents a night in the early 1900s). The more adventurous could sleep in a tent at the campground.

A myriad of eating establishments served up meals to the hungry. The Casino's specialty was fresh seafood dinners served in the large dining room and on the surrounding verandas. Captain Freedly's provided ample shady groves for those who brought their own picnic baskets. The Park Café, or Park Lunch Room, was well known for its first-class lunches. Another popular spot was Bentley's Pavilion, which housed an ice cream garden and lunch parlor. Guests strolling on the boardwalk could sit down for a coffee at Joe Franks' café. Other desirable eateries included the dining room at the Maryland House Hotel and the Rustic Café, which was located on the bluffs above the train station, practically guaranteeing a refreshing breeze on a hot day. Billing themselves as "The first and last word in wholesome eats"; Sniders offered slices of pie, sandwiches, and milk or coffee, each for just a nickel.

Bosley expended a fair amount of capital in improving the *Dreamland* for the summer of 1914. Two moonlight cruises a week were announced, on Monday and Friday evenings. A new pier and several new amusements awaited excursionists at Chesapeake Beach.[12] A new hardwood dance floor was installed aboard the *Dreamland* in time for the 1915 season.[13] Looking to supply beachgoers with a more thrilling attraction, the Great Derby roller coaster was erected for the 1916 season. This ride was quite a bit higher than the scenic railway and was situated on a pier which extended out over the bay. Trouble arrived at Chesapeake Beach in June of 1916, when the Calvert County sheriff and six deputies raided a building housing several slot machines, seized eight machines and arrested two men in the process. Acting on a tip that the illegal slots were in operation, the sheriff organized the raid. The two men arrested tried to prevent authorities from removing the machines via wheelbarrow.[14]

The women of the Broadway Relief Club organized a special excursion for Baltimore soldiers in July of 1918. Several camps and hospitals, including Holabird, Fort Mead, and Fort McHenry, sent their soldiers to the harbor to board the *Dreamland*. Several of the soldiers in attendance were wounded or had been blinded by poisonous gas during World War I. Over 1100 servicemen boarded the steamer and were entertained by a vaudeville performance and treated to lunch during the cruise down the bay. The men in uniform also received tobacco, cigarettes and boxes of candy, and the amusements were waiting for the soldiers to enjoy upon arrival.[15]

A funhouse-type attraction, the Bug House, was in operation by this time. A Dodgem ride, an early bumper car attraction, was installed in the early 1920s. More Maryland and District of Columbia residents began to take a greater interest in the Chesapeake Beach area in the mid–1920s. Many beachfront lots were purchased and summer cottages erected to offer beach residents attractive seaside views. On the night of July 13, 1921, a fifteen-square-foot section of boardwalk collapsed, dropping dozens of people ten feet into the bay. Fortunately, the water was shallow, and all were able to make their way out of the debris safely. The nearly three dozen injured were loaded on a train and transported to hospitals in the Washington, D.C., area.

The Chesapeake Beach Railroad announced plans in the winter of 1922 to allot $100,000 in funds to make improvements to the railway and to reconstruct portions of the pier and boardwalk. A fire on October 31, 1926, decimated the original Dentzel carousel and the building in which it was housed. Mamie Jahn of Baltimore held a four-year lease agreement to operate the carousel at that time, but she did not renew the lease after the fire. It's believed that a replacement carousel operated for the next few seasons.

New management undertook a large, expensive renovation for the 1930 season, adding new attractions, buildings, and concessions. The group, known as Seaside Park, Inc., ensured that the grand opening of the new Seaside Park attracted much attention. The improvements were contracted out to Harry C. Baker, Inc.[16] Baker was a former business partner of amusement industry veteran John Miller. Baker's company offered expertise in amusement park design and layout, and conceived and built various park structures, including ballrooms and halls, carrousel buildings, miniature railways, old mills, airplane swings, and roller coasters. Patrons were treated that season to a spectacular ballroom and a large saltwater swimming pool, which was claimed to be the largest north of Miami. Several new rides were relocated inland away from the old boardwalk, which was ripped out to provide a new landscape of the beach.[17] The park added a miniature golf course and also expanded the parking facilities to handle some 1200 cars.

Among the new rides to debut included a Whip, miniature railway, coaster dip, Skooter, airplane swing, and Custer cars.[18] A refurbished Dentzel carousel, which was relocated from another amusement park, would become a permanent replacement for the model lost in the fire a few seasons earlier. Thousands made the trip over the opening Memorial Day weekend to experience the new Seaside Park at Chesapeake Beach. "Everything New but the Beach" was the promising slogan for the 1930 summer season. Expanded bus and railway service was available from Washington, D.C. Joe Lorell and his orchestra were booked for the season to provide music for the nightly dances.[19]

The pool would be a summer favorite for several decades; it allowed bathers to safely continue water activities when the sea nettles became active in July. The large pool measured approximately 100 feet long, and the park stated it could handle up to 12,000 swimmers daily. Floodlights and music were added for nighttime swimming. (The pool finally closed in 1971.) However, the new owners had gone into debt with the park's ambitious transformation, and the lingering depression wasn't helping matters. In October of 1930 the railroad management team resigned, and a new course for Seaside Park's future was planned.

Various scenes of young people enjoying a day at the beach in July 1923.

A lone man stands on the deck of the *Dreamland* during a cruise to Chesapeake Beach in August of 1925.

This unique miniature train ride skirted the length of the pier. It shuttled Bay passengers to and from the excursion boats.

A circa 1930s view of the roller coaster from the ride's station. The ride had several names over the years, including the Blue Streak and the Comet. The structure would be razed towards the end of World War II (from the collection of the Chesapeake Beach Railway Museum).

As the park's railroad patronage had begun to drop off, an attempt was made to reintroduce steamer transportation to the resort. Beginning in May of 1931, the Wilson Line steamer *State of Delaware* began departures from Pier 8 in Baltimore's harbor down the bay to Seaside Park.[20] A round-trip cruise during this time cost just 75 cents

A c. 1941 postcard view of the *Bay Belle* docked at Chesapeake Beach.

for adults and 40 cents for children. This steamer operated through the 1935 season, to be replaced by the steamer *Dixie,* which would make the bay voyage until the end of the 1941 season.

For the 1931 season, Bill Strickland's Orchestra was booked to provide jazz for beach visitors, and the Blue Streak coaster was one of the advertised thrills for that summer.[21] (The roller coaster was named the Comet in later years). Jazz performances in the ballroom were a consistent draw at Chesapeake Beach. Bernie Jarboe's Nite Hawks would open the 1932 season, along with a floor show.[22] A unique addition to Chesapeake Beach that May was the miniature railway, which traveled the length of the pier to the steamships. This fun ride for all ages spared ship passengers the lengthy walk to the beach. The garden section of the park was updated with 1200 new plants and shrubs. During the opening weekend, it was announced that nearly 50 organizations had booked an outing at the beach, with the first being a contingent of newspapermen and their families from the National Press Club.[23] In an attempt to increase patronage of the rail service from Washington, it was announced in the summer of 1933 that round-trip rates would be reduced to ten cents for children and twenty-five cents for adults. The new summer attraction was a spectacular circus, featuring performers from the Great DeRizkie troupe.[24]

Sadly, with declining numbers of riders, April 1935 marked the end of the passenger train service from Washington, D.C., to Chesapeake Beach. In its summer heyday, the train station at Chesapeake Beach handled up to six trains a day, but now the station would be converted to a bus depot to handle visitors. A local business man commented that the beach trade was just as good or better with guests arriving via bus than by train.[25]

Between World Wars I and II, Stephen Gambrill, a House Democrat, called for the improvement of the Fishing Creek, a stream which meets the bay at Chesapeake Beach. The Army Corp of Engineers spent a generous sum of money dredging and developing break walls to shape a harbor here. This allowed for the introduction of a protected area for the fleet of fishing boats.[26] Improvements announced for the 1939 season included upgrades to the bathhouse and beach facilities. Additional amusements were added, and motion pictures on the moonlight steamer trips were offered after dark.[27] Later, in November of that year, Chesapeake Beach would be the recipient of nearly $7,000 in additional Public Works Administration (PWA) funds to extend the beach bulkhead an extra 200 feet. A timber bulkhead was in place from a previous PWA grant, but the town requested additional funds in an effort to better protect the shoreline.[28]

On May 30, 1941, the reconditioned steamer *Bay Belle* was christened at Baltimore's Fort McHenry. Mayor Howard Jackson and a host of notable locals helped launch the

Crowds fill the large pool at Chesapeake Beach. The pool was a popular alternative to the Bay waters during the times when sea nettles descended on the beach (from the collection of the Chesapeake Beach Railway Museum).

Crowds board the miniature train for a ride through the picnic grounds in this photograph (from the collection of the Chesapeake Beach Railway Museum).

updated steamer into the Wilson Line's fleet, accompanied by curtains of water launched into the air by harbor fireboats, all to the sounds of the Star Spangled Banner. The four-deck vessel could reach 17 knots, making her the fastest steamer to sail out of the port of Baltimore. Veteran skipper Captain William T. Munton would be at the helm, as daily summer excursions to Seaside Park would start a week later, on June 8.[29] Sadly, war restrictions put an end to the bay steamer voyages to Chesapeake Beach in 1942, and the long wooden pier was left to deteriorate, never to be used again. The unique miniature railroad that carried passengers from the ships to the beach would roll no more.

In December of 1943, the Seaside Park Corporation passed the land it had acquired in 1930 back to the Chesapeake Beach Hotel Company, and dissolved itself shortly thereafter. The park remained closed through a portion of the war years.[30] Jim Angle-meyer leased the struggling beach park for the 1945 season, which was referred to that one summer as Chesapeake Beach Amusement Park and Fishing Wharves. He completed major renovations and repairs to the park's structures and attractions; and the roller coaster was razed. However, the Beach Hotel Company repossessed the park and sold the amusement park land outright, about 20 acres in all, in August of 1946. The buyer was a new company, Chesapeake Beach Park, Inc. Attendance increased in the postwar years at the park, now referred to as Chesapeake Beach Park again. Slot machines were legalized in Calvert County in 1948, which contributed to the larger crowds. Crowds numbering over 4,000 were common on hot summer weekends in the 1950s, filling the town's cottages to capacity.[31]

Popular rides and attractions at that time included the carousel, the funhouse (a ride-in-the-dark), Ferris wheel, miniature train, and several kiddie rides, including a roller coaster, teacups, and a helicopter. Joan Kilmon fondly recalls her childhood days of summer spent at Chesapeake Beach. "My grandfather (Wesley Stinnett) ran the park. My first job was at the bingo hall, helping with the bingo games. My favorite rides were the carousel, especially the Palomino horse, and the funhouse. The Rod-n-Reel and the Beachcomber stand were great places to grab a bite to eat." A long-time favorite, the Rod 'N Reel restaurant, has been a gathering spot for decades at the beach. For the 1955 season, management offered special arrangements for group outings, which could include access to one of the fleet's 26 fishing boats. F.J. Donavan was general manager of the beach park at that time, under president/owner Stinnett.[32] Stinnett would be tapped to be the mayor of Chesapeake Beach in 1955 and would serve in that capacity until August of 1963, when he died of a heart attack.

The late 1960s and early 1970s proved to be a difficult period for the Chesapeake's

Little ones hang on for dear life on the kiddie coaster (from the collection of the Chesapeake Beach Railway Museum).

Chesapeake Beach's Ferris wheel takes riders for a spin (from the collection of the Chesapeake Beach Railway Museum).

varied resorts. Maintenance of the beach properties tended to be a full-time battle. Chesapeake Beach's Brownie's Hotel burned to the ground in May of 1967. It had been a popular meeting place over the years but had been reconditioned to private quarters a few years earlier.[33] Sadly, Chesapeake Beach Amusement Park closed on Labor Day 1972, and all of the park's rides and equipment were purchased by Fairfax, Virginia,

The bingo hall, shown here filled to capacity, was a popular pastime at the beach (from the collection of the Chesapeake Beach Railway Museum).

A crowd lines up to brave the unknown in the funhouse dark ride (from the collection of the Chesapeake Beach Railway Museum).

Enjoying a meal in the park's dining hall. Note the bottles of Rock Creek brand soda, a regional favorite for decades (from the collection of the Chesapeake Beach Railway Museum).

resident and noted carousel dealer Jim Wells. Wells had purchased, restored, and then sold several carousels in the area, including the rides at Glen Echo Park in Washington, D.C., and Lake Fairfax, Virginia. Wells soon placed an ad in a Washington newspaper announcing the weekend sale of much of the park's items, to be held in February 1973, including the arcade and its contents, the carousel, and the remaining rides. Wells' asking price for the unique carousel was $60,000.[34]

The Maryland Historic Trust attempted to add the carousel to the National Register of Historic Places, but the nomination was returned by the Department of the Interior. The National Register noted that the carousel comprised parts from various other carousels, and that the impending sale and potential removal of the ride from Chesapeake Beach did not bode well. Realizing the importance of the antique treasure, local residents and carousel buffs convinced the Maryland-National Capital Park and Planning Commission (M-NCPPC) to consider purchasing the ride. The M-NCPPC soon contacted noted carousel historian Frederick Fried to inspect the ride at Chesapeake Beach. Fried was the author of the outstanding pioneering volume *A Pictorial History of the Carousel*, which was considered to be the only complete work on carousels produced up to that point. After a thorough examination of the three-row carousel, Fried noted the following in his report to the M-NCPPC:

The carousel, 52 feet in diameter has on the outside row 14 horses, 1 large lion, 1 large tiger, and 2 double-seated facing chariots. The middle row consists of 8 horses, 2 goats, 1 bison, 1 ostrich, 1 stag, 1 kangaroo, and 1 hippocampus (seahorse). Inside row consists of 10 horses, 1 small lion, 1 small bison, 2 donkeys, and 1 small tiger. The upper outer rim is an old replacement as is part of the inner rim and scenery screen. The platform is in excellent condition as is most of the upper and inner scenery. The machinery consists of a wooden centerpole and bearing in good condition as is the fluid drive and hydraulic brake. However the vertical drive shaft and some of the bearing will need repairs or replacements. Current was not available to run the carousel but by pushing it manually I found that the main bearing was in good condition.

Building—The building represent[s] the style made popular by the Philadelphia Toboggan Company and is all wood with glass lights in the upper section and removable doors for light and ventilation. Structurally it is sound but in my opinion it would take as much to remove it in sections to rebuild it as it would to replace it completely. I regard this carousel as one of the fine production made by the Gustav A. Dentzel company of Philadelphia and although there is the deterioration that comes from lack of care and maintenance, it still is one of the outstanding carousels of its kind in the country [Fried valued the carousel at approximately $65,000].[35]

A bill was introduced, and passed, to purchase the carousel in April of 1974. The Chesapeake Carousel Fund was set up to accept donations to help pay for the purchase; the

View of the midway, c. 1950s (from the collection of the Chesapeake Beach Railway Museum).

The classic Dentzel carousel, which operated at Chesapeake Beach until the park closed in 1972, still provides rides today at Watkins Regional Park in Largo, MD.

carousel's price tag was $55,000, with an additional $15,000 in funds set aside for relocation and site preparation costs.[36] The M-NCPPC would relocate the antique treasure to nearby Prince Georges County and restore it. It operates today at Watkins Regional Park in Largo, Maryland.

Today, the Chesapeake Beach Railway Museum operates in the original railway station building. It houses a fantastic collection of Chesapeake Beach photos and memorabilia, including an old delivery truck and a rare Kangaroo figure from the carousel. Those who are further interested in exploring Chesapeake Beach's history can join the Friends of the Chesapeake Beach Railway Museum, Inc., group. Their *Chesapeake Dispatcher* semiannual newsletter is a valuable and fun publication to enjoy.

Electric Park

Baltimore's Electric Park opened to much fanfare in June of 1896, under the direction of August "Gus" Fenneman. The 30-acre park was located just south of Belvedere Avenue, near Reisterstown Road. It was named for the blazing lights that outlined nearly all of the park's buildings, including the landmark pavilion entrance. When the park was introduced, throngs crowded the place and gazed in awe at this electric wonderland. Baltimore's Electric Park was one of several Electric Parks that were developed in the U.S. around the turn of the century, others being located in Albany, Kansas City, Tulsa, Detroit, and Indianapolis, to name just a few.

A feature attraction during Electric Park's early years was a large harness racing track, which operated as Arlington Park prior to the amusement park's debut in 1896. A dance hall offering moonlit dances was a prime draw at the site as well. An impressive theater offered musical programs and motion pictures. One exciting, but unplanned, event at Electric Park occurred in the late 1890s when a lion escaped from the animal show in the casino building. Luckily, no one was hurt, as the lion was soon recaptured.[1]

The casino, which was opened in June of 1896, was perhaps the park's main gathering place. This large, two-story structure was situated on the infield of the half-mile racetrack, and included an auditorium that could hold at least 2000 guests who enjoyed the vaudeville performances. During intermissions, Edison's Vitascope showed moving pictures. Following a performance, the auditorium was cleared of chairs and couples would dance to the sounds of Professor Fischer's twenty-piece orchestra.[2] For its grand opening, under the guise of Charles E. Ford (owner of Ford's Opera House), one thousand reserved seats were placed directly in front of the stage. Tables and chairs covered the remaining space of the main floor.[3] Electric Park's appeal could also be attributed to the popular amusement devices that were soon added. The park offered a carousel, Ferris wheel, and boat rides in the early years.

Summer was not the only season at Electric Park. During the park's early years, Gus Fenneman would hold a winter carnival on the night of the first measurable snow in Baltimore. Billed as the "Snow Carnival of the Horsemen," it attracted up to two thousand men with horse-drawn sleighs to participate in a spin around the horse track. Judges awarded a substantial prize for the best equipment. Dancing followed the event, lasting late into the night.[4] Vaudeville and various new acts were a popular draw at Electric Park in the early 1900s. Comedians, acrobat acts, and storytellers were booked for week-long appearances. "Phroso" the mechanical doll appeared at the park in July of 1902, straight from New York City's Hammerstein's Roof Garden. The doll's appearance and movements were said to be so lifelike that many thought it was a real child.[5] Electric Park would benefit from a United Railways announcement in May of 1903 that reduced the fare to Electric Park, from any location in the city, from ten to five cents. Also, the Garrison Avenue line was extended all the way out to Electric Park, allowing for greater numbers of visitors to the park.[6]

Misfortune hit the park on January 6, 1904, when the landmark clubhouse, deck, and grotto were leveled in a swift-moving fire. Firemen from the Arlington Fire Company quickly arrived on the scene, but they could do nothing to save the tinder-like structure. The clubhouse portion of the building was a three-story, 90-foot × 60-foot structure; attractions housed on the first floor included a 10-pin bowling alley, bar, billiard tables, and cigar counter. A dance hall, café, and music stand comprised the second floor. The third floor housed a large kitchen and several dining rooms, complete with elaborate furnishings. Fenneman believed the total loss to be approximately $40,000; however, insurance was estimated to cover only about one third of the loss. The adjoining deck and grotto had occupied approximately 60 feet × 200 feet. It was reported that hundreds of curious Baltimoreans took sleigh trips to the park to view the charred remains.[7] Eager to rebuild, Fenneman had plans drawn up by the end of the month for an elaborate new clubhouse, deck and grotto. A target date for completion was set for May 1.

Grand opening for the 1904 season would be Decoration Day. The beginning of the vaudeville season kicked off on this day, along with a special 10-mile road race that started and ended at the rebuilt clubhouse. The Royal Band of Italy was booked to play concerts twice a day on the clubhouse deck. Two new attractions that were added included a new dance pavilion, and Ye Old Mille, whose boats would travel a circular course around the exterior of the casino building.[8] The $50,000 clubhouse opened on schedule, and featured 15,000 colored arc lamps and incandescent lights. The large one-story structure was reported to be 70 feet × 100 feet, built of steel and concrete. A dance area, stage, billiard room, and several dining rooms were in operation. The deck and roof garden were situated on the roof of the clubhouse; a stage and plenty of room for an audience were at the far end of one end of the roof. Four ornamental towers, two at either end of the building, were outlined in electric bulbs, and the roof garden, deck and grotto were bathed in a blinding white light.[9]

Published Vaudeville updates from May 1905 included details of Signor Phillipini and the Banda Savola appearance at Electric Park. The popular band was a nationally recognized act that had recently performed for an entire season at Atlantic City's Steel Pier.[10] Quite a few workmen were on hand during the spring months performing remodeling on the clubhouse. The billiards area in the clubhouse was being transformed into a large summer dining room. The old dining room was converted into a billiard and stag room. Drop lights were added over each of the dining tables, and paneled mirrors were placed throughout the eating area. Other improvements to the park included new private bathrooms at the swimming pool, and the "Streets of Venice." Similar to stage sets at Coney Island's immensely popular parks, Venice was placed near the main entrance at the boat lake. A New York artist was commissioned to create and paint several sets depicting an impressive re-creation of Venice.[11] The well-attended

"Irish Day" was a popular celebration during the first week of June that season. Bicycle and automobile races were held at the track. Motorcyclists were also matched up against racehorses as part of the day's racing activities to witness. Signor Phillipini and his Royal Crown Band performed two programs for the masses to enjoy. A new amusing attraction, the House of Trouble, was a popular draw.[12]

The most exciting time at Electric Park that season, however, was a mid–August incident in which Prince the lion (appearing at the park for Lafayette's "The Pearl of Bhutan" show) escaped from his handler while being transferred from his traveling cage to the performance stage. Frightened bathers at the swimming pool ran for shelter in the dressing rooms, save for one gentleman who remained trapped at the top of the high dive platform. As the lion attempted to ascend the platform ladder at the edge of the pool, Lafayette, the lion's trainer arrived just in time and was able to coerce the beast into his cage. Lafayette commented that this was in fact the second time the lion had escaped. In the previous scare, which had also been in Baltimore about five years earlier, Prince "devoured a valuable horse belonging to Mr. H.M. Little, the Howard Street liveryman."[13]

Constantly looking to improve his Electric Park, Fenneman divulged his ambitious plans for the upcoming summer season in January of 1906. Over $40,000 was allotted to contract with various amusement providers, in an effort to add modern amusements to his popular resort. A large space behind the casino building was designated to be the site of the new amusement devices. Fenneman also decided to remodel a portion of the clubhouse deck to include a two-story portable stage, complete with orchestra pit, and balcony and lodge seating.[14] However, Fenneman soon received and accepted an offer to sell Electric Park. In May of 1906, Fenneman sold the park to Philadelphia attorneys Crain and Hershey for approximately $115,000. The two then entered into a ten-year lease with Schanberger and Irvin just a few days later. These businessmen planned many improvements, including a "cuisine service" featuring traditional Maryland specialties.[15]

Frederick Schanberger was the manager of the Maryland Theater at that time and was closely involved with Baltimore entertainment man James Kernan. Kernan was well known in Baltimore's theater community, getting his start at the early age of 12, and worked at both the Academy and Auditorium theaters over the years. Upon signing the lease, Schanberger readied plans to travel to New York and line up exciting new attractions for Electric Park. With Coney Island's wildly successful Dreamland and Luna Park in mind, he set out to bring Electric Park up to the next level.

Schanberger and Irvin's Greater Electric Park would open on May 28. A Coney Island-inspired attraction—Fighting the Flames—would make its debut. Firemen entered a burning two-story building to rescue actors strategically placed at various windows, while others dowsed the flames. The popular Keith vaudeville company was booked to perform at the casino, which was enlarged and equipped with new scenery and lighting effects.[16] The half-mile track was converted for speed contests.[17] Two of the more thrilling acts to perform at Electric Park's open air venue that summer was Lunette, who performed a dangerous 1000-foot slide hanging only by her teeth, and a wrestling bout between the famous grappler Shad Link—billed as "the modern gladiator"—and an annoyed young bull.[18]

"The most pretentious of any exposition ever attempted in the South" was organized for the closing of Electric Park's 1906 season under the Travelers and Merchants Association, a local business organization. This event was intended to help the city along on the recovery from the Great Baltimore Fire. The Baltimore Home Product Exposition and Jubilee was held from September 8 to October 6. Several well-known attractions were booked for the grand event, including Mundy's Big Animal Show, Beachy's Airship, Bostock's Gondola's, Roltaire, a South African ostrich farm, the Red Dragon, Pharaoh's Daughter, Chiquita the living doll, a German Village, and the Baby Incubators.[19] An army of workmen descended on Electric Park to prepare for the exposition. Track from the Western Maryland Railroad station in Arlington was extended into Electric Park to allow old locomotives and other train cars to be transported and placed on display. The floor of the casino was ripped up and reinforced with large heavy timbers in order to support the weight of the Baltimore and Ohio Railroad exhibit.[20] Much fanfare was evident on the nighttime opening; the mayor and a local congressman gave speeches to the large crowd.

Electric Park's management may have been heavily influenced by the attractions on display at the Jamestown Exposition of 1907. Commemorating the 300th anniversary of the founding of the Jamestown colony, the exposition would operate for most of 1907, drawing less than expected numbers, however. Amusements which no doubt caught the eye of Baltimore amusement operators included Fairy Land, Baby Incubator, Hale's Tours of the World, Destruction of San Francisco, Paul Revere's Ride, miniature railway, Shooting the Chutes, and re-creations from battles at Manassas, Gettysburg, and the *Monitor* vs. the *Merrimac*. Many of these were situated on the "War Path," the designated midway area at the exhibition grounds.[21]

One of Electric Park's main attractions for the 1907 season was bandleader Vincent Del Manto's hair. Recognized as the youngest maestro in the city, the twenty-seven-year-old Italian with the long hair was constantly approached by young women. Many requested permission to pull on his hair, thinking that it must be a wig. Del Manto was a favorite of the ladies, who often left boxes of candy at the bandleader's podium.[22] Gennaro and the Royal Venetian Gondolier's Band also performed during the summer season.

This 1902 ad touts a Saturday performance of a concert band and acrobatic act at Electric Park (courtesy Hearst Newspapers LLC/*Baltimore News-American*).

An early view of the landmark Pavilion. Its open-air upper level was a great spot for a couple to share a meal.

Schanberger had 10,000 additional lights installed on the deck and park grounds, providing an unsurpassed nighttime view of an electric wonderland. A new theater and adjoining dining room were added to the clubhouse building, along with a bar. A return attraction was the famous Russian artist Suchorowsky's unique painting *Nana*, which was owned by the Sutton family at that time.[23] The casino's auditorium was outfitted to accommodate both dancing and roller skating. The skating session was open each evening from 7:30 to 10:00, with dancing following until 11:30.[24]

Attractions at Electric Park at that time included the large roller skating rink, the miniature railroad, and the Double Whirl, a revolving Ferris wheel-type ride.[25] One of the most popular outdoor features offered at the park that summer was the appearance of the daredevil Norin. Doused with gasoline, Norin would set himself afire, then leap from a high tower into a tank of water which had flames atop the surface.[26] At the end of the successful summer season, the park was the site of the county fair for the first time. An expanded horse race line-up, agricultural and livestock exhibits, and shows in the German Village were available to patrons.[27] In late October of 1907, Schanberger announced preliminary plans for the Electric Park Company, to be formed by businessmen from Baltimore, New York, and Cleveland. The company planned to take over Electric Park and transform it into a Luna Park. New York lawyer Holmes Jones was one of the key players of the new company, which reportedly would be capitalized at $1,000,000.[28]

An ugly confrontation played out in February 1908, when Schanberger sold the park to the new Electric Park Company, over which George Finch was appointed a receiver due to an unpaid bill. A race to Electric Park to claim possession of the place ensued between recently assigned general manager Holmes Jones and Finch, the new

A c. early 1900s photograph of Electric Park's Ferris wheel; notice the well-dressed crowd (*Baltimore Sun* photograph archives, Nathan Marsh collection).

receiver. They were met at the park by W.H. Gore, who had previously been secretary of the company. Gore believed that he had been appointed to represent the receiver. Jones was denied admission to the park, and a fight broke out, with pistols drawn. Police arrived on the scene and arrested Jones. Jones would claim that Schanberger had filed for a receiver, not because he couldn't pay an electricity bill, but in an attempt to remove Jones from the position of park manager. Schanberger countered with the statement that he had leased the park to Jones for $22,000, but only $5,000 had been paid.[29] The matter was resolved in May of that year when the courts ruled that the park be turned over to the Electric Park and Exhibition Company, which would take up the outstanding indebtedness of the present sublease. This essentially nullified a ten-year lease that Schanberger held, as well as his sublease to the Electric Park Company.[30]

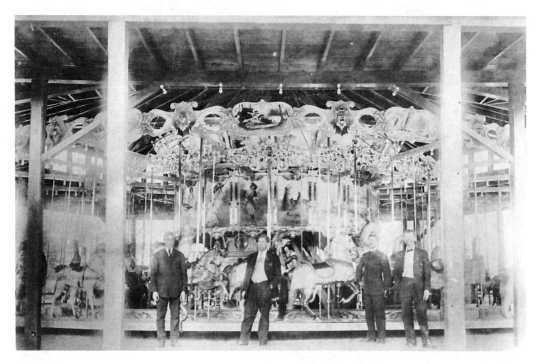

An early view of the Electric Park carousel (courtesy Historical Society of Baltimore County).

Vincent Del Manto and his band strike a pose on the casino deck in this 1907 photograph (*Baltimore Sun* photograph archives).

In April of 1908, the United Amusement Company, headed by Lloyd L. Jackson, entered into a fifteen-year lease with the Electric Park and Exhibition Company. Thomas L. Waters was president, and Harry Gilmor was secretary and treasurer of the United Amusement Company. Schanberger would stay on board and help achieve the company's vision of an amusement park on the scale of the renowned parks at Coney Island. Many attractions were included in the April announcement; a Scrambler (six cars on a platform which spins and moves the cars in all directions), the Helter Skelter bamboo slide, and a bicycle track were just the tip of the iceberg.[31]

General manager Max Rosen was also on hand to oversee the ambitious expansion plans that were drawn up for Electric Park. Architects Copeland and Dole were commissioned to design and construct the novel attractions for Electric Park. This pair had designed many of the larger buildings at the recent Jamestown and St. Louis exhibitions, and had a hand in the design of amusement parks in Boston, Providence, and New London. The on-site builder was Thompson V. Moore of New York, who was responsible for many Coney Island amusement park structures. It was reported that a workforce of over 600 men were on-site to ready the park by opening day. The summer of 1908 also saw the addition of a new ballroom, and it was hoped this would become one of the most popular dance venues south of Coney Island. To achieve this, the old casino was gutted and rebuilt, complete with a 100-foot × 200-foot dance floor. Concession stands were erected near the casino offering candy, refreshments, and curios to purchase.[32] Kennedy's Indian Show and Wild West Ranch was booked to present cowboy and Indians battles twice daily to the large grandstand crowd. Attractions unveiled in June included the carousel, Dazy Dazer roller coaster, the Infant Incubators—where the curious were willing to pay a quarter to view newborn babies under a doctor's care—and the Johnstown Flood.[33]

The Dazy Dazer roller coaster was constructed by the Breinig Construction Company of Terre Haute, Indiana. The ride covered approximately 9,000 square feet, and was 2900 feet long and 50 feet tall at its highest point.[34] The spectacle of the Johnstown Flood was re-created in a theatre several times daily. This attraction was first seen as one of the popular midway draws at the Pan-American Exhibition that was held in 1901 in Buffalo, New York. A scale model of Johnstown was built on an elaborate stage set, housed in a building approximately 112 feet across. A narrator would give a detailed talk describing the city, only to be interrupted by thunder and lightning effects. It wasn't long before all hell broke loose as a deluge of water flooded the set. Buildings seemingly collapsed, and Johnstown lay in ruins.[35] Backstage, a few switches and levers were reset, and the spectacle was ready to be presented to the next eager crowd. Another new attraction was the Awakening. A new large carousel was among the many additions to the midway.

Two additional new attractions erected in the park during this aggressive expansion were the $25,000 Shoot the Chutes ride, and the It. The thrilling Chutes ride consisted of 8–10 passenger wooden boats which were hauled up a high incline approximately 75 feet high, and released to speed down the slope ending in a wet splashdown in the lagoon. A boatman stood in the back of each boat and steered back to the loading station.[36] "'It' is a device in which the passengers ride in imitation eggshells, which are placed in a rapidly revolving circular disc. By the force of the moving disc, they are thrown off one tangent with the circular edge of the disc. Around the circular edge is a heavy railing constructed of rubber, which causes the eggshell-like cars to rebound back on the disc, only to be thrown against the rubber railing again."[37]

Electric Park became the center of attention in 1908 when Lincoln Beachy ascended from the park grounds en route to the first dirigible flight over Baltimore. The sausage-shaped aircraft was about 25 feet long, and was propelled by a small motorcycle engine. Beachy made it all the way downtown, landing on a rooftop at Lexington and Liberty streets.[38] About two years earlier, the boy aviator, just seventeen years of age, had attempted to fly his homemade dirigible to Washington, D.C., for a demonstration in front of 50,000 schoolchildren, with the goal to circle the Washington Monument. Strong winds kept him making the trip, however. Famed amusement park inventor/designer/builder Frederick Ingersoll, who had an interest in nearly 50 amusement parks at that time; including a chain of "Luna Parks," expressed interest in helping Beachy. When he learned of the difficulties encountered with the strong winds, Ingersoll replied, "That's all rot; I'll furnish the money if you furnish the airship that will tackle a 40-mile wind."[39] Beachy accepted the offer, and Ingersoll completed plans for two new flying machines. A later flight attempt from Park Heights Avenue by Beachy's brother Hillery resulted in the craft's rising approximately 30 yards in the air before crashing to earth. The landing gear was wrecked in the process.[40] Beachy would continue to experiment with various flying machines over the years, attaining wealth and fame as 'the man who owns the sky." Tragically, he would lose his life attempting a difficult upside-down maneuver in his stunt plane during the Panama-Pacific International Exposition in March of 1915, when he plunged into San Francisco Bay.

Other acrobatic events at Electric Park included a high dive act, and a hot air balloon ride. Fifty cents bought passengers a brief ascension in a wicker basket to several hundred feet, with a cable tethered to control the lift-off and descent.[41] Nelson, a high-wire acrobat; performed daring feats that season. He would wear a special costume outfitted with electric lightbulbs to illuminate him during nighttime performances.[42]

With the wildly popular park hosting large crowds sampling the large variety of new attractions, however, the surrounding neighborhood wasn't pleased with the elevated noise levels at the park. In June of 1908, the Law and Order League of Arlington was granted an injunction against the United Amusement Company from disturbing the neighborhood with its attractions. The group claimed that the noise emanating from the Wild West Show, switchback railway, and band performances was just too loud and had even interrupted local church services on Sundays. The group also alleged that the noise levels were depreciating property values in the area. Manager Rosen refuted the claims, stating that Baltimore citizens demand that places like Electric Park should be kept open on Sundays; he also suggested that the park's aggressive expansion served to increase property valuations in the area.[43]

The 1909 season saw several more improvements to Electric Park, which was still managed by Max Rosen. The boardwalk, which led guests through the grounds; was expanded and new concession buildings erected. The casino received a fresh coat of

The cover of a July 1904 newsletter/program from Electric Park. Details on the park's band concerts were included along with various ads from Baltimore businesses.

paint, and a new manager was hired from out of state to handle its catering and events. Rosen would throw the switch on opening night to illuminate the park with a reported 43,000 incandescent electric lights. A shaft of light that was produced could be seen for miles."[44] Attractions that debuted included a motion picture screen, the flying machine ride, and the "Human Laundry" funhouse-type attraction. Guests had to nav-

The Shoot-the-Chutes attraction allowed guests the opportunity to cool off during hot Baltimore summers (*Baltimore Sun* photograph archives).

Two men stroll along a path in Electric Park in this early 1900s view. The Johnstown Flood attraction can be seen in the background (*Baltimore Sun* photograph archives, photograph by Walter R. Miller).

Lincoln Beachey lifts off from Electric Park in the first attempt to fly a dirigible over Baltimore. The famed aviator was hired to appear at many amusement parks in the early part of the century to showcase his skills on his flying machine (*Baltimore Sun* photograph archives, photograph by William Boettinger).

igate moving platforms that were situated above water and get up and over steep barriers. This challenging walk-through culminated with the guest being pushed through a pair of giant rollers. A unique carousel debuted, replacing the existing one. It featured two separate revolving platforms, each rotating in a different direction, reportedly just the fourth such device to operate in the country.[45] Also, Professor Cockey held his annual grand May Ball, marking the opening of the dance hall for the season.[46]

Rosen would arrange for quite a few free attractions to appear at Electric Park that summer. Polar, the daredevil performing on a swaypole, and the Johnstone troupe; a comedy cyclists' group, drew crowds in June. Aeronauts Strobel and Hillery Beachey presented dirigible races during a two-week engagement. Their flying machines were outfitted with electric lights so spectators could enjoy nightly ascensions.[47] The Tub of Fun and Jingle Jungle rides were additions that summer as well. A swim instructor was hired on to help give lessons to kids, and the locker rooms were renovated.[48] In July, a German Festival night was held. Governor Crothers and Mayor Mahool were invited by President Walters of Electric Park aboard the streetcar *Lord Baltimore* for a journey to the park. Speeches were given and song and music provided as well.[49]

A view looking down a dusty Belvedere Street towards the rear of the park's pavilion shows a horse-drawn carriage sharing the street with an automobile. A trolley car can be seen towards the rear of the photograph (from the Maryland Rail Heritage Library, courtesy Baltimore Streetcar Museum).

The most popular meeting places in the park included the casino, which housed plays, vaudeville acts, band concerts, and boxing matches. The landmark pavilion was covered with electric bulbs, and provided a spectacular backdrop at night. It was a prime spot to drink a beer or two and enjoy the ever-popular crab sandwiches. Below the open-air roof was a popular restaurant with a cavernous appearance, which was sometimes referred to as "the Cave." By 1910, Electric Park was one of Baltimore's most popular entertainment destinations. Management installed a zoo and animal exhibition, and also offered free vaudeville and moving picture shows. Sparing no expense, new attractions including the Trip to the North Pole, the Oriental Village, and the Temple of Mystery were added to the park's expanding lineup of exciting diversions.[50]

Fenneman took control of the park again in September 1910 and planned to expand its offerings.[51] Quite a bit of money was put into the park for the spring opening. Advertised attractions debuting for the park's 1911 season included an open-air theater, the Squeezer, the Palace of Mystery, and the Circle Swing ride. Another new feature was the City of Destruction, an electrical display of the San Francisco earthquake.[52] Vaudeville performances were planned on the main deck, which could seat 5,000 people. A new hurricane deck overlooking the stage was erected; that could seat an additional 1,000.[53] Music was provided by the popular Royal Venetian Band. Fenneman also tried to restore the park to its original appearance. The boardwalk was removed, and the racetrack was refurbished; it offered harness and trotter racing, as well as the occasional auto race.[54]

Fenneman's success would be short-lived, however, as the Electric Park and Exhibition Company took possession over the park in June of 1911. Fenneman was reportedly not able to meet the demands of owning the company. (Fenneman had disposed of his interests in the Suburban Hotel the previous year.) The plan was for Electric Park to continue to operate as an amusement park for the remainder of the season.[55] It was sold again, in April of 1912, to a horse racing concern. The amusements at Electric Park would not open again, as horse racing would be the park's primary attraction over the next couple of years. Sadly, fighting poor health for the past several months, a despondent Fenneman attempted to take his own life on August 6, 1914, at his sister's home in Baltimore. Suffering from a razor cut to the throat, he was rushed to the hospital, where doctors were able to save him. Friends reported that financial setbacks had contributed to his depressed state. Fenneman previously had operated a restaurant in West Baltimore and an ice business before moving in with his sister.[56]

The sprawl of the suburbs soon began to encroach on the land occupied by Electric Park, however. The 24-acre park was sold for the final time in February of 1916 to the Electric Park Improvement Company for the sum of $100,000. A demolition agreement was reached shortly thereafter, with the idea of future real estate development in mind. August "Gus" Fenneman would pass away at the age of 63 at the home of his sister on December 23, 1917.[57]

8

Enchanted Forest

A seasonal highlight for many Baltimore and Washington children was a trip to the Enchanted Forest theme park. Opened in 1955 (the same year as Disneyland's debut), this popular family park initially occupied 20 acres and eventually encompassed approximately 50 acres. The result of a dream conceived by Howard E. Harrison, this land of make-believe would bring fairy tales to life, for all ages to enjoy. Harrison, a father of five at that time, created the $250,000 playland with the help of his son, Howard Jr., along with designer Howard Adler and Charles Brandt of the Bonnet and Brand architecture/engineering firm.[1] "There are no mechanical rides in the park," commented Howard Jr. just prior to the park's opening. "Instead, we hope the children will enjoy the make-believe figures that are before their eyes. I say children, but actually, we think that many grown-ups will enjoy seeing the famous old figures that they knew when they were children."[2] Admission for that first year was just 50 cents for children and one dollar for adults.[3]

Just a few steps beyond the impressive castle's drawbridge entrance awaited a fairy tale land of attractions for kids of all ages to experience. Scenes from several nursery rhymes and children's stories lined the wooded paths in the front portion of the Enchanted Forest, including the Three Little Pigs (who could be heard singing "who's afraid of the big bad wolf"), the Dish and the Spoon, and the Tortoise and Hare. Kids could go down the slide in the Old Woman's Shoe, peer through the windows of Little Red Riding Hood's house, and step into the mouth of Willie the Whale as he floated at the edge of the pond. Kids could also talk to Rapunzel, Peter Rabbit, and Humpty-Dumpty by dialing them up on an antique hand-crank telephone.[4] The park's attendance for that first shortened season was reported to be around 145,000 guests; including 20,000 just during the first week of operation.[5]

One of the park's main attractions was Cinderella's Castle. Kids could navigate the dim passageways and watch the animated story figures within each chamber. For the park's second season, the Merry Miller display was added along with an animated mouse band. (Little ones could also pet the bunnies in their egg-shaped home near the Merry Miller's house.) Returning guests found an expanded parking lot and additional picnic areas to handle the increasing crowds. In July, the large Robin Hood's Barn was opened to offer snacks and gifts to the public. The Gingerbread House also made its debut that summer. The unique architecture of the whimsical structure was inspiring. Fronted by an oversized ice cream cone, kids could grab a bite to eat inside, and parents could also choose to reserve the festive place for catered birthday parties.

Howard Adler, the man primarily responsible for the design of the Enchanted Forest's unique buildings and figures; owned Adler Display Studios. His company designed parade floats, television props, 3-D signs, and animated displays that could move and speak. Just a few short years after his initial work at the Enchanted Forest, he would move on to help conceive the popular Frontier Town Theme Park in Ocean City, Maryland. He designed the unique 22-foot-high horse and cowboy that would guard the entrance to Frontier Town, which is still in operation today.[6] As the park grew in popularity, mechanical attractions were added. You could arrive at the castle by riding Cinderella's Pumpkin Coach if you chose to do so. The large orange pumpkin coach was pulled by six white mice. Many a child's first driving experience was behind the wheel of the Antique Car ride. These gas-powered cars didn't run on a single rail like most versions of this theme-park staple. Instead, it ran between two guiding side-walls, which allowed for a fair amount of bumping between two cars as well as the guard-rails. Other fun attractions included the Crooked Man's House, and the Three Bears' House.

The rear portion of the park offered perhaps the most thrilling diversions. A large expansion in 1962 added a half-dozen captivating attractions that included Alice in Wonderland, Snow White and the Seven Dwarfs, Robinson Crusoe's Island, Mt. Vesuvius, Little

A c. 1977 brochure from the Enchanted Forest.

The Enchanted Forest is filled with exciting places to visit and familiar nursery rhyme characters to see. Watch the Three Pigs build their house of bricks and thwart the Big Bad Wolf and stop and pet the rabbits at the Easter Bunny's House. Listen to Willie the Whale laugh as you tickle him under the chin, and visit Goldilocks and the The Three Bears in their beautiful little house.

You will love the pony rides and the playground, as well as the delicious snacks served by The Merry Men in Robin Hood's Barn. Gift shops at both entrances are filled with special remembrances of a delightful day.
There are tame deer, goats, bunnies, ducks and a lamb that you can pet. A large free picnic area and plenty of free parking space are available.

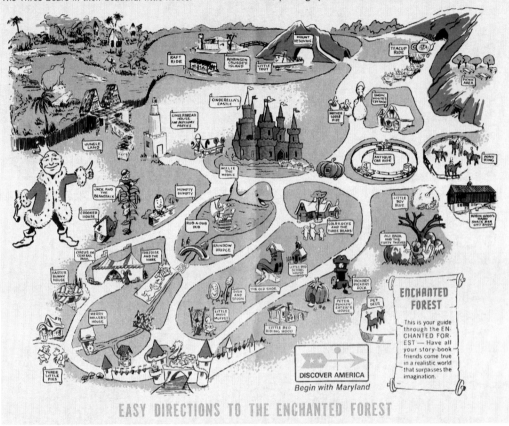

EASY DIRECTIONS TO THE ENCHANTED FOREST

Map detailing the layout of the Enchanted Forest. Quite a few unique attractions awaited children of all ages.

Toot, and the Mother Goose ride. An adventurous ride in the dark could be experienced on the unique Alice in Wonderland attraction. The voyage began on a Teacup ride resembling a miniature train, with alternating teacups and standard benches providing seating for guests. The lead car was a large teacup, where the conductor sat that pulled the rest of the "train." After a brief ride through the trees, the train entered an underground tunnel, and passengers would disembark to explore the mysterious world of Alice in Wonderland. Several tableaus could be enjoyed here, including the Mad Hatter's Tea Party, complete with the March Hare and the Dormouse.

The raft ride to Robinson Crusoe's Island fortress was a fairly quick trip; you could explore his island home and also spot his Man Friday in the lookout tower. But a tempting site awaited children just a few yards away. Kids could hurriedly exit the island fort by crossing over a footbridge to reach Mt. Vesuvius. The giant 65-foot slide down from

Two of the most popular attractions at the Enchanted Forest were Robinson Crusoe's island fortress (bottom), and Mt. Vesuvius (top), with its exciting high slide.

The Safari ride allowed guests to encounter "wild" animals up close.

Mother Goose leads her ducklings past Robin Hood's barn.

Kids could cruise around the park's lake on the Little Toot boat ride.

the top of Mt. Vesuvius was arguably the biggest thrill at the park. Arriving safely at the bottom of the slide, kids could run around to the rear of the mountain and slide over and over again. The Little Toot Tugboat ride was a fun cruise around the lake and through a tunnel that passed through the mountain. Kids and adults alike enjoyed the Snow White and Seven Dwarfs house, where a walk through the cottage led to a trip down into the diamond mine where the dwarfs sang while they worked. Along with the Mother Goose ride, where kids could ride in the goslings that followed Mother Goose through the park, these were experiences that provided additional cherished memories. Another favorite was the Safari Ride (also called Jungleland). Added around 1964, the jeep-propelled tram navigated through jungle-type terrain past primitive huts and friendly natives. Passengers' favorite scene on the tour tended to be the vine-clinging monkey, who would narrowly avoid a fast-approaching crocodile by "climbing" out of reach. Elephants, crocodiles, and other "wild" animals lurked around every bend.

The driving force behind the Enchanted Forest, Howard Harrison, passed away in April of 1967 at the age of 73. His family would continue to preserve the Enchanted Forest experience for the next generation of families. Adler Display Studios was on-site that same year to reproduce the Cinderella Story in 3-D animation inside Cinderella's castle. Additional diversions at the park included the Circus in Central Park. This was a miniature mechanized carnival housed under a circus tent comprising over 100,000 pieces. Also, a gentle water ride through a dark cave was in store for youngsters at the Ali Baba and the Forty Thieves attraction. Over two dozen 3-D Arabian Nights-inspired figures, including at least 14 of which were animated, could be found along the way during the search for Ali Baba's treasure.

At the end of a fun-filled day, it was naturally nearly impossible for a child to leave the Enchanted Forest without a stop at Robin Hood's Barn. The large red structure housed a snack bar and gift shop. Here, a vast collection of park souvenirs were available for the taking. Pennants, postcards, pencils, hats, plastic weapons, and numerous other trinkets were considered must-haves for departing kids. Of course, if you happened to be on a school field trip, teachers and chaperones tended to have a different view of these tempting toys, particularly if a nun caught sight of a child hurling a jungle spear at a schoolmate.

Yearly attendance at this venerable playland was around 300,000, during the peak of the park's popularity.[7] Although business remained strong, the mid-to-late 1970s presented some difficult challenges for park ownership. In 1974, the park was hit by a rash of after-hours thefts. Howard E. Harrison III worked with Howard County police to circulate 3000 fliers to houses in the nearby neighborhoods. The fliers clearly stated that park management would prosecute anyone arrested for theft of park property. This proved to be a successful deterrent for a few seasons, but the problem arose again in the summer of 1977. At least 15 burglaries took place between April and September that year. Thefts included stereo equipment, several hundred dollars in cash, 400 pounds of meats, and one-of-a-kind fiberglass figures. Mr. Harrison lamented that "all these burglaries are bad for business. We have no insurance coverage on some of the landmarks in the park, including the lighthouse and the wishing well where the thieves have struck. It's a gang of kids. We have problems with youth unemployment in the

Alice in Wonderland—postcard view. The trip to the underground fairyland offered children a view of the Mad Hatter's Tea Party and the Court of the Queen of Hearts.

The landmark castle at its new location at Clark's Farm in Ellicott City.

county, and you can see kids hanging around the streets at night with nothing to do. The thieves have nothing personal against us. The park is an attraction—a kind of place for kids. It is not like a gas station. They come in here and look for something they can sell or eat."[8]

The park did add two new attractions for the 1977 season; Huck Finn's fishin' hole and the Enchanted Auto Museum both debuted. Admission to the park at the time was still a very reasonable $1.50 for adults and children alike, with each mechanical ride costing only 30 cents. The park would continue to add new attractions when possible. The animated Chicken Little Trio, an eight-minute show featuring three animated characters, was presented at the Enchanted Forest Playhouse in the mid–1980s.

Sadly, with attendance dwindling, the park closed in 1988, and it was sold to JHP Development, Inc., who soon developed the Enchanted Forest Shopping Center on a portion of the park's land. JHP opened a family entertainment center, the Family Fun Jungle, in 1992. A portion of the park did reopen for one season in 1994, but no rides were in operation.[9] Many of the attractions remained but were deteriorating in the woods, attracting the occasional Enchanted Forest fan, longing for just one more glimpse of their favorite playland. The shopping center went on the market in 1997, and was purchased by the Mid-Atlantic Realty Trust.[10]

The Kimco Realty Corporation purchased the Mid-Atlantic Realty Trust Company

A fruit column very similar to this one (from Philadelphia's 1903 Cannstatter festival) was the centerpiece of the annual fall Cannstatter Volkfest in Baltimore.

in 2003, thus acquiring the park and shopping center. They kindly donated Cinderella's Pumpkin Coach to an interested group of workers in the strip's Coldwell Banker office, who restored the almost forgotten attraction. It was sold at the group's annual charity auction to two Essex businessmen for $2,300.[11] An agreement was later reached with Martha Clark to relocate the pumpkin coach to Clark's Elioak Farm in Ellicott City. Kimco realized the importance of retaining the Enchanted Forest's artifacts in Howard County and allowed the Clarks to remove almost all of the Enchanted Forest pieces to their farm.[12] The restored coach is now available for children to play in at Clark's Elioak Farm.

Fans of the park have formed preservation groups in recent years in an attempt to keep the park's rich history alive. The Friends of the Enchanted Forest and the Enchanted Forest Preservation Society have both lobbied to preserve the Enchanted Forest site.

9

Frederick Road Park

One of the most obscure of Baltimore's old amusement parks was Frederick Road Park, which enjoyed a brief yet intriguing lifespan. It was situated at what today is the meeting point of Frederick Avenue and Hurley Avenue, across from the Mt. Olivet Cemetery. Originally the residence of Mr. Jacob Lerian, it was recognized as one of the handsomest sites in Baltimore.[1] Frederick Road Park was initially referred to as "Cannstatter Park." This spot was, for a time, the site of the annual Cannstatter Volks-fest, a popular German fall celebration noted for its traditional giant wooden monument some 30 to 40 feet in height, which was adorned with fruit and other produce. The monument served as a symbol of thanks for a successful harvest season. The fruits and vegetables were replaced during the nearly week-long festival as they became rotten, and any fresh produce remaining at the end of the celebration was donated to local charities.

Many booths and food stands were erected for this fall festival, offering carnival-type diversions and cold beer, drinks, sausages and sauerkraut. A dining hall was on hand to feed the masses. Several types of crab dinners, Maryland fried chicken, and sour beef and dumplings were popular items on the menu.[2] German doughnuts and other goodies could be sampled while one walked through the various amusements. The first volksfest held at the Frederick Road location was in 1914; for the previous seven years it had been located at West End Park. Renovations were conducted at the park to help create a reproduction of parts of the German city Cannstatt for that first festival.[3]

Christian Riegger, a contributing writer to the *Baltimore Sun*, related in one of the *Sun*'s popular "I Remember …" columns the spectacle of the Cannstatter festival: "One of the attractions which fitted in perfectly with the carefree tone of the festival— was a two-story, box-like milling contrivance called the "youth machine." Its operators would coax some old lady out of the crowd and ask her to climb the stairs to the top of the machine and enter a door there. After the old lady disappeared, the machine produced a series of squeaks, grinding noises, humming and whirring. A minute or two later, the lower door of the machine would open, and out would walk a beautiful young girl. The crowd would howl with laughter.[4]

Frederick Road Park was formally opened by a local group of businessmen, the Frederick Road Park Company, in 1915. Frederick Road quickly established itself as a popular family park, serving the western and southwestern sections of Baltimore. Located in a heavily populated middle-class residential area, it was also served by three city streetcar lines which ran alongside the park. The dance floor afforded a good time for just 5 cents a dance.[5] The Monastery Parish at Irvington held its popular annual picnic here for several years.[6] A popular athletic tournament headed by the Philadelphia District of the German Turn Vereiners was held for several years also. Hundreds of athletes from that city, as well as Baltimore, Washington, Newark, and Jersey City, gathered to compete in various activities, including gymnastics, running, shot-put, pole vaulting, and other track events.[7] For a time, starting around 1918, the site was known as Monumental Park.

In August of 1919, Monumental Park hosted Hibernian Day, which attracted a large crowd numbering an estimated 15,000. Politicians and Irishmen alike enjoyed the picnic and amusements that were offered. The Sons of Irish Freedom sponsored a booth and handed out the flag of the Irish Republic. Irish dancing demonstrations rounded out the evening.[8]

In 1919, the Frederick Road Park Company, headed by Arnold Aiman of the Philadelphia Toboggan Company (PTC), entered into a lease with the Cannstatter Land and Park Company and began developing an amusement park. A thrilling roller

A rare view of the classic three-row PTC Carousel (#52), which was delivered to Frederick Road Park in 1920. It operated in at least three other amusement parks during its lifetime (from Philadelphia Toboggan Coasters, Inc./Tom Rebbie, president/CEO).

A panoramic view of some of the park's attractions, including the Circle Swing, Coaster Dips, and Old Mill (from Philadelphia Toboggan Coasters, Inc./Tom Rebbie, president/CEO).

coaster, the Deep Dipper, or Coaster Dips, debuted for the 1920 season. A work by famed designer/builder John Miller (and built by PTC), the ride utilized some of the park's hilly terrain to include an exciting double-dip. It was one of the largest coasters in the city and commanded 10 cents per ride. Other attractions erected in the early 1920s included the Dance Pavilion, the Dodgem, the Hilarity Hall funhouse, a bowling alley, a penny arcade, the Old Mill Chute ride (also referred to as Lovers' Lane), the Circle Swing, the Whip, a rifle range, and other games. The park was also fortunate to operate a Philadelphia Toboggan Company carousel (PTC #52). This classic subsequently appeared at several other amusement parks, including Gwynn Oak Park.

George Gaul, billed as "Baltimore's best trombonist," occasionally performed with his jazz orchestra in the dance pavilion. A special annual treat for public school children each June was a large picnic hosted by Mayor Broening. Tens of thousands of children celebrated the end of the school year at Frederick Road Park at these picnics, held over several days with free tickets distributed to them to enjoy the exciting rides. Twenty thousand school children crowded the park during the rainy outing in June of 1922. The local police captain, who had brought eight of his patrolmen to maintain order, soon had to call for additional reinforcements.[9]

Just prior to the start of the 1923 season, Frederick Road Park's string of bad luck began. An early April fire ruined the Old Mill ride and partially destroyed the Coaster Dips. The cause was thought to be a discarded match or cigarette. Five firemen were hurt in the $100,000 blaze, as they were caught under a section of the roller coaster as it collapsed. Members of Baltimore's Cross Country Club, who had just finished a footrace with its finish line in the park, formed a bucket brigade to help prevent the spread of the fire.[10] However, the park did manage to open for the season on schedule a week later. Park manager C.D. Bond made good on their promise to rebuild what they claimed to be the fastest roller coaster in the country, to now be renamed the Wildcat, and had it up and running within two months' time.

The Frederick Road Park Company (one of many PTC subsidiaries) decided to go ahead and formally purchase the park from the Canstatter Company for the sum of $500,000 in May of 1923.[11] They planned to erect a plant that would build amusement devices on the site. In July, a second fire wrecked the open-air theater, but was brought under control before it could spread. Luckily, the fire started before the park was opened for business.

After the 1923 season's end, PTC employee George P. Smith put together a report on the park's overall status and forwarded it to the board of directors. It painted mostly a grim picture of the parks' physical state. General park maintenance had not been undertaken on a regular basis, and the parks' infrastructure was beginning to decline. The Dodgem cars and funhouse were both in poor shape. The Whip platform and the Airplane swings, as well as the older sections of the roller coaster, also required major repairs. One of Smith's recommendations was, "If we are to improve the park and put it on a real competitive basis we will require the expenditure of from $35,000 to $45,000

A view from the Coaster Dips shows the twisting layout of the Old Mill, under construction in this early 1920s view (from Philadelphia Toboggan Coasters, Inc./Tom Rebbie, president/CEO).

Crowds lining up to traverse the Hilarity Hall Funhouse (from Philadelphia Toboggan Coasters, Inc./Tom Rebbie, president/CEO).

Passengers enjoy a thrilling drop on the Coaster Dips (from Philadelphia Toboggan Coasters, Inc./Tom Rebbie, president/CEO).

Opposite bottom: Ecstatic riders coast back into the station of the Coaster Dips in this early 1920s shot. Note the second coaster train sitting in the storage shed just to the right of the track (from Philadelphia Toboggan Coasters, Inc./Tom Rebbie, president/CEO).

at least. The wisdom of such an expenditure is the serious question. The investment of $50,000 in a good coaster in a suitable location in my opinion (would) net a better return. Baltimore, in my opinion, is overparked and until some of the others close I believe it would be better to mark time, either operating on that basis or leasing."[12] Smith may have had a valid point, as far as the number of Baltimore parks in operation at that time. At least 6 local parks were open for business, as well as several other beachside parks. To survive in such a competitive market required consistent infusions of cash to satisfy the public's increasing appetite for thrills and entertainment.

To this end, the park's last season of operation would be 1924. The Philadelphia Toboggan Company dismantled several of the rides after the fall closing and had no plans to open the park for the 1925 season. A string of nearly a dozen fires in 1925 helped seal the short-lived park's fate. Arson was suspected in nearly every case. A small fire was set under the dance hall in February. A fire in the field next to the roller coaster was set in March, followed shortly by a blaze set to one of the park's fences. The largest fire struck on April 15 and gutted half a dozen buildings, causing an estimated $60,000 in damage. Park assistant manager Benjamin Esley blamed the local police for the latter fire, as he had pleaded for a uniformed officer to be positioned on

The comical exterior of the funhouse was inspiring (from Philadelphia Toboggan Coasters, Inc./Tom Rebbie, president/CEO).

The charred remains of the Coaster Dips after the April 1923 fire. Note two Baltimore landmarks towards the top of the picture: the old St. Agnes Hospital to the left, and the St. Mary's Industrial School (later the Cardinal Gibbons School) to the right (from Philadelphia Toboggan Coasters, Inc./Tom Rebbie, president/CEO).

the park grounds to help deter further incidents. Destroyed in the fire were the dance hall, bowling alleys, penny arcade, rifle range, and funhouse.

The park land was sold on August 13, 1925, to a local developer, a transaction believed to be in the neighborhood of $55,000. A number of two-story brick buildings would soon replace the charred amusements, closing the chapter on Frederick Road Park's brief existence.

10

Gwynn Oak
Amusement Park

Perhaps the best remembered and most beloved of Baltimore's amusement parks, Gwynn Oak Park, opened its gates in 1894. The real estate can trace its roots back to a land purchase in 1892 by William Schwartz and Nicholas Smith. Their intentions were to build houses on the large plot of land but soon realized that without a trolley line extending to the area their plan might not be feasible. They opened the Gwynn Oak, Walbrook, and Powhatan Railroad, which ran past their 65-acre park-land. Realizing the potential for the beautiful lakeside setting, Schwartz and Smith formally opened Gwynn Oak Park on July 1, 1894. A pavilion near the railway landing, a few booths for picnickers, picnic tables, and the lake with its surrounding woods were the trolley park's only offerings in the early years. A few problems were experienced on opening day with the new cars and tracks, but delays were held to a minimum.[1]

In spite of quickly developing a good reputation for being a "dry" family resort, Gwynn Oak encountered problems with maintaining Sunday operations. Just three weeks after opening, members of local Presbyterian and Methodist churches registered protests with the county commissioner and sheriff to "request that the Sabbath be properly respected."[2] A ballroom was soon added, the house band directed by John D. "Professor" Farson for many years. Gwynn Oak hosted the first of a series of jousting tournaments in September of 1894. Various prizes were awarded to the "knights," including best-equipped knight. Jousting involved riders on horseback navigating a course where suspended rings could be "speared" using a lance. Jousting is still recognized as the state sport of Maryland. The dance pavilion hosted the crowning of the queens and maids after the riding competition had completed.[3]

The Baltimore Traction Company took over the line in December of 1894. Schwarz would stay on the board of directors, but Smith resigned. Gwynn Oak Park was now under the control of the traction company. The park had recently expanded by 25 acres to a total of 76 acres, with the idea of additional park improvements being considered.[4] In February of 1895, at the annual meeting of stockholders for the Baltimore Traction Company, President Frank Brown would present his yearly report to the assembly, and it offered more than a hint of a profitable future. Noting that twenty-four miles of railway had been constructed or purchased over the last year, Brown declared:

> It is well recognized that the business of the city railroads can be largely increased during the summer months by furnishing resorts and amusements for the public. The Traction

Company is now the owner of Gwynn Oak Park, which has recently been purchased, and which is one of the most attractive resorts in the suburbs of the city. Next season, we will offer to the public additional amusements which must attract, and, we believe, add largely to the company's receipts. In the constructions of track in 1894, one of the most important additions was the building and extension of the Edmondson Avenue line from the eastern city limits, on Fayette Street, across the city to the western boundary in the vicinity of Walbrook, connecting at that point with the to the Gwynn Oak, Walbrook, and Powhatan Railroad, which furnishes direct connection to Gwynn Oak Park.[5]

In March 1895, President Brown announced the Traction Company's plans to run "palace trolley cars," to be leased for group trolley parties to Gwynn Oak. Music and luncheons were provided on board for these special outings. Brown also announced his hopes to establish a military encampment on recently purchased property at the park. Large stands were to be erected to allow spectators to view morning and nightly drills. It was noted that after the drills the men would be given the opportunity to take a bath in the lake, where numerous bathhouses were already under construction.[6] Later that month, Brown sent a letter to the county commissioners to warn them of any applications that they might receive for the sale of liquor in the general vicinity of Gwynn Oak Park: "You are no doubt aware that it is the intention of the Traction Company to keep this park as a resort for ladies and children, and we will not allow any spirituous or fermented liquors to be sold on the property."[7] Brown would go on to report later that summer that he intended to introduce legislation to the next Maryland legislature that citizens living along the Gwynn Oak and Parkville trolley lines be allowed to reach Baltimore city without having to change cars:

> It is an annoyance to have to change cars anywhere, and we frequently have complaints of the change which has to be made at Walbrook for Gwynn Oak and at Francis and Retreat Streets for Pimlico and Pikesville. But it is not generally known that we have to take this step by law. The law on the subject expressly says that the street railway can only charge five cents for a passenger upon any one car within the city limits.... We would lose money if we were to carry passengers for five cents through from Patterson Park to Gwynn Oak or Pimlico, and so we have to run two separate cars and charge five cents upon each of them. The law was intended for the old city limits. We have a much larger territory in the city now, and so many persons live in the outlying districts that conditions are quite different.[8]

Like many trolley parks developed around the turn of the century, Gwynn Oak offered a wooded, tranquil setting; affording a relaxing getaway from the stifling summer heat of the city. Boating and fishing were popular activities on the lake. In time, tennis courts and athletic fields were available for picnickers. Ample picnic grounds drew throngs of guests, who could marvel at high-wire acts, balloon ascensions, or enjoy a show at the park's amphitheater. The large, rustic dining café catered to those park-goers who didn't bring a picnic meal, and it sold ice cream as well.

Baltimore residents celebrating July 4th in 1896 were treated to a double balloon ascension, manned by Jack Reynolds and Madame Zitta. An all-day lawn concert was presented as well.[9] The Flying Horses, an early carousel, was in place by 1897. Smith and Schwarz would sell 50 acres of their original land purchase to the Washington and Baltimore Land Company in June of 1898 for just over $20,000. The street railway company decided in August of 1898 to apply some changes to the Edmondson Avenue line to route every other streetcar up to Gwynn Oak Park. The company had booked a circus at the park that summer and was planning on a large increase in patronage.[10] One of the unique attractions offered for the 1899 season was Knechle and Linders Wonderful Firegraph, which provided moving pictures featuring the "most realistic fire scene; also, the Sunset Limited Express, going 70 miles an hour, etc."[11] The Passion Play pictures also appeared at the park for a week-long exhibition at the beginning of the summer.

In June of 1900, the fraternal order of the Royal Arcanum hosted a picnic to celebrate their 23rd anniversary. Farson's Military Band gave an afternoon concert, and several sporting events were held, including a baseball game, sack race, tug-of-war, foot races, climbing the greased pole, and a tub race in the lake.[12] The café and confectionary stand were upgraded for the 1902 season; the shooting range, photo gallery and swings were also ready for patrons to enjoy. A covered stage was in place at this point to present short vaudeville features free of charge. During this time, admission to the dance pavilion was free during the afternoon hours. However, the price for night-time dancing was 25 cents for men; women were admitted free of charge.[13]

In May of 1904, the first annual Memorial Day gathering of the Patriotic Order Sons of America were held at the park. Various races and a baseball game were held. A program of songs and recitations, including Lincoln's address, soon followed.[14] Arrangements were made with architects Simonson and Pietsch to place a new carousel and building at the park in the spring of 1906. The carousel was said to be one and a half stories tall, and approximately 78 feet square. The pair also added a large 25 by 50-foot addition to the dancing pavilion.[15] A 1906 *Street Railway Journal* article spoke of the park's high-class patronage, numbering between 4000–5000 guests on an average Sunday afternoon: "Rules were strict during this time. Cigarette-smoking women were taboo. Dancing partners had to keep a certain distance between them or get off the floor. The lancers, waltz, and quadrilles were the fad. The sight of a bottle of beer or whiskey flask was enough to send the park attaches into quick action, except on such occasions as German Day."[16]

The Improved Order of Red Men held their reunion at the park in July of 1907. The large gathering of Indian tribes presented a unique program, including the capture and torture of a spy, arranged by members of the Potomac Tribe No. 51; the presentation of the Indian play *Oneta, the Little One*, by members of the Tecumseh Tribe No. 108; and the capture and saving of Capt. John Smith.[17] Vaudeville acts that appeared that summer included comedy act Prince and Diston, who spoke in a German dialect, and Walters and Everts, Hebrew humorists.[18] Visitors to Gwynn Oak in 1909 were treated to the thrilling high-wire performances of Calvert, who performed difficult stunts in mid-air that many could not do standing on solid ground. Calvert appeared at the park over a period of several seasons, frightening crowds while performing on a wire 100 feet above the ground.

Two exciting attractions would debut at Gwynn Oak for the 1910 season. The Deep Dip Racer, a double racing roller coaster built by John Miller, offered a thrilling ride through the treetops at a cost of 10 cents. Thomas Luther (T.L.) Stine's spinning Double Whirl ride was also added. Stine was a dealer and operator of carousels and had ride concessions in many Maryland resorts; including Gwynn Oak, Woodland Beach, Altoona Beach, and Tolchester Beach. His unique Double Whirl ride operated at Gwynn Oak for approximately five seasons. A new pony circle was added, with the ponies supplied from a nearby farm.[19] During that successful season, two vaudeville shows were offered daily. A *Sunday Sun* ad from May 1910 boasted of several Gwynn Oak offerings: "Baltimore's Garden Spot. Family Day Today. Get them together—bring them all out. 2 sacred concerts by Prof. Farson's military band. A "sensational bicycle act—75 feet in mid-air" was the special attraction for the week.[20] Other amusements in place at that time included the miniature train and the Aero Swing, which whirled riders at dizzying speeds. Under the leadership of James Pratt, the park was recognized in 1911 as having one of the finest dance floors in the United States.[21] The four Due sisters were booked that summer to provide swimming and diving exhibitions in the lake.

Balloon ascensions were becoming popular draws to amusement parks at that time. Gwynn Oak booked popular balloonist Fred Owens for a week in June 1912 to perform his daring feats twice daily. The balloon would ascend with a parachute and cannon in tow, Owens carefully placed inside the cannon. After reaching a dizzying height, he would shoot himself from the cannon and descend to safety under the parachute.[22] Another popular events of the 1912 season was a nighttime carnival held on the lake. Various lights and lanterns were placed around the lake, with a large, well-lit electric fountain in place in the lake's center. All of the park's rowboats were outfitted with lanterns; the flotilla of two dozen boats circled the lake as visitors gazed in awe. An estimated crowd of 12,000 was on hand and enjoyed a fireworks exhibition at the end of the evening.[23]

The United Boys Brigade held their annual field day exercises as part of a large program for the park's spring opening in 1913. Gwynn Oak presented the play *Hiawatha* that same year. The outdoor pageant featured Native Americans, some actually floating in canoes down the stream that separated the audience from the performers.[24] The production received excellent reviews from impressed viewers. June 12, 1913, marked a special record-breaking banquet at Gwynn Oak which featured an outdoor dinner and cabaret show. Attendees from the Advertising Club Convention held at the Fifth Regiment Armory earlier in the day were shuttled to the park via special trolley cars. Reportedly, it took sixty full carloads to deliver all of the guests. Thousands strolled through the park grounds, nearly all wearing the customary badge and ribbon decorations that were distributed for notable group outings. A circular stage was erected on the baseball field with tables arranged around it, and thousands of light bulbs were strung above the tables. Fireworks were presented after the dinner, at which over two dozen uniformed policemen helped maintain order. The cabaret show followed to close out the night's festivities.[25] "Toyland" was the theme at the park for a week in August. Toys were handed out to children at all of the rides, including the goat and pony tracks and the motorboat ride.

Gwynn Oak Park was decorated in fresh green and white paint for the 1914 season. The popular rowboats were rehabbed and ready for picnickers, and the perennial Farson's band supplied the soft orchestra music for guests.[26] Park managers during this period were Herb Walters and Daisy Stine, a married couple who helped the park grow in the early 1900s. Ms. Stine was the daughter of T.L. Stine.

Aeronaut George Owens presented a unique aerial display at Gwynn Oak in July of 1916. Simulating the aerial bombing that was underway by European aviators in World War I, Owens twice a day, dropped harmless bombs from his biplane on safe areas designated within the park with the nighttime performances carried out with illuminated bombs.[27]

New offerings at Gwynn Oak's 1920 season included a roller coaster that replaced the original double racing coaster. Other attractions advertised for that summer included the Kentucky Derby, Walking Charlie, Whip, Ferris wheel, Sea Wave, and bowling alleys. The daring Azimas Brothers displayed their Whirling Propellors acrobatic act 50 feet in the air.

Gwynn Oak's 27th season in 1921 was marked by a series of improvements intended to offer guests an even more enjoyable visit. New roads were constructed, and additional landscaping was added, along with the placement of the ever important park benches and new picnic pavilions. New tennis courts were also built, while a new amusement device—the Frolic—was installed. The old restaurant building was renovated, with a new paint scheme and pink and yellow shades covering the lights. Chicken and seafood dinners were just $1.25 at that time. A complete list of amusements in operation for the 1921 season included the Double Dip Racer, Whip, Sea Wave, carousel, Palmist, shooting gallery, goat and pony track, bowling, baseball, swings, and photographer.[28] Sadly, the dance pavilion was destroyed in a June 1921 fire. Plans were immediately drawn up by United Railways for a larger pavilion to be erected near Gwynn's Falls, in the center grove section of the park.

GWYNN OAK PARK, BALTIMORE

Early postcard view of the trolley crossing over the bridge at Gwynn Oak Park.

Postcard view of the rustic dining room.

The park attracted much local attention that same year when park superintendent John Cullen persuaded United Railways to purchase an elephant as a park attraction for the kids to enjoy. At that time, local schoolchildren were pleading with City Hall to bring an elephant to the zoo at Druid Hill Park. Mayoral candidate Howard Jackson decided to include Mary Ann the elephant as part of his campaign agenda, and promised a permanent home for her at Druid Hill Park if he were elected. After defeating incumbent William Broening, he made good on his promise, as United Railways donated the animal to the zoo.[29]

The United Railways Company would occasionally gauge the success of a new attraction that they placed at their Bay Shore Park, and then arrange to purchase that same ride or game to operate across town at Gwynn Oak. The crowd-attracting Balloon Racer game soon appeared at Gwynn Oak, one year after opening at Bay Shore in 1921. A street car (the Jolley Trolley of the Monkeyshine Line) very similar to the one installed at Bay Shore was added to the kids' playground in 1922. The popular Custer Cars would debut at Gwynn Oak in 1926 after enjoying earlier success at Bay Shore.

Several improvements were made to Gwynn Oak prior to the 1922 season opening. Besides a new dance floor to replace the one that burned, a soda fountain and checkroom were installed towards the front of the park, and the nearby ladies' rest room was upgraded to accommodate mothers with small children. The lunchroom expanded to include a small dining room. Also, the men and women's checking areas in the dance pavilion were enlarged.[30] An exhibit of live monkeys appeared at Gywnn Oak for the kids to enjoy during the summer of 1923.

The 1920s and early 1930s proved to be a difficult period for the park, however, as

The old Cagney steam train enjoyed a sprawling layout around the park (courtesy Historical Society of Baltimore County).

The Double Dip Racer coaster began operation in 1909. It offered guests a thrilling ride for just one dime (courtesy Hearst Newspapers LLC/*Baltimore News-American*).

A trolley rounds a bend outside of Gwynn Oak Park (courtesy the Baltimore County Public Library).

it suffered through two major fires, the Great Depression, and a decrease in attendance. John D. Farson managed the park for several years during the 1920s, and was succeeded by D.C. Turnbull. In 1930, a large group of citizens with the backing of the city council formally requested that the municipality purchase Gywnn Oak Park for use as a public park. A large gathering was held in May at Forest Park High School, spearheaded by community groups from Howard Park, Gwynn Oak Uplands, Gywnndale, Arlington, Forest Park, and Larchmont. They suggested that the park and surrounding valley be purchased using the Leakin Estate fund.[31] Their request was not granted, although it was presented several more times over subsequent years.[32]

Three hundred local residents signed a petition in May of 1934 objecting to the issuance of a liquor license to sell beer in Gwynn Oak Park. The Baltimore County Liquor License Board was in the process of reviewing an application from a Mr. Walter Joyner to obtain a license to sell beer in the park. The board decided that the park owner, United Railways, would have to petition the board for the request to move forward. Siding with the local residents, the United stated that they did not expect to seek a beer license for the park. The residents signing the petition, however, added that "they had no objection to the sale of beer on days when Germanic groups held their outings. These groups, it was asserted, knew how to handle their beer."[33] Several thousand people attended the two-day picnic of the Independent Retail Grocers' Association

Concession and game stands were shaded by Gwynn Oak's ample supply of trees (courtesy Hearst Newspapers LLC/*Baltimore News-American*).

T.L. Stine's Double Whirl ride. Stine placed many of his attractions and concessions at several Maryland amusement parks, including Gwynn Oak and Tolchester Beach (courtesy Historical Society of Baltimore County).

at the park in August that year. Activities included vaudeville shows, a baseball game, and fireworks.[34]

A late season picnic in September of 1934 attracted 15,000 people of German birth or descent. This was the annual outing of the Independent Citizens Union of Maryland, which comprised mostly all the German singing organizations in the city. Relay running teams made up of members from the First German Sport Club, the Vorwaerts Turnverein, and the German Turnverein were driven a distance of five miles from the park where they were given a letter of greetings from the German ambassador. This special letter was then delivered to the main podium at the picnic by the relay runners.[35] Longtime Gwynn Oak bandleader and dance hall manager John D. Farson would pass away in late December 1935. The "Professor" had spent forty-one years managing the dance floor at Gwynn Oak. He left behind a wife, a daughter, and two grandchildren.[36]

The Baltimore Transit Company (which replaced the United Railways and Electric Company in 1935) leased the park to Arthur B. Price in 1936. Price, a local movie house operator and city councilman at that time, hired several workmen to renovate and redecorate much of the park, including rebuilding the dam. Several name bands provided music for the ballroom dancers for the 1936 season.[37] Over 23,000 German-Americans enjoyed the annual German Day celebration at the park in September of 1937. However, two "hangovers" were reported the following day. Evidently someone gained entrance to the groundskeeper's home and made off with $1,000 belonging to the park's concessionaires that was stored in a locked strong box. In addition, more than 70 motorists had been issued parking citations during the festival, for illegally parking in restricted zones in the nearby neighborhood.[38]

Several new attractions were unveiled for the park's May 1939 opening. New roadways were constructed and buildings redesigned to accommodate larger crowds. Additional parking spaces were added as well. It was reported that Mal Hallett's band would be the first in a series of recording artists to perform at the park that summer.[39] In November of 1939, a fire destroyed the park's ballroom, reportedly the state's largest. The loss was estimated at $30,000 and was not insured.[40] (A carelessly discarded cigarette may have been the culprit.) The ballroom had recently been enclosed in glass to allow the dance hall to operate during the cold winter months. A few rooms, including a machine shop, had also been constructed underneath the hall to store machinery and other park equipment. These rooms were a total loss as well. The large Spanish-style structure which could hold up to 1000 dancing couples, was quickly rebuilt; this would be the fondly remembered Dixie Ballroom. Many Baltimore residents attended dances at the park, where nationally acclaimed "Big Bands" like Benny Goodman, Tommy Dorsey, Glenn Miller, and Artie Shaw played. Various ethnic celebrations were held there over the years, including German, Polish, Irish, Lithuanian and Italian festivals.

Despite war-time restrictions, Gwynn Oak managed to add new attractions during this period. The grand 4th of July celebration in 1942 featured Jungle Land, presented by Captain Roland Proske, the distinguished animal trainer. Captain Proske offered an impressive display of wild animals, including Bengal tigers, a lion, a chimp, monkeys, alligators, and a selection of exotic birds. The Dobas family, an aerial acrobatic team, was on hand to present their amazing high-wire act. The holiday crowds also enjoyed the park's latest amusements—a miniature railroad and the magic carpet funhouse.[41] The miniature train came to Gwynn Oak from Pen Mar Park, located in the Catoctin Mountains in western Maryland. This fondly remembered coal-burning steam train is believed to have operated from 1904 to 1943 at Pen Mar. One of the repeat performers at the park during the late 1930s to early 1940s was Bernice Kelly's Circus Review, which consisted of performing ponies, dogs, and monkeys and was a free show for all to enjoy.

The summer of 1943 was extremely profitable for Baltimore's amusement parks, in spite of wartime restrictions. The parks were able to overcome a cold and wet spring which would lead to many sunny, hot days in achieving the best summer season in a decade. Park men credited not only the weather, but also the park's accessibility, and the excellent streetcar service for contributing to a 20–25 percent increase in attendance over the previous year. Park operators estimated that approximately $4,000,000 was spent at the fun parks for the 1943 season, with servicemen comprising a large portion of the crowds. Concessionaires would go on to estimate that 10,000,000 hot dogs and 1,200,000 gallons of soft drinks were consumed at Baltimore's amusement parks that summer.[42]

Arthur Price exercised an option and formally purchased the park in 1944 as the park quietly celebrated its 50th birthday season. The park's formal opening for the 1944 season reportedly drew a record-breaking crowd of 25,000, who enjoyed the rides and a pop concert. Price introduced Mayor McKeldin, who presided over the grand opening.[43] The 1945 NAAPPB Buyer's Guide listed Gwynn Oak's offerings: twelve major rides, two kiddie rides, one walk-through, nine games, seven refreshment stands, a ballroom, two penny arcades, a shooting gallery, and a large athletic field.[44]

For the park's 1948 season, a new merry-go-round debuted (believed to be Philadelphia Toboggan Company model #52, which originally operated at Frederick Road Park, and was then later relocated to a park in St. Paul, Minnesota). This large four-row machine contained sixty horses. Additional rides unveiled that summer included the Moon Rocket, the Looper, and the Sea Cruise. Power boats were added to offer brief rides on Gwynn Oak's lake. The postwar baby boom was the driving force behind the addition of the "Babyland" section that opened that year. Scaled-down versions of favorite adult rides were built for the kiddies, including mini-autos, boats, and a miniature railroad.[45] Similar kiddie lands sprung up at amusement parks across the country for the next 15 years or so. Newly expanded picnic groves and parking areas greeted returning guests for the 1949 season. The postwar years also saw a decline in the popularity of traditional ballroom dancing. Interest steadily dropped after the war and this longtime guest favorite was discontinued in 1950.

A kid could never run out of things to do at Gwynn Oak. The always popular Kiddieland contained many rides; including a kiddie coaster, boat ride, Ferris wheel, merry-go-round, and a car turnpike ride featuring 1950s style T-Birds. Kids could also enjoy the pony and goat rides. One of the carousels that operated at the park spins riders today at the Smithsonian Castle on the Mall in Washington, D.C. This ride was built by the Allan Herschell Company in 1947.

Gwynn Oak management put quite a bit of time and money into rehabbing the park for the 1950 season. Visitors were greeted by fresh paint, new rides and games, enlarged facilities, and an upgraded Kiddieland, which was boasted to be one of the best in the nation. "Big" kids remember the more thrilling rides, like the Deep Dipper or Double Dip roller coaster, which operated at the park from the early 1920s to about 1955. It was replaced in 1956 with a coaster that Baltimore natives remember the best, perhaps—the Big Dipper (or Racer Dip). This thriller boasted a first hill of about 60 feet high, with a track length of just under 3000 feet. It was constructed by the National Amusement Company of Dayton, Ohio. Gwynn Oak proudly advertised its new thriller—"Ride the all new jet streamlined Big Dipper with jet streamlined cars—greater speed-thrills-and safety."[46]

The first annual "All Nations Day" was held at Gwynn Oak on September 9, 1951. A variety of groups from different nations wore their distinct costumes, and food from the country of each participating group was served. The Baltimore Colts marching band performed as well.[47] The annual festival would become a huge success; 25,000 guests representing nine foreign countries were in attendance for the next celebration in 1952. An exhibition hall allowed for guests to view art objects and costumes from the various countries. Groups represented the countries of Greece, Poland, Russia, Israel, Ukraine, Italy, Norway, China and Czechoslovakia.[48] By the 1954 season's festival, the number of different local nationality groups, embassies, and cultural missions in attendance numbered thirty-six.

The Aero Swing ride operated for several years; the park's band shell can be seen in the background (courtesy Historical Society of Baltimore County).

Long-time Baltimorean and former park employee Bob Thorn relates what it was like to live near and, later, work at Gwynn Oak:

We moved just behind the park in the summer of 1955, after the 32 streetcar line was eliminated. I was ten years old when we moved there and had no idea how important that move was and how it would impact my entire life. I remember the first time I saw the park. I was walking along the Gwynn Falls entrance, when all of a sudden I walked around a curve and there in front of me was the rear entrance to the park. I couldn't believe my eyes. Here in my back yard was a dream come true. I entered the park not really knowing if I were dreaming or if this was for real. Here I am, ten years old with my own personal playground. I used to cash in empty bottles for two cents each and do odd jobs for the neighbors just to get some

A 1940s view of the roller coaster during the annual Baltimore Gas and Electric summer outing (courtesy Baltimore County Public Library).

A c. 1950s view of the kiddie boat ride. This popular ride made its debut in Babyland for the 1948 season.

This is believed to be a Baltimore celebrity greeting and signing autographs for park visitors during an appearance at Gwynn Oak in the summer of 1955 or 1956—a Baltimore Oriole perhaps?

money to go to the park. Where else could a young guy go and have so much fun? I would take my hard earned money and buy ride tickets. My first ride was the "Butterfly," which was an airplane-type cockpit attached to a cable that swung you around in a large circle. Immediately I was transformed from a young kid to a fighter pilot hunting down the Red Baron, diving and swooping my trusty airplane getting ready to shoot down my enemy. When the ride slowed to a stop, the culprit had gotten away this time, but tomorrow would be different.

I would then run over to the go-carts. Now I was a race car driver speeding around and around leading the rest of the carts to the finish line, to be the first ten year old to win the Indy 500. I would get out of the cart, take my bows, and be off again, this time to the "Rifleman" stand where I would plunk down 25 cents and actually be able to shoot a real gun; not just one, but twenty shots. Now, I was a famous cowboy shooting down the bad guys. I would pretend they were running away and shooting on the move, never missing, always hitting my target, preserving law and order in the Wild West. This was a typical day at the park during my early years.

Soon I wasn't ten anymore. I was a teenager. Suddenly I had a different outlook on the park. I had met a lot of friends over the last few years. The park had become a great place to hang out. We would play the pinball machines in the Arcade all day long; it only cost a penny a game. A decent player could stay on the machine all day for a quarter. There were claw machines, Skee-ball, wheels to spin for candy or cigarettes, golf, and most of all, the horse track. Just outside of the Arcade was a nickel pitch game where you could win a stuffed bear. This was my favorite place to be. All you had to do was pitch a nickel onto a plate and you won a bear. I actually became so good at winning bears that Mr. Hulsey (the head honcho), barred me from winning more than one bear a day. I would win a bear spending ten or fifteen cents on that game, then I would leave to go to the horse track. Before reaching the track I would always find some little girl that looked like she needed a bear. Needless to say, hardly any bears ever made it to the horse track. The bear pitch operator estimated that I was winning about 140 bears a season. That surprised even me, but he said he was keeping count. There must have been a lot of happy little girls out there, because I never kept any of the bears.

As a teen, I worked at the horse/pony track, and was paid 75 cents an hour; a pretty good wage at that time for a young man. Around noon, we would close the track, and walk the ponies through the park, across the bridge, and up to the horse barn. We'd feed and water them, and then lead them back around 2:00 p.m.

One of the horses, Goldie (the other three horses were Joe, Dusty, and Geronimo), became so familiar with this daily routine that she could walk through the park back to the pony track unattended, drawing the occasional surprised look from park guests.

Mr. Thorn has many other fond recollections of Gwynn Oak, details such as each of the ride operators picking up the small red cans to collect the individual ride tickets at the beginning of a shift, the sock hops at the Dixie Ballroom, and scaring unsuspecting kids on Report Card Day by hiding inside the Laff in the Dark. At the end of a long workday, he would sometimes hitch a ride on the park's miniature train for the short trip home.

Other attractions that spun, scared, and dizzied willing riders included the RotoJet, Laff in the Dark, Ferris wheel, Caterpillar, Whip, Tunnel of Horrors, Wild Mouse, Butterfly (Flying Scooters), Tilt-a-Whirl, Space Rocket, and Looper. Baltimore resident

Nothing could beat the taste of a hot dog and a Coke on a summer's day at Gwynn Oak. A snack stand is seen here in this 1956 photograph.

Betty Cook recalls the good times at Gwynn Oak: "We'd see Bozo the Clown walking thru the park, and yell to him; hey Bozo, what time is it? Bozo would lift up his pants leg to display a clock he had strapped to his leg. 'It's half-past' would come his reply. We would yell back 'Half-past what?' 'Don't know ... only got one hand on this clock' was Bozo's comical answer." Ms. Cook's fondest memories included the Pretzel ride and the nearby mechanical fat lady, and the annual fireworks display on the 4th of July. The amazing ground displays that typically included an illuminated American flag were a crowd favorite.

The late 1950s and early 1960s would be a troubling period for the park. The demise of the streetcar's popularity was affecting Gwynn Oak's attendance by the late 1950s. Arthur Price's three sons—David, James, and Arthur—formed Gwynn Oak Amusement Park, Inc., in 1957. Arthur Sr. passed away unexpectedly in December of that year, leaving the park operations entirely under his sons' control.

The park endured through some disturbing incidents. December of 1958 saw a melee break out in the Dixie Ballroom during an event where the dance hall had been rented out by local teens. Three policemen and six detectives were injured before order could be restored. At least five teens were arrested.[49] Also, as early as 1955, members of the Baltimore Committee on Racial Equality had demonstrated against the park's "whites only" policy, as blacks were not allowed to attend the popular All Nations Day

Kid band performing on stage at Acme's "In the Money" Day.

March against the park's segregation policy held at Gwynn Oak in 1963 (courtesy Hearst Newspapers LLC/*Baltimore News-American*).

Festival at the park. Cardinal Sheehan soon forbid local parochial schools from holding their annual outing at Gwynn Oak, which reportedly resulted in over 50 school picnics being cancelled, a huge blow to the park's group outing business. The park's landmark outdoor events stage was destroyed in August of 1962 when a weakened 75-foot oak tree fell on it. Luckily no one was hurt.

On July 4, 1963, Gwynn Oak attracted nationwide attention when hundreds of integrationists and clerics staged demonstrations against the park's whites-only policy. Two hundred eighty-three demonstrators, many from as far away as New York, were arrested, and most were cited for violating Maryland's Trespass Act. Among those arrested included a chief executive of the United Presbyterian Church, an Episcopal bishop, and several Catholic, Protestant, and Jewish clergy. Many were loaded onto school buses and taken to various police precincts for processing. Another demonstration at the park followed three days later, resulting in additional arrests.

A new committee was soon formed, the Baltimore County Human Relations Commission, to help resolve the tense stand-off between the park owners and the demonstrators. An agreement was reached in the next two weeks, as Baltimore County executive Spiro Agnew stepped in and asked David Price to reconsider the park's admittance policy. An eleventh-hour agreement was reached between the two sides on July 19, and it was then announced that Gwynn Oak Park would be integrated on August 28. Civil rights leaders agreed to discontinue any further demonstrations, canceling a massive protest march scheduled for the next day that would have resulted in further arrests and possibly violence.[50]

The park decided to try to operate daily, for the two weeks following Labor Day, and planned to hold a large parochial school outing during the first week of September. Local clergy were now trying to encourage Baltimoreans to head out to Gwynn Oak and support the park. Crowds were less than the numbers hoped for, although it was reported that there were no disturbances in the weeks following integration.[51] The park would limp through the later portion of the decade, as patronage dropped off. The park would receive quite a bit of positive publicity in August of 1964, when a 14-year-old Boy Scout from Edgemere, Maryland, named Walter Stone set out to break the world's record for the most consecutive hours riding a Ferris wheel. While it was not exactly known what the world record was, Stone was ready to stay on the ride for 64 straight hours, which would eclipse what was thought to be the world record of 54 hours. Gwynn Oak provided all of his food for the duration of his marathon ride, in addition to pills for motion sickness and a harness to hold him in place while sleeping.[52] Six years later, in July of 1970, Gwynn Oak would be the site of the new world record, which was set by 13-year-old Bobbie Kemp. The son of the district director of the Maryland Muscular Dystrophy Association managed to stay on the wheel for fifteen days and nights, raising approximately $2,000 that was donated to support the fight against Muscular Dystrophy. The youth braved several large storms, plus the queasiness of watching a few of his friends get sick after climbing aboard to support him for a few spins.[53]

In 1965, an unfortunate accident marred the Memorial Day fireworks display, sending 30 guests to the hospital. Two errant shells landed in the crowd, causing several injuries.[54] Gwynn Oak's ride line-up in the late 1960s to early 1970s was expanded with the addition of rides like the Roundup, Giant Slide, Twister, Cortina Bob, and the Sky Wheel (double Ferris wheel).

Gwynn Oak did survive to celebrate its 75th season of operation in April of 1971. Coowner David Price was not very optimistic about the park's future, though. A *News-American* article conveyed some of Price's thoughts on the business, as he admitted the park had been operating in the red for the past few seasons and that there wasn't much hope for a major improvement for the 1971 season: "I would prefer to stay in the amusement park business, since I've been in it for 27 years, but I won't throw good money after bad." A drop-off in patronage over the last several years necessitated the raising of ticket prices on popular rides. This also helped cover the cost of rising employee salaries and park maintenance costs: "The company spends between $14,000–15,000 each week during the summer season in these areas. We're spending all that money and on a given day we might only have three people on a ride."[55] To help alleviate the park's financial problems, management closed the park down one day during the week and cut the daily operating hours back as well.

In late May of 1972, the county ordered the park to be closed due to unsafe conditions on two of the rides. The owners obtained an injunction, requesting just cause for the park's closing. The circuit court ordered a formal inspection that was carried out soon afterward. County officials would allow the park to open during the first week of June under the condition that 14 of the rides would not operate until the required repairs were completed. The county inspectors commented that it was believed to be the first time the park had been threatened with a stoppage in operations due to ride safety.[56] However, no one was prepared for the havoc that Hurricane Agnes would wreak in the summer of 1972. Gwynn Oak Park was literally washed away, never to fully recover. Damages to the park grounds amounted to close to one million dollars; thirteen of the parks' 31 rides were lost in the flood. When the park attempted to open

Kids could somewhat control their flight on the Butterfly, a thrilling spin through the air.

Sign atop the park's thrilling Laff in the Dark ride (courtesy Baltimore County Public Library).

A sad view of Gwynn Oak's Dixie Ball Room after the devastation caused by Hurricane Agnes in the summer of 1972 (photograph by Jeff Morgenstern, courtesy Baltimore County Public Library).

for the 1974 season, the county would not issue an operating permit, due to several structural repairs that needed addressing. The park's mortgage holder, Yorkridge Federal Savings and Loan, soon sent David Price a letter of foreclosure and the park's fate was sealed.[57]

June 25, 1974, marked a sad event in Baltimore's history, as Gwynn Oak Amusement Park was sold at auction. A large crowd attended the auction, including carnival and amusement park operators from around the country; each hoping to find rides and equipment at bargain prices. Most left disappointed, however, as Yorkridge Federal Savings and Loan purchased the park as a block for the sum of $415,000. David Price was extremely frustrated with the outcome, as the final price paid for the land ($325,000) should have been about three times higher (the park's appraisal value in 1971 was over $1 million). Price felt that the park sale could have brought in a higher take if the rides and other park assets had been auctioned off individually, as the "block" sale shut out all of the smaller bidders.

The Price brothers did try to fight Yorkridge S&L on the park's foreclosure. In the meanwhile, the park continued to decay and became a prime target of vandals. Crumbling buildings, broken glass, and miscellaneous junk were a common sight at the park; and weeds began to overgrow all of the structures. Sadly, the park's landmark Dixie Ballroom was destroyed by a suspicious fire in February of 1975.[58] Another arson was

Opposite bottom: Workmen prepping the Twister ride for the upcoming season (courtesy Baltimore County Public Library).

committed within the week, leveling the penny arcade and damaging Pistol Pete's shooting gallery. In an effort to enforce the county laws on building code violations, Baltimore County entered into a long fight with Yorkridge, in an attempt to get the remaining park structures removed. Finally, in March of 1976, the savings and loan agreed to hire a demolition crew and set a start date of April 1. County building inspectors had originally cited the decrepit buildings as fire hazards in January of 1975 and had ordered them to be removed. Buzz Berg Wreckers agreed to remove the remaining rides and buildings as part of a $75,000 contract agreement.[59]

A sad sign board from Gwynn Oak. The park is closed forever in this photograph taken after Hurricane Agnes devastated the area (courtesy Mike Taylor).

When the park land was finally cleared of the abandoned buildings, different uses for the old Gwynn Oak property were discussed. The Baltimore County Council approved a measure to purchase the 63-acre property for $565,000 to be used as a county park. Residents would be able to stroll through Gwynn Oak Park once again, but with only the memories to keep them company. Much of the property was located in the Gwynn Falls watershed, so no buildings could be erected in any flood-prone area.[60] The county estimated that perhaps only 19 acres of the property could be used for common parkland.[61]

A walk through the county park today provides a mix of emotions among those who were fortunate enough to spend time at Gwynn Oak years ago. Bob Thorn relates his heartfelt thoughts:

> It is now over 40 years later, the park has long disappeared and all that is left is a large, empty field. At the end of the field are three white concrete steps that used to lead the way to the boat lake. They are still there, remnants of a time long since passed. If you drive down Gwynn Oak Avenue and park your car, you find yourself drawn to those steps. You walk to them as if in a trance. Climb up the steps, turn around, and sit down. If you close your eyes and listen

The trackage of the Wild Mouse lies in disrepair after the park's closing (courtesy Mike Taylor).

Pistol Pete's had seen better days by the time this photograph was taken. The game stand would be the target of arsonists soon afterward (courtesy Mike Taylor).

The Big Dipper sits quietly, hoping to run roller coaster trains along its track again (courtesy Mike Taylor).

A view of the destruction at Gwynn Oak Park. The forlorn cafeteria can be seen in the rear (courtesy Mike Taylor).

ever so carefully you can still hear the clickety-clack of the Big Dipper, the sounds of the Whip, the organ music coming from the merry-go-round, the screaming of the little kids running from ride to ride shouting, 'hurry mom, hurry dad let's ride again!' If you take a deep breath you can still smell the aroma of cotton candy, French fries and hot dogs. Times seemed a lot easier back then, and with eyes still closed you wish times could be like that again. But you know way down in your heart it will never be the same. You don't want to open your eyes, at least not yet. With your eyes closed, you are still that ten year old kid again, discovering that small piece of land with rides and games that was called Gwynn Oak Park. Reluctantly, you slowly open your eyes and are suddenly transported to the present. You come to realize you are not ten years old anymore, but a sixty-five year old man, and a little tear comes to your eye knowing that it is the end of a way of life.

11

Hollywood Park

Hollywood Park generated plenty of publicity and controversy over the years it operated on Back River at Eastern Avenue. "Down the road to Hollywood" was a common destination for sailors arriving in the port of Baltimore. During its existence on Back River, one investigating grand jury labeled it a place "where drinking, reveling, gambling, singing, dancing, and general misbehavior prevailed." Its humble beginnings can be traced to a country club that was established by James L. Kernan, with the intent of providing a meeting place for the Eagles fraternity. In May of 1899, Kernan opened the Hollywood Inn on the spot of the former Manhattan Beach.[1] He soon added a pier for boating and fishing, and refurbished an old dance pavilion into a rustic casino, with an enlarged stage and opera chairs. Vaudeville and opera performances were presented to the masses. A carousel was operating by the end of 1899. The pavilion was soon expanded, in 1901, to accommodate the increasing crowds.

Kernan would help the Baltimore Aerie, No. 50, Fraternal Order of Eagles (FOE), open the Eagles' Country Club at Hollywood on May 12, 1901. The streetcars and transfer stations were overwhelmed by the great numbers of Baltimoreans looking for a pleasant day's activities near the water along the Back and Middle rivers. Music, songs, and refreshments were enjoyed by over 600 members of the new organization.[2] A new carousel with galloping horses began providing rides for children that month. A five-cent fare transported guests to and from Hollywood daily, after 1:00 p.m.[3]

With his auditorium business booming, Kernan decided to lease out the park operations of Hollywood and River View at the beginning of the 1902 season. Frederick Schanberger and George Irvin were tapped to manage Hollywood Park and announced several new features and attractions for the upcoming season. A gypsy camp, confectionery booth, and rifle range were in place for guests to enjoy. Yet another carousel was to be in operation, and a steamed crab concession was introduced as well.[4] The new managers were held to appear in front of a grand jury that summer, however, when the Society for the Protection of Children accused them of hiring an underage girl to dance and sing in the park theater. The Back River area was hit by a fierce windstorm on July 3, 1902. At least a dozen trees were blown over at Hollywood, with one damaging the casino. The wind whipped up waves on Back River to the point where they washed over the connecting bridge for a time; motormen chose not to run the streetcars across the bridge until the storm passed.[5] Kernan would again lease the park to the pair for the following season, and local businessman Joe Goeller, the proprietor of nearby Goeller's Back River Park, would assume control by the 1904 season.

Rare view of Hollywood Park from Back River, July 1900 (Maryland Historical Society, Item MC2307–1).

Joe Goeller was one of the more colorful individuals in Baltimore's history. Born in Germany in 1859, he immigrated to America as a young boy, and soon found work in a shoe factory. Goeller gained recognition as an amateur boxer, and he decided to open his own gymnasium downtown on Chester Street, where he helped train fighters and promote the occasional match. By 1896, he was operating the saloon and surrounding grounds on Gay Street known as Standard Park (named for the nearby Standard Brewing Company). When this venture proved unsuccessful, Goeller focused on purchasing land along the Back River.[6] "The whitewashing of its tree trunks and the painting of its beaches a brilliant green were certain signs of approaching spring when all other signs failed. The figure of Joe Goeller, short and stout, never with a coat, always with a straw hat, a short stick in his hand, and his trousers trussed up with heavy 'galluses' [suspenders], was as familiar a sight as the river itself."[7] Drinking appeared to be the most popular pastime at Hollywood Park, however, even on Sundays.

Goeller immediately went to work and contracted to have the pavilion expanded to contain amusements and arranged for additional concessions to be brought into the park. Goeller had a rude awakening at Hollywood Park, literally, on a warm August night in 1904. While napping under a tree on the park property, two armed robbers attempted to steal his valuable jeweled eagle, which he wore as a member of the FOE. Goeller fought back, and called out for help. Several patrons found their way from the pavilion to the scene of the fight, and they eventually subdued one man and caught the other after a brief chase. Towards the end of the 1906 season, Goeller had a two-story hotel under construction at the park. The 60-room structure was approximately 60 feet by 150 feet, and included a palm garden.[8] A June 1907 *Baltimore Sun* commentary on a Sunday spent at Hollywood Park provided an interesting look at how Baltimoreans spent their free time away from the daily grind at the workplace:

> Their attention is engaged from noon until midnite by the show in the casino, the soft crabs, the popcorn, the fried fish, and the beer—particularly the beer. Hollywood, indeed has taken on its perfume. The whole place smells beery.... All of these Patapsco Neck breathing spots smash the Sunday laws into smithereens, but it is questionable if the county police, even if they were sincere—which they most certainly are not—could enforce it. It would take a regiment of cavalry, with two regiments of foot and a battery of field artillery, to make Back River "dry" on Sunday. The people who go there are utterly unable to picture an outing without its attendant keg. To them, pleasure and beer are synonymous.[9]

An unnamed county commissioner was quoted as stating, "To enforce the Sunday law on the 'Neck.' ... would be impossible and useless. Take a place like Hollywood, for example. Here we have 5,000 people enjoying themselves in the best manner they understand. They are not damaged, and they are damaging no one else. If the Sunday law were enforced, they would be driven to Spring Gardens or to the sidedoor saloons of Highlandtown. Isn't it better to let them come here and pass the day harmlessly?"[10]

It wouldn't be long before the law did start to take a closer look at the activities underway at the various Back River resorts, though. Goeller's Hollywood Park would face numerous fights over the next several years. Police would raid Hollywood Park in June of 1908, and again in March of 1909. In both cases, Goeller appeared before Justice Thompson at the Canton police station and pleaded guilty. He was convicted of selling liquor on Sunday and fined. Several of his employees were fined by the magistrate for working on Sunday.[11] Police raids would soon become commonplace at the riverside resorts. An April 1909 incident on a streetcar heading back to the city after a Sunday evening of drinking at Hollywood didn't help matters. A large fight broke out aboard the car, prompting the conductor to lock all of the troublemakers inside the car upon arrival at the Highlandtown carbarn while the police were summoned. A frustrated Justice Thompson levied stiff fines against all 18 of the arrested participants, sending the message that disorder on the Back River line would not be tolerated.[12]

Attempts were soon made to attract more families to Hollywood by adding popular amusement devices. Plans were announced in the spring of 1910 to transform Hollywood into a Coney Island-style park. The 30-acre park would be outfitted with the latest amusement devices and expanded facilities to handle up to 25,000 people a day. Three rides were added: a roller coaster one-half mile in length, the Circle Dips, and the Tubs. The Tubs ride was 1000 feet long, and featured eight-passenger upholstered tubs which traversed a gravity incline. Riders experienced drops, climbs, and spins while constantly being jostled about. Plans were unveiled for additional attractions including $5,000 in improvements for the beach, a Japanese Garden, Philippine Village, Monmouth Caves, a pony track, and a large children's playground.[13] The dance pavilion was expanded, which was advertised as the largest in the South.

Improvements to the tune of $125,000 were announced for the 1911 season, which included a new, handsome archway, extensive landscaping, and the addition of 100,000 incandescent lights. Many of the park's existing structures were torn down, and new amusements erected in their place. These included the Ben-Hur racing coaster, Venice by Moonlight, carousel, Third Degree, ballroom and casino, and Shooting the Dips roller coaster.[14] Other attractions in place at that time included the Human Roulette Wheel and the Trip to the Alps.[15]

Setbacks would be frequent for Goeller, though. In February of 1912, a circuit court jury found him guilty of selling liquor at the park on Sunday. Being the second offense within a year's time, he was fined $250 and his liquor license suppressed.[16] The following month, state's attorney George Hartman ordered the sheriff to close down Hollywood Park. Goeller had not yet paid the $250 fine previously imposed on him, and had filed a writ to take his case to the court of appeals.[17]

The park would open for the 1912 season on May 14, however. Harry Peters was the acting manager and brought in several new features. A large $40,000 merry-go-round with 1,600 electric lights offered rides for the kids, and the roller coaster was remodeled. New shows included the Oriental dance, Turkish combat, and the Hindu magic show. General park improvements included concrete walks beginning at the park entrance.[18] Other billed attractions included the Diving Girls show, Jack Chisolm's Wild West Show, Russo's 12 Opera Singers, and the new Teaser ride. Dancing in the new ballroom cost just a nickel; the large structure could reportedly hold 500 couples. Two men who operated concessions at Hollywood, including the Walking Charlie game, the astrology booth, and an eating booth, filed an injunction against Goeller to prevent him from interfering with their business. They claimed that he was threatening to tear down the buildings that housed their operations.[19] Goeller actually rejected a sale offer of $175,000 for the resort from the United Railway Company that same year. In spite of the park's questionable character, the URC may have viewed the expanding park as a growing threat to its trolley parks.

Fifty new amusements were boasted for Hollywood's May 1913 opening. Many of them made their way from Coney Island, and a large vaudeville show debuted as well. Prompted by reports of "wide-open" resorts at Back River, a July raid at two Back River resorts gained mixed results for Marshal Mahle and the county commissioners. Nine employees were arrested at "Spot" Mitchell's establishment, where close to 1000 patrons had gathered for Sunday drinks. Goeller was evidently tipped off about the second raid of the evening, which had targeted Hollywood Park. Approximately 300 patrons escaped from the drinking hall through a back passageway, crawled under a fence and scattered. Someone punctured the tire on a new police vehicle after the authorities had entered the pavilion. Marshal Mahle suspected there were leaks within his office, as this was the second consecutive Hollywood raid that produced no solid evidence of illegal gambling and alcohol on the premises.[20]

In a somewhat vague *Sun* article in August 1913, it was disclosed that the United

Women of Maryland were close to selecting a social worker to be assigned to a new position at Hollywood Park. A conference had been recently held between Goeller and the women's union, in which Goeller agreed to allow a social worker to be placed at the park. In addition, it was stated that the new hire would be provided ample protection. United Women's goal was to undertake changes at Hollywood park and present to other proprietors how to elevate the status of their resorts while keeping patronage levels up: "The members of the United Women group feel that there is a great opportunity for them along this line of work in transforming all of the river resorts into places of amusement and recreation that can be enjoyed by the residents of the city and suburbs without their having to be subject to conditions that now keep a great majority of the people [away] from them."[21] There was no mention of what the "line of work" for women was at Hollywood, but one can draw his own conclusion here.

Irresponsible actions on the part of an amusement park's guests while on a ride are a thorny issue today. Not much has seemingly changed over time in that respect. Several disturbing Baltimore newspaper accounts from the early part of the 20th century document ride accidents that were caused by riders' improper actions. In August of 1913, a 41-year-old man riding in the third seat of Hollywood's roller coaster stood up and attempted to strike a Negro passenger in the front seat with his hat while the train was in operation. He lost his balance and was pitched out of the car, landing on the ground and fracturing his skull.[22] Also in August, it was reported that the United Railways and Electric Company was again interested in acquiring Hollywood and some additional property on Back River. Goeller confirmed this, but was said to have been asking for the price of $200,000, which the railway company was not willing to meet. At that time, Hollywood Park and other resorts were under fire from the Lord's Day Alliance, and the Society for the Suppression of Vice. Some thought this was the perfect opportunity for Goeller to sell, but he had other plans: "When they get Joe ... they will have to fight. I am not anxious to sell—in fact, I don't care to; but if anything does turn out, they will have to meet me on my own terms. The company has been after me for about two years for the place, but I don't see any need for getting out of business. You'll hear from me when I do."[23]

The sticky issue of enforcing the Sunday liquor law—banning the sale of alcohol in the county—would continue to raise its head. On August 12, 1913, fourteen Baltimore County police officers were suspended. They were accused of not enforcing the Sunday ban. The county commissioners had recently leveled accusations against Marshal Mahle, passing down a directive that he and his men crack down on the liquor law violations. The commissioners had grown weary of repeated reports of incidents near the city where saloons and other establishments were selling beer and whiskey to large crowds of men on Sundays, and policemen within yards of the premises "looking the other way." Mahle had no choice but to discipline those suspected, who were termed to have "shaky" records while on the force.[24]

Another suit was brought against Goeller during this same week by a park concessionaire. Robert Livingston, the operator of the "Hell's Kitchen" game, sought $3,000 in damages after Goeller allegedly placed another individual in charge of the popular game. For the cost of just one nickel, men could purchase three baseballs and attempt to break as many kitchen dishes as their pitching aim would allow. Under a two-year agreement with Goeller, Livingston was to keep 75 percent of the receipts, while Goeller would receive 25 percent.[25]

A March 1914 report stated that the Hollywood Park Amusement Company was being sued for $10,000 in damages for injuries allegedly suffered in September of 1912 on the park's Racer Dips roller coaster. The court would eventually rule in favor of the New Hollywood Park. The park suffered further negative publicity two months later when two men were severely beaten by a group of unidentified men.[26] The park did advertise a new attraction for 1914; "Lingerman's Children" was "an enjoyable amusement for the youngsters, and many others."[27]

A large ad in the morning *Sun* on May 8 trumpeted the grand opening of Hollywood Park for the 1915 season. Billed as "Baltimore's Coney Island," it boasted 50 new amusements, and claims of "Greater—Grander—Better than ever." Trying to soften the park's image, the ad proclaimed that "no intoxicating drinks would be sold on Sunday, or to minors on any day," and that there was no gambling. The ad went on to state that the resort was geared "towards the ladies and children, with several amusements in store, including the pony track, carousel (complete with a new $10,000 band organ), and two roller coasters; the nearly mile-long Ben Hur Races, and the Shoot-the-Dips, a Ferris wheel, the Teaser, and the Tub Races. Two big musical comedies daily under the special direction of Guy Johnson"[28] were touted as well. (Another article mentioned that the new carousel organ cost $7,500, and was covered with 1500 multicolored electric bulbs (Goeller spent at least $15,000 on improvements that season).[29]

Hollywood Park would again receive unwanted negative publicity in May 1915, when two men were shot at a park pavilion. Evidently a Baltimore County deputy sheriff paid a visit to the park shortly before 1:00 a.m. and began questioning why the park appeared to be open past its midnight closing time. Words were exchanged, guns drawn, and both the sheriff and a patron suffered minor wounds. The patron took a streetcar to the Lombard Street carbarn and awaited a patrolman to take him into custody. He was charged with shooting the sheriff and released on $2,000 bond. The accused claimed that the Sheriff was "trying to put the screws on the business at Hollywood" and claimed that the Sheriff had drawn his weapon first, accidentally shooting himself in the process.[30]

Long time local Joseph Oronson, recalls two enterprising young men, who set up a concession at Hollywood; "Herb and Joseph Bruner sold popcorn and peanuts at the park. They'd ride the streetcar to Jeppi Brothers' on Sharp Street and purchase 90 lb. bags of peanuts. They'd put together single bags of the snack to sell; their take for a good week was $25–30 dollars."[31]

In a March 1958 newspaper column, Ralph J. Siebert related some tales of the early days at Hollywood Park. He remembered Frank Tinney and Jimmy Barton getting their start on the park's open-air vaudeville stage, working for the spare change that was tossed at them. He also related his tendency for finding trouble at the park:

> On an early occasion I was in a party of four young fellows who seated our selves at a table in the large pavilion. One of our party got into a trivial altercation with a man at a nearby table and they stood up as if to trade punches. There must have been a couple hundred men

at the surrounding tables, and as the pair squared off, a roar as if from a million angry bees arose. Alas, the party of the second part to the impending fight worked at the Baltimore and Ohio Railroad's Mt. Clare railroad shops. Practically all the other men worked there, too, it seems, and they were his friends. With yells of "Throw 'em out," they made for our table in droves, and we lost no time in reaching the door. It was at that point that Goeller's 'secret police,' a corps of bouncers headed by Herman Miller, one-time pro fighter, took over and added momentum to our going.[32]

Siebert would later be part of an MP detail assigned to the park to enforce the "off-limits for military ban," with somewhat mixed results.

Back River residents massed a protest against the city of Baltimore in 1917 claiming that the real estate surrounding the city's sewage disposal plant on Back River was being affected by foul odors and was a health menace. Meetings set up by Goeller at Hollywood's hall to organize the property owners' claims eventually led to a successful suit, with monetary damages paid by the city.

May 1919 would start another difficult chapter in Hollywood Park's checkered history. Prohibition was now in force, and while many a Baltimore saloon would close their doors, Hollywood would stay open and offer amusements and food with soft drinks, according to their local ads.[33] The park's seedy reputation prompted one local writer to recall years later "the old wild days ... when blood ran hot and the beer ran cold. And, the only prohibition at Hollywood, was on smoking opium in the Old Mill, and the only responsibility was to bury one's own killings."[34]

Hollywood Park was just one of several Baltimore amusement parks to debut a roller coaster for the 1920 season. An early June ad in the *Sun* announced the new "Dip the Dippers; the greatest Racer Dip ever built this side of New York."[35] This was believed to be another John Miller design. Miller had a hand in building four new roller coasters in the Baltimore area alone during his busy winter of 1919–1920.

A costly fire in March of 1921 signaled the beginning of the end for Hollywood Park. A stove in the kitchen of the hotel is believed to have been the source of the blaze. It soon consumed the roller coaster, the dance hall/cabaret, Old Mill, shooting gallery, several concession stands, and the park entrance as well. The total loss was estimated at about $200,000. Sadly, Goeller's park was uninsured, as he had let the park insurance policies expire two years earlier. Initial reports indicated he was quitting the business. A few structures did survive the blaze, including the Ferris wheel, carousel, billiards hall, the large vaudeville/dance pavilion, and one of the shooting galleries.

A breakdown of the major damage was as follows: "Hotel, dance hall, cabaret—$80,000; Racer Dips—$60,000; Old Mill—$25,000; four concession stands—$2,000; shooting gallery—$1,000; transformer house—$5,000; park entrance—$2,000, hotel furnishings, racer dip cars, gondolas, etc—$20,000."[36] This was just one of several Back River parks to suffer a major fire over the years, though Hollywood Park managed to outlive Jack Flood's popular park at Curtis Bay. Upon arrival at the smoldering ruins to help console her father, Joe Goeller's daughter Josephine was heard to declare, "Many a tongue will wag in Baltimore when they hear that Joe Goeller's place has burned."[37]

Goeller did manage to stay open and reconstructed some of the park's buildings. However, in October of 1921, Prohibition agents raided Goeller's Hollywood Park again.

Inside the rebuilt hotel they found several quarts of whiskey (many of them hidden under Goeller's bed) and almost 500 bottles of home-brewed beer. Nearly 80 cases of the home brew were found in a shed on the property. Goeller admitted to selling the illegal drinks and paid a $250 fine.[38]

A grand jury for the circuit court released a report the same day the raid hit the news, that essentially attributed the various violations of the law in the Back River section of the county to inattention on the part of the local police: "The grand jury feels that if the people of these sections would co-operate with the Police Department and report in detail such violations as come to their notice it would help in a great measure to wipe out the conditions that exist. The geographical outline of the county affords along the water front opportunities for vice and immorality. In these secluded spots, barricaded by woods and water, disorderly houses are maintained and the destruction of this class of vice requires a fearless and untiring vigilance of the Police Department."[39] The park never recovered from the disastrous 1921 season.

In January of 1922 it was announced that the resort would be permanently closing, as Goeller was being sentenced to serve six months in jail for maintaining a disorderly place at Hollywood Park. Park rides were soon put up for sale. Talk of the park reopening in May of that year surfaced; however, state attorney H. Courtney Jennifer denied the reports. Mr. Jennifer had been assured by Goeller and his attorney that Hollywood Park would never operate again as a resort. Goeller hired an engineer to subdivide the large holdings around the Hollywood Park property into lots in preparation of new homes being built.[40] Goeller would eventually retire at his home in the exclusive Homeland area of Baltimore. He died at the age of 81 on June 3, 1940, survived by his wife, Julia, six children, and one granddaughter.[41]

12

Luna Park/Paragon Park

Baltimore residents who read their *Sun* paper the morning of January 28, 1910, were treated to a pleasant surprise. The Luna Park Amusement Company was announcing detailed plans for a new amusement place to be erected in West Baltimore. Luna Park was to be built on the site of the old Shipley estate, at the corner of Garrison Avenue and West Baltimore Street previously referred to as the Calverton Heights area. The land was purchased by James Keelty from the Mercantile Trust Company and was being leased to the Luna Park Amusement Company. Harry Geiglein was the park operator, with George N. Bryan managing. The company's attorney was James J. Carmody.[1] Capital stock of $50,000 was authorized, with 500 shares at $100 each.[2]

A proposed diagram of the park, at an area of slightly more than five acres, showed a large auditorium with a bandstand to the rear. A carousel stood nearby, and an automobile track circling the park was in the plans as well. Several amusement devices were anticipated to be added, including a bowling alley, shooting gallery, and a Ferris wheel. Auto and carriage sheds would be erected to allow for repairs and maintenance. Plans were also in the works to operate a moving picture concession year-round. The owners visualized the park as operating on the same scale as the famous Luna Park at Coney Island. To help achieve that vision, many incandescent lights and 50 Tungsten lamps were to be placed on tall light poles, providing the spectacular nighttime illuminations associated with its Coney Island namesake.

Surprisingly, the gentlemen who had erected the original Luna Park at Coney Island, Frederick Thompson and Elmer Dundy, did not protect the trademark name or design of their wildly successful Luna Park. This allowed many businessmen to open their own Luna Park not only in the United States, but also in various locations around the globe. Luna Parks opened between 1905 and 1920 in many U.S. cities, including Pittsburgh, Cleveland, Detroit, Indianapolis, Denver, and Houston, as well as Europe.[3]

Groundbreaking for the $50,000 Park took place on March 1. A *Sun* article noted that the park site was "about the highest to be found in or around Baltimore."[4] (The park stood just across the street from Gustav Graubner's West End Park, which offered dancing and drinking for the city's west side. This site also hosted the Cannstatter festival for several years.) Shortly after the groundbreaking, Luna Park gave the Pennsylvania Railroad the approval to remove a gigantic poplar tree that had stood on the park property for many years. At nearly 200 feet tall and 21 feet in circumference, it absorbed plenty of lightning strikes over the years.[5] The large carousel, measuring approximately 70 × 70 feet, was built by James W. Koontz at a cost of $800.

However, Luna Park encountered a major setback just prior to its grand opening. Park officials would second-guess their recent decision to remove the enormous poplar tree, as lightning would strike the nearly completed double racing coaster on May 24. The structure collapsed across the Philadelphia, Baltimore and Washington railroad tracks. The ride's builder, Harry Brienig, had only the running rails remaining to attach to the coaster at the time of the accident; he estimated the damage at $7,500. He was confident that the ride could be up and running in 30 days, however. (This severe thunderstorm also flooded Electric Park, and forced the bay steamer *Emma Giles* to undertake an emergency rescue. The schooner *Briscoe* had become disabled during the storm, and the steamer's captain, Lee Woolford, guided the *Emma Giles* alongside and towed the schooner into the Poplar Island narrows.[6])

Opening day for Luna Park "the Beautiful" followed on Decoration Day, May 30. The Fourth Regiment Military Orchestra was booked to play in the dance hall, as well as E. Dell Arcipreti's Royal Roman Band. Mayor Mahool and the city councilmen were on hand for the bash, and Baltimoreans had yet another amusement park to enjoy.

Unfortunately, Luna Park suffered another serious impediment which deprived many would-be patrons from experiencing Luna's offerings. A two-alarm fire leveled a significant portion of the park just after midnight on July 6, 1910. Virtually every building with the exception of the carousel was destroyed. Damage was estimated at approximately $35,000. Boiling grease in the restaurant kitchen was the culprit in the fire, discovered by policemen on patrol. Employees Brian, Carmody, and Geglein were in an upper room of the main building counting the day's receipts when the fire started and were forced to jump from a window when they could not reach the stairs to escape. They survived the leap unharmed, with the day's take intact. Besides the large dance hall/restaurant building, other losses included the soda fountain, ice cream stand, popcorn stand,

GRAND OPENING

Luna Park

"The Beautiful."

MONDAY, MAY 30TH, DECORATION DAY.

FREE ADMISSION.

BEAUTIFUL DANCE HALL.
FOURTH REGIMENT MILITARY ORCHESTRA.

LARGE AIRY DINING-ROOM,
CUISINE A LA MARYLAND.

SIG. E. DELL ARCIPRETI'S ROYAL ROMAN BAND.

FREE ADMISSION.

The park's 1910 grand opening attracted much attention, but, sadly, Luna would suffer from many an amusement park's long-time nemesis—fire. Shortly over one month after the grand opening, a large blaze devastated the park (*Baltimore Sun* photograph archives).

and shooting gallery. About 30 other employees that were present in the park helped save the carousel from destruction.[7] Graubner's West End Park suffered some minor damage from the blaze, with damages estimated at $500.[8]

Surprisingly, Luna's owners reopened the park the following night. A large number of people were in attendance, many just curious to observe the smoldering ruins. Dancing was held in the new moving-picture theater, which was only partly constructed at that time. Plans were immediately laid out to construct new buildings, but it would be difficult for Luna Park's owners to completely recover from this blow. Receivers were appointed for the Luna Park Amusement Company later in the season, on August 28.

The park did open on schedule in the spring of 1911. Several new attractions were added in the hopes of boosting Luna Park's fortunes. A photo gallery, and several new game concessions including Hoop-La, Walking Charlie, the Electric Ball Game, and others were added to the midway. The feature act at the park for the season was the Boston Orchestra, directed by Signor Castellucci.[9] The park managed to limp through the 1911 season, but operated at a loss. Receivers again were appointed in August of 1911, and Luna Park's fate was soon sealed.[10]

The demise of Luna Park, however, was not the end of an amusement park in this desirable West Baltimore location. On April 28, 1913, the Paragon Amusement Company took over Luna Park with the intention of retaining the amusement park. Much publicity was evident for the first event at the new Paragon Park as the Elks' Exposition and Social Session Association opened in mid–May. The feature attraction was the Bostock-Ferrari Wild Animal show at the fete, a spectacle included trained performances by nearly 200 exotic animals. The opening day parade featured two elephants, Gyp and Judy, pulling what was believed to be the world's largest band chariot. Judy had already gained some notoriety in the Baltimore news. After a performance in Chester, Pennsylvania, the prior week, the large beast became agitated when hearing the occasional roar from nearly a dozen lions cordoned off in a separate pen in the same railroad car. Judy literally raised the roof of the car at least half a foot by using her head, and then proceeded to kick out the end of the transport car.[11]

Attractions and shows imported for the exhibition included Dreamland, the Crystal Maze, merry-go-round, Ferris wheel, and a Broadway musical comedy, *Follies of the Day*. The thrilling Motordrome show featured four modified racing autos reaching speeds up to 90 miles per hour on a tight track.[12] Paragon Park would hold its formal opening on May 30. Poor weather kept the large crowds away on opening day, but the park showed great potential. A feature attraction of the park was the cabaret show. Vaudeville shows were changed weekly, as the show could be held outdoors in a grove, or brought indoors to the German Village, in case of rain.[13]

An event prior to the park's formal opening generated much unexpected commotion when aviator S.J. Crossley took off from Paragon Park in an attempt to fly his biplane over Baltimore city. Crossley was under contract to appear at various carnivals and exhibitions to demonstrate his flying skills. Strong winds however, forced him to land in the Gwynn Falls Valley when he was not able to pilot the craft safely back to the park. A large crowd gathered to gawk at the flying machine. Crossley was able to fly the plane back to the park later in the week.[14]

The roller coaster and carousel were still in operation, and several new bowling alleys were added. Newspaper ads stressed that admission was free to Paragon Park, which was managed by W.J. Crowley that first season. A special lineup was offered on the 4th of July. An aerial act, a contortionist, a comedian, and other entertainers were booked for the anticipated crowds. The day was capped off by a large fireworks display in the evening.[15] An August 1913 *Sun* ad touted Paragon Park as "this week better than ever … pleasure for all." Emphasis was placed on the open-air vaudeville programs.

An early season *Sun* paper ad in 1915 featured moving pictures and bowling contests for the ladies. No intoxicating liquors were sold at Paragon, as management tried to promote a high-class image for the park, which was now managed by Michael Luber. But Paragon Park would face the same inevitable fate that Electric Park would meet, and it was soon closed. A local company was contracted to purchase and remove the buildings at the park in January of 1916. The land was then later sold to a developer in 1918 with the intention of "building on" to an expanding Baltimore city.

13

River View
Amusement Park

Although it experienced a relatively short run as a full-blown amusement park, River View Park can trace its origins back as a popular meeting place for more than 60 years. Originally known as Point Breeze, this area was developed as a beer garden in 1868 by John Lowery. Initially, it consisted of nothing more than a one-story brick building in a grove full of picnic tables. "Lowery's Place," as it was sometimes referred to, had some success and established a reputation as an ideal gathering spot.

In 1876, Harry McGowan purchased the property and operated it as a picnic and retreat grounds, featuring his Point Breeze Hotel by 1879. McGowan hosted a variety of outings, sometimes offering hot air balloon launches and fireworks. Initially, McGowan's Point Breeze was served by the Highlandtown and Point Breeze Railway, which operated a small two-car train that shuttled visitors to the grove from High-landtown.[1] McGowan may have been keen on generating publicity for this ideal spot; he planted 100 trees, and named each for a different friend of his. He also kept two black bears on the property, which evidently developed a habit of consuming large quantities of beer.[2] E.B. Adams, the assistant superintendent of plant and factory engineering at Western Electric, would later compose a history of the Point Breeze site. He noted that McGowan "served his patrons a breakfast, consisting of a half-chicken, two fish, 2 soft-shelled crabs, and all the coffee and cakes one could eat, for 1 dollar. A mint julep cost 15 cents."[3] McGowan ran the resort until 1885, when William Folk took over.

Improvements began at Point Breeze in April of 1895. A bulkhead was added with a long promenade placed alongside it. An 800-foot pier was constructed with bath-houses placed at the far end. A new sewer system was constructed, and paths were laid about the grounds. A large pavilion was constructed to provide shelter for picnics and gatherings.[4] Large crowds began to frequent this spot to partake in bathing, diving, fishing and crabbing, followed by a sumptuous crab dinner in the evening. Children had free reign to run about the picnic grounds and could gaze intently at the bear enclosure to follow the animals' antics.[5]

The Point Breeze Company began making sweeping improvements to the site in spring of 1898, and the spot was named River View Park. This stock company's directors included John Hiltz, J.G. Wright, Louis Illmer, Lawrence McCormick, and Milton Offutt. Additions included a vaudeville theatre, casino, and revamped waterfront board-walk that was illuminated at night. The casino could handle up to 2000 patrons. At that time the Consolidated Railway Company ran passenger cars out to River View. A bandstand was erected in the center of the park, at which Steinwald's Military Band performed on many occasions. A carousel and shooting gallery provided thrills and entertainment as well.[6] The Great Divide (a scenic railway) was erected, complete with tunnels and electric lights at various points along its course.[7] It was built by L.A. Thompson of New York, who was recognized as the inventor of the first "modern" roller coaster, and responsible for several thrilling Coney Island attractions. The "Scenic Railway," a common term used in naming many early roller coasters, was thought to have originated from the Mauch Chunk Gravity Railway, a nearly nine-mile-long downhill railroad track constructed by a Pennsylvania mining company to deliver coal to the town of Mauch Chunk in 1827. Many scenic railway coasters offered painted scenery and dark tunnels to further enhance the ride's mystique.

The park was purchased later that year by United Railways. Local showman James L. Kernan would lease the park shortly after, in March of 1899. Kernan was a well-known operator of several local theaters and the owner of Hollywood Park. He announced plans to replace the existing restaurant with a large hotel-style structure which would feature wide verandas on the first and second floors for guests to enjoy meals. He went on to state that United Railways had promised 24-hour transportation to the park from any part of the city, for a 5-cent fare.[8] He labeled the park as "The Coney Island of the South" and embarked on an aggressive expansion plan. In July, the L.A. Thompson Scenic Railway Company was reported to be disassembling a carousel which they had erected on some property at Middle River with the intent to ship it to Coney Island. River View's success had prompted Thompson's company to establish a new resort at Middle River; but it soon abandoned the effort, to the disappointment of local residents who had hoped for employment opportunities.[9]

For the 1900 season, Kernan converted the casino building into a German Village. A large midway was erected between the casino and the scenic railway. Over 75,000 yards of canvas was used to decorate the site, which employed twenty different nationalities of people. Several different types of animals that afforded rides to the young ones were situated here as well. Kernan's brainstorm to develop the space situated beneath the casino resulted in the "Rathskeller" pub, which featured bark covering the interior and exterior walls to provide a rustic effect. The popular miniature train would also make its debut that year. The 10-car train provided a scenic trip for 20 passengers over a 1200-foot track layout.[10] Other offerings on the midway at that time included the Hindoo Theatre, Crystal Maze, gypsy camp, Essau the snake-eater; the Moorish Maze, and electric gondolas.[11] The park added a large museum full of curiosities for the 1901 season, along with new features to view in the American biograph and the theatre.[12]

In April of 1902, it was announced that James Kernan would not renew his lease, and Michael J. Fitzsimmons was brought in to manage the park. Early attractions in place at that time included the Mountain Gorge, the Cave of the Winds, the Katzenjammer Castle, and Ye Old Mill ride. After a successful 1904 season at River View, the Royal Artillery Band of Italy was booked to return for the 1905 season. The popular band had performed over 270 concerts during the season.[13] In November of 1904, the

L.A. Thompson Scenic Railway Company brought a suit against Mr. Fitzsimmons in an attempt to prevent him from installing another roller coaster at the park. The Thompson Company evidently had caught wind of River View's plans to add a roller coaster that would compete with Thompson's Scenic Railway; this was viewed as a violation of a previous agreement with River View Park.[14]

New amusements and attractions were unveiled in the spring of 1905 amounting to nearly $40,000 and included the Circle Swing ride, comedy acrobats, and a trained-horse act. Billiard and pool parlors were added below the pavilion. Captain Edwin Wilson, the lion tamer, was also featured, preceded by tantalizing ads of his dangerous foray into the cage of Cronje the untamed lion. Fitzsimmons would also order a new miniature train during the season; this newer model could "handle thirty passengers without a wreck." A Shetland pony concession was brought in for the season and quickly became a popular stop for the young ones. Strangely enough, fearing that people from foreign lands would visit River View and not be in a position to enjoy a familiar form of travel, Fitzsimmons ordered several camels to provide rides for children and adults.[15] The dining pavilion was extended to create a new shelter building which extended about 135 feet along the river bank.[16] The Royal Artillery Band left immediately after the season and traveled to New York to play at Pabst Garden.

A published report from February 1906 noted that a large music pavilion and an elaborate entrance arch were being added for the upcoming season. The arch was 105 feet wide and 60 feet tall, with the top lit by 2000 electric lights. Approximately $50,000 was spent in all on improvements, which included a new lake. A portico on one side of the lake was 170 feet long and nearly 50 feet high. Columns on either side were outfitted with electric bulbs.[17] Fitzsimmons also erected a fountain with electric lights in the middle of the lake.[18] Reported to be a copy of the newly installed electric fountain at Washington Park, New Jersey, its pumps could handle 1200 gallons of water per minute. The illuminated fountain would be activated at 10:30 each night, drawing large crowds to marvel at the array of lights, which were enhanced by a display of fireworks. The park was filled with so much light after dark that management decided to hold an amateur photography contest; the best night photograph snapped would net a $10 prize.[19]

Other attractions added at this time included the Hall of Laughter, the Electric Theatre, Down and Out, Ferris wheel, House of Mirth, pony farm, bandstand, and new roller coaster, believed to be a figure-eight model. The exciting Tours of the World offered a ten-minute tour to various parts of the world over mountains and streams while viewing spectacular vistas.[20] George Hale and Fred Gifford patented the illusion-based attraction, which debuted in 1906 and eventually appeared in hundreds of amusement parks around the world. A typical Tours of the World setup involved "passengers" entering through the rear of two Pullman railroad cars. At the other end of the car was a large movie screen where a projected film of various travel scenes appeared. Passengers enjoyed a simulation of a trolley car or train ride with a point of view showing the tracks laid out in front of the audience. Bells, whistles, and other sounds enhanced the experience, along with the shaking and shifting of the actual seats in the cars.

Signor Tasca and the Royal Artillery Band were brought back to River View for the 1907 season. This would be the band's first appearance in Baltimore since they were involved in a serious train wreck near Atlantic City in the fall of 1906. A special July 4 program was presented by Signor Tasca. The *Civil War* was a "realistic tone-picture of the hostilities between the North and the South. This production is a musical panorama through its various movements from beginning to end." The re-creation of the battle included the fife and drum, and musket and artillery fire.[21]

Fitzsimmons unveiled a successful promotion in August of 1907. He placed ads in the *Sun* to announce that kids could enjoy all of River View's attractions free of charge each afternoon between 1:00 and 2:30. He would go on to relate his appreciation to park guests: "We have had a large family patronage this season. Mothers have brought their children here freely, and at times the park has the appearance of a playground. I appreciate the value of this patronage, and I have determined to give the kids a good time free of all expense."[22] The Baltimore Lodge of Elks held their summer outing at River View in May 1908. The highlight of the event was the crab soup contest, which was held under the watchful eye of C. Ross Klosterman. Two dozen cooks competed for a prize for the best or most popular cook.[23]

This rare c. 1898 photograph of the L.A. Thompson Scenic Railway is believed to be from River View Park. Thompson was recognized as the premier designer/builder of the early scenic railways in the United States and abroad (courtesy Jim Abbate collection).

Shortly after the 1908 season, Fitzsimmons decided to step down from his position as the president of the Maryland Biscuit Company (considered to be the largest independent biscuit company in the region). It was believed that Fitzsimmons, with an impressive reputation for business matters, was looking to free up additional time to devote to River View and various other business ventures.[24]

Improvements for the 1909 season included a double roller coaster—the Ben Hur Racer, more commonly known as the Racer Dips. Built near the park entrance adjacent to the Roland Park streetcar loop, this racing coaster boasted a height of 75 feet. It offered a twisting "double-s" layout that measured nearly a mile and a quarter in length. The park claimed it was the longest amusement ride ever built. The proximity of the dual tracks encouraged some who desired to be on the "winning train" to reach out and attempt to hold back the other train, which resulted in several serious accidents over the years.[25]

Management also decided to rebuild the Scenic Railway, adding six new dips, some as high as 60 feet.[26] Another new attraction was a "Tour of the Alps" (which replaced the Tours of the World) which offered moving pictures depicting scenes from the Alps. The casino building received a fresh coat of paint. In addition, a Human Laundry funhouse concession, similar to Electric Park's, would debut here this season.[27] A wooden boardwalk a mile and a quarter in length was also erected to replace the old path to the waterfront. Benches were placed at dark corners along the walk to provide couples with a romantic spot to enjoy the view of the water and take in the sounds of

MINIATURE RAILWAY. River View Park. Baltimore, Md.

The ten-car miniature train departing the station to travel its 1200-foot track layout. This family friendly ride made its debut at River View for the 1900 season (courtesy Baltimore County Public Library).

One of many Old Mill rides built in the early part of the 20th century, River View's Ye Olde Mill ride floated guests through its darkened course; a water wheel created the gentle current which propelled each boat. It culminated in an exciting chute drop into the water (postcard view).

the band.[28] The new Park Theatre was opened to present vaudeville shows and motion pictures.[29]

Misfortune beset the park at the end of the 1909 season, as a costly fire wrecked a large portion of the park on September 30. The fire, of unknown origin, started in the stables below the casino building and quickly spread to several other buildings and attractions. Among those destroyed were the figure eight (Scenic Railway #1), Old Mill, casino (including the Human Roulette Wheel), photograph gallery, bandstand, miniature train station, pony stable, Katzenjammer Castle, and a half-dozen concession stands. Structures that suffered damage included the Great Divide (Scenic Railway #2), the rest house, and part of the boardwalk and pier. United Railways' powerhouse, located just outside the park, was, fortunately, left untouched. A few boats were hurriedly pressed into service to fight the fire, including the fireboat from the Maryland Steel Company and a couple of nearby tugs, which helped douse the flames on the park's long pier.[30] Only four rides were left standing, the Racer Dip, Great Divide, Scenic Railway, and carousel. Despite the extensive damage, River View was ready for its May opening for the 1910 season, as Fitzsimmons had the bandstand rebuilt over the water for the new season.

A day at River View Park was not complete without a concert by the Royal Italian Artillery Band. Concerts were held in the landmark band shell, which stood near where Colgate Creek joined up with the Patapsco River. A 1910 issue of the *Riverview* weekly newsletter lists Salvatore Oriunno as the head bandleader. Later ads refer to Oriunno as the "world's greatest trombone soloist." Musical numbers came from a wide range of selections, including operas, waltzes, two-steps, and marches. The band's noted interpretation of Giuseppe Verdi's "Anvil Chorus," which featured a sledgehammer-wielding musician bashing an anvil, signified closing time at River View. This would sometimes trigger a mad dash for a seat on the long trolley ride back home.

A visit to the funhouse was a highlight of a summer's day at Point Breeze. A steep slide led to moving floors, distortion mirrors, rotating barrels, and of course, air jets to raise the skirts of unsuspecting ladies. Also located in the funhouse was the Human Roulette Wheel, where several persons would be seated in the center of a large bowl. Once set in motion, upon achieving a sufficient speed, they were flung at high speed in various directions.[31] Another popular attraction was the Postal "Foto" Gallery. Patrons could get their pictures taken in front of an eye-catching and sometimes whim-sical backdrop, a keepsake souvenir to carry home at the end of the day.

Of course, eating and drinking at River View were an integral part of a day's visit. A dozen crabs could be had for about 75 cents. "Charlie the Crab Man" served up steamed crabs on paper-covered tables; hungry guests were each provided a wooden

A lone man stands near the rear of the exciting Racer Dips roller coaster. Riders reaching out to grab riders on the parallel racing train resulted in several serious mishaps over the years.

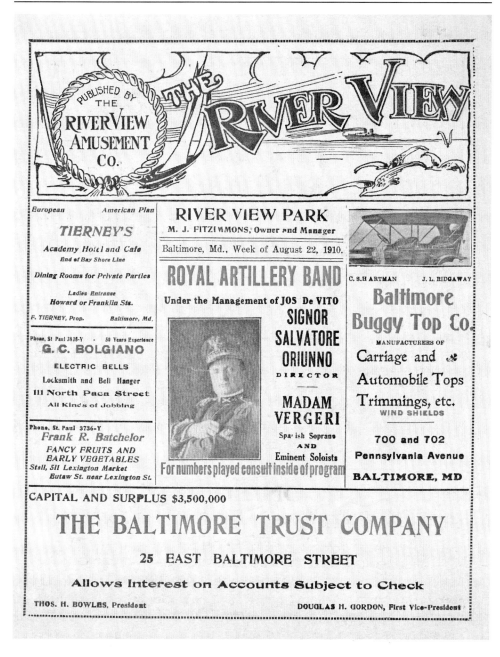

The *River View* ad/newsletter shown here from 1910, provided details on the park's concerts and other attractions.

chair leg to crack open the shell and dig out the succulent crabmeat.[32] The man operating the hot dog stand had an unbeatable pitch: "A loaf of bread, a pound of meat, and all the mustard you can eat …. for a nickel."[33] Chicken, seafood, and roast beef dinners cost 50 cents, usually accompanied with a large mug of beer.[34] Gottlieb-Bauernschmidt-Straus was the park's choice of beer for a time. Local organizations hosted annual picnics at the park, bringing their own traditional tastes; the German Singing Society dined on sour beef (sauerbraten) and dumplings, while the Ancient Order of Hibernians (Irish) favored corned beef and cabbage.[35]

Under William Gaban's watch for the summer of 1911, a new small lake was created to present a special diving act. Several bathing beauties were recruited to dive and swim about; it afforded quite a spectacle, especially at night with the multicolored incandescent lights in place.[36] A *Sunday Sun* ad from 1913 listed several of River View's attractions: "FREE FREE for children … every afternoon this week, starting Monday 1:00 and 3:30 p.m.: Not one ride, but as many as you want on the: Racer Dips, Canals of Venice, Scenic Railway, carousel, and Human Roulette Wheel. Take the children for a days pleasure. Costs you nothing but the 5-cent fare."

River View came under public scrutiny in August of 1913 when it was found to be one of several Baltimore businesses that were cited for employing minors in violation of the Child Labor Act. Park management faced four counts of employing underage workers, one being under 11 years of age. The remaining three youths were actually of legal age for employment but did not have the proper permits from the Bureau of Statistics, whose agents had led the investigations.[37]

For the park's 1915 opening on May 8, a newspaper ad highlighted River View's new dance floor, new Ferris wheel, famous steamed crabs, and "the only Racer Dips." The new 100-foot tall Ferris wheel that debuted that summer contained 3500 electric lights. A new miniature railway was purchased by Fitzsimmons at a cost of $7,500. The engine weighed just under three thousand pounds and was said to have the strength to pull two full-size freight cars. A string orchestra, along with singer Eddie Nelson, was booked to perform in the new Vienna Palm Garden, which was erected near the water's edge to enhance the nighttime views.[38] Free daredevil attractions were popular at River View during this period. A man would take off in a balloon, and, after achieving sufficient height, would leap from the basket, hoping that his parachute would open. High-dive performers would perform a death-defying plunge from a platform 75 feet above a shallow tank of water. The most infamous daredevil moment occurred on July 5, 1920, when a stunt pilot appeared at the nearby Dundalk Flying Field. Excited crowds gathered at River View's pier to watch the aerial exhibition, but they were soon horrified when the pilot crashed his biplane and was killed.

Upgrades to the park for the 1916 season included a new promenade built near the water front, complete with nighttime illuminations. Nearly $15,000 was required to replace the bulkhead which was swept away by a severe fall storm.[39] It was also noted that Professor Schwaber had been hired on to direct dancing at the park, offering free lessons to kids during selected afternoons, and contests with prizes being awarded to the winners.[40] River View suffered two separate mishaps on June 25, 1916. The miniature train derailed on a curve and overturned, injuring five passengers. Then an unidentified man decided to stand up at the highest point of the Racer Dip and fell to his death as the train descended the first drop.[41] During the 1917 season, the Children's Carnival was held three days a week beginning at 4:00 each afternoon. Professor Cockey's Famous Dancing Dolls provided character impersonations and dancing for the kids, who each received a souvenir for attending.[42]

One of River View's large group outings for the 1918 season was for the men of the Army's Camp Holabird. The camp was in need of an auditorium to be constructed. Sgt. E.P. Ramey devised a plan to hold a Holabird Day at River View on August 3. All proceeds from the day's outing, which was attended by 3000 men from Holabird, as well as 1000 from Fort Howard, and the general public, would be put towards the $30,000 goal needed for the project. A few Civil War veterans were on hand at the crowded park, as well as thousands of pretty young Baltimore girls. After a full day of enjoying the rides and eating and drinking, the Camp Holabird Band and the park's band both put on concerts. Local boxer Kid Williams closed out the evening with an exciting 10-round exhibition bout.[43]

Later that month, the public service commission declined a protest from Michael Fitzsimmons, who was seeking to have the United Railways place the five-cent excursion fare to River View back into effect, rather than the regular 10-cent fare that had been carried over into the summer season. Fitzsimmons naturally wanted the eager public to pay just the nickel fare to reach River View, thus ensuring steady attendance at the resort. The commission ruled that United continued to charge the ten-cent fare in order to lessen the traffic to the resort, which also allowed them to utilize their transportation resources that could be better used for war industries. The commission also contended that patronage at River View had not dropped significantly; therefore Fitzsimmons had not experienced a serious loss in revenue, in their opinion.[44]

Sadly, Michael Fitzsimmons passed away in January of 1919, after battling illnesses for several months. One of his eight children, William, would step up shortly to assume control of River View. In June of 1919, Captain Phillip Hembold, commander of the Provost Guards for the city of Baltimore, rescinded a previous order he had implemented, which essentially outlawed admittance to River View Park for any soldier, sailor, or marine in uniform. This order drew heavy criticism from a variety of groups and individuals, as it had also created a prohibited zone in northwest Baltimore for military personnel in an effort to reduce disorder and vice in certain areas that were frequented by men in uniform.[45]

In March of 1920, the general manager of the United Railway Company, Herbert Flowers, announced that the company would no longer manage their amusement resorts at Bay Shore and Gwynn Oak. A new company, the Amusement Parks Company, headed by William J. Fitzsimmons, assumed the responsibility of managing the popular parks. Fitzsimmons would soon become a very busy man, closely following in his father's footsteps.

Huge expenditures of cash marked the opening season of the 1920s. River View was faced with the prospect of stiff competition from the competing Baltimore amusement parks, particularly with the emergence of Carlin's Liberty Heights Park and Frederick Road Park. A new large illuminated entrance was constructed, and Valeno's Concert Band was booked for daily concerts. A huge new carousel (costing six cents per ride) replaced the early model which had been in operation for quite some time. Two new roller coasters would make their debut—the Cannon Ball and the Coal Mine Dips. Carl Hulsey of the Grand Rapids Amusement Company of Atlanta helped lay out the exciting Cannon Ball ride. (He would soon transfer over to Carlin's Park to act as foreman on the erection of the wild Mountain Speedway coaster.) The Coal Mine Dips featured a long dark tunnel at the top of the lift hill, simulating a trip through a coal mine. Other thrilling new attractions included the Rapids Gorge, Crystal Maze, funhouse, Ride the Rapids, and Kentucky Derby.[46] In addition, the park offered hydroplane rides from the pier, and it also added a new bandstand and revamped the bathing beach for the 1920 season.[47]

The park offered many rides and attractions to choose from in the Roaring Twenties, including Captain Louis Sorcho's Submarines and Deep Divers show, the Mysterious Woman, Devil's Hall, Oriental Hall, Harry Hunter's Wild Animal Circus, the Hopi Indian Village, the Whip, the Frolic, and the miniature train. Professor V.P. Wormwood, billed as the "World's Greatest Animal Trainer," operated the Monkey Theater. Other diversions included the shooting gallery, billiards room, flying horses, giant Ferris wheel, Chair-o-Plane, swimming pool, Caterpillar, and roller skating rink. Children could enjoy the pony rides, the carousel, and the goat carts. Boxing and wrestling matches were presented at River View on occasion, drawing sizable crowds.

Unfortunately, River View experienced more than its fair share of roller coaster accidents over the years. Most appeared to be the fault of the rider, though. In an incident on June 18, 1922, a 27-year-old man stood up as he rounded a curve on the Coal Mine Dips. He was tossed out of the car, fell over 30 feet to the ground, and died of his injuries at the hospital the following day.[48]

The United Italian Societies held their annual picnic at River View for several years. The August 1922 celebration saw more than 4000 members take part in boat races and athletic events. The featured speaker was Governor Ritchie; the day was capped off by a dance and a fireworks display.[49] Sadly, an 11-year-old boy drowned in River View's pool in September of 1922. The boy's father would win a $5,000 settlement against the park the following January, as the court ruled negligence in that the pool was not properly safeguarded.[50]

Several old newspaper accounts describe wild gang brawls involving the early trolley routes to River View. The Number 10 car line carried passengers from Roland Park through downtown to Highlandtown and lower Canton. When two "rival" streetcars (one usually occupied by the notorious Sandy Bottom Gang) would pull alongside one another, a broadside "battleship"-type fight would ensue, with beer bottles as the weapon of choice. Law-abiding fare-paying customers had to fend for themselves. Fitzsimmons announced several new additions to the park in April of 1924. An expanded parking lot awaited those who chose to make the drive; and the road leading in to the park was improved as well. The dance floor was enlarged, and new rides installed included a skooter car and airplane swing.[51]

On Labor Day of the 1925 season, the largest gathering of Baltimoreans for the holiday weekend was credited to River View's 36th annual Labor Day picnic, hosted by the Baltimore Federation of Labor. Governor Ritchie and Mayor Jackson were the honored guests of the federation. Many field events were held for the youngsters in attendance. Governor Ritchie's address included a tribute to the late Samuel Gompers, who had served as president of the American Federation of Labor (AFL) until his death

River View generated quite a bit of income by selling whimsical souvenir photographs. Various backdrops were offered, including boats, airplanes, and the stylish automobiles of the time.

in December 1924. Ritchie commented that the "national prosperity and welfare are dependent on the contentment and happiness of the workers of the country."[52]

New attractions for the 1926 season included a modern miniature railroad and a new Ferris wheel. However, one popular park hangout, the Penny Arcade, was lost in an early-season blaze. Admission to dance in the park's Crystal Ballroom that summer was fifty cents. The park was noted for its spectacular Independence and Defender Day fireworks displays. Local resident Charlie Echols recalls a visit to River View in the late 1920s as a 12-year-old. The park's three exciting roller coasters stand out in his mind. He remembers sitting on the front steps of his house on Sundays, across the water from the park, watching the balloonist perform the dangerous parachute jump. (Charlie's memories from this period also include roller skating undisturbed on the nearby newly constructed Broening Highway, which carried virtually no auto traffic for the first couple of years after completion.)

River View Park's existence at Point Breeze soon came to an end, succumbing to both the widespread use of the automobile and the inevitable industrialization of the area. On October 30, 1928, Western Electric purchased 125 acres of land, including River View Park, and announced plans for a $15 million plant that would manufacture telephone cable and wire. Western Electric had essentially run out of space to expand

Interesting view from the water's edge of the rebuilt band shell. Daily concerts were a highlight of a visit to River View (from the Maryland Rail Heritage Library, courtesy Baltimore Streetcar Museum).

A c. early 1920s detailed aerial view of the park. Note the proximity of the band shell to the water, in the upper left portion of the photograph next to the pier. The park's three roller coasters and the old mill chute can clearly be seen here (photocopy by Holmes I. Mettee Studio).

at their other plants. United Railways president C.D. Emmons confirmed that the park would be razed. It was believed that the first phase of the construction project would be complete by December of 1929, with an estimated need of up to 1500 workers. A local wrecking firm advertised the need for 75 men to tear down River View, but nearly 700 men answered the ad, and crashed the gates when they learned there weren't enough jobs for all. Police were called in, and the situation was peacefully resolved.[53]

A fondly remembered piece of River View Park was kept on display in Baltimore after the park's closing. J. Roland Stolzenbach purchased the beloved miniature train locomotive and displayed it at his electric equipment store on Frederick Street, and also later at his new location on Pratt Street for several decades.[54] There was a brief resurgence of interest in River View Park in 1961 when, during a Western Electric expansion project, the park's old swimming pool was unearthed, fully intact. There were some efforts to convince the company to

Captain William C. Eliason, who helped form and then managed Tolchester Beach for many years (courtesy Tolchester Beach Revisited Museum).

restore the pool for employee use, but, sadly, this fell through. Several years later, in 1969, the Baltimore Streetcar Museum would complete a restoration of the only streetcar remaining (#1164) from the Number 10 Riverview Line.

14

Tolchester Beach

Among the finest of the old Chesapeake Bay resorts, Tolchester Beach outlived many of the Baltimore area amusement parks. Believed to have opened around 1877, this venerable beach resort survived until 1962. The development of the site can be traced all the way back to 1659, when Lord of Maryland Cecelius Calvert granted several hundred acres of land to William Toulson. The land was divided and sold several times up until the early 1800s when John Thomas Mitchell acquired a large tract which included Tolchester and Gresham Hall, built in the mid–1740s. The Mitchell family sold just over 1000 acres to the Ambrewster family in 1876. The Ambrewsters met up with Philadelphia steamship operators Calvin Taggart and his son E.B. Taggart, who were running a steamship line on the Delaware River and were looking to expand their operation to include the upper Chesapeake. The two families, along with one of Taggart's former deckhands, William C. Eliason, formed the Tolchester Improvement Company. At that time, Eliason was working on the steamer *Pilot Boy*, a 600-passenger steamer.

Eliason spent his childhood years in Delaware and lost both parents when he was still a young boy. He decided to leave school at the age of fourteen and started working on a farm. He was not cut out for the farmer's life, however, and soon heeded a call to the excursion business. He landed a job as the clerk of the Philadelphia and Chester Steamboat Company. After three years, he was promoted to the position of ship's purser on the side-wheeler steamer *Ariel*, which plied the waters of the Delaware River. After another three years of work experience, he then opted for the Tolchester enterprise.[1]

Plans were drawn up to connect the steamship line with a new railroad being laid across Kent County. However, the rail line folded, and the plans were scrapped. The group soon leased a wharf in the Baltimore harbor, and formulated a plan to open an excursion route that would take Baltimore residents on a two-hour cruise to a fine summer resort down the bay. Initially 10 acres, Tolchester Beach eventually grew to encompass over 150 acres.

At first, the site was essentially a simple picnic grounds. It contained a small wharf, only one building, a few sheds, and a hand-propelled carousel.[2] On one of the initial steamer trips to Tolchester, the *Sarah K. Taggart* ran aground near the Tolchester wharf. Excursionists were safely brought to shore and hasty arrangements were made to accommodate the throng of 200 for the night, if it became necessary. Finally, around midnight, passengers were returned to the ship, which was freed by the tide around 3:00 a.m.[3] The Tolchester Steamboat Company, as it came to be known, announced at the resort's opening that the operation would be under temperance management, meaning that no alcohol would be served on the boat or at Tolchester Beach. This was in marked contrast to many of the other gathering places at that time, as many amusement parks began their lives as beer gardens. Most speculated that the Tolchester Beach venture would fail to turn a profit, but they were soon proved wrong. Approximately 30,000 guests visited Tolchester in its first summer of operation.

The steamer *Nellie White* would replace the *Pilot Boy* for the 1881 excursion season.[4] The Tolchester Steamboat Company would soon purchase the steamer *Louise* from the York River Line. The popular steamer had undergone a recent rehab, including a new coat of paint, and was capable of carrying up to 2000 guests. The expanded dining room could accommodate 75 people. The expansive grounds at Tolchester would experience continual improvements. Four large pavilions were in place to host group outings for the 1883 season.[5] A pair of alligators and different species of fish were on display for the 1885 season. They were accompanied by a small collection of caged animals for visitors to observe. The younger guests spent quite a bit of time in the new skating rink or taking endless spins on the new merry-go-round. The steamer *Louise* was upgraded to include a new stairway, an enlarged saloon, and the addition of sixty electric Edison lights to enhance the ship's appearance after dark.[6]

A special attraction at Tolchester during the 1887 season was a balloon ascension by eighteen-year-old Grace Levere of Cincinnati, Ohio. Her much-anticipated flight, which was launched from behind the shooting gallery on a warm June evening, ended shortly afterward in a tall cherry tree, about a mile and a quarter away from the beach.[7]

The new steamer *Tolchester* began its runs to Tolchester in late May of 1899. This increased the capacity of families wishing to make the journey down the bay. A multitude of improvements were made to the resort that year, including a new shooting gallery, a sledding hill, and several new bathhouses. An Oriental music stand and a new dining room were placed atop the bluff above the beach. A large bridge stretching across the ravine which separated the restaurant from the park was erected. In addition, a snack stand was opened near the wharf to offer visitors additional eating options.[8]

However, the most popular new attraction for that summer was the Whale At Tolchester. Bill Betts, the curator of the Tolchester Beach Revisited Museum, which is located in Rock Hall, Maryland, on the Eastern Shore, relates the story detailing one of Tolchester's most curious exhibits. In 1889, a large whale, about 70 feet long and weighing approximately 65 tons, was captured alive off of Cape Cod, Massachusetts. Entrepreneurs saw a chance to make a few dollars on the behemoth, and transported the whale to Boston. They pumped it full of embalming fluid to help keep the carcass intact, to extend the period of viewing by the general public. When they ran out of embalming fluid, whiskey was used as a substitute. The whale was then placed on a barge to embark on a tour of seaside cities for the masses to gawk at. It eventually made its way up the Chesapeake Bay, for a well-publicized visit at Tolchester Beach. For a fee, guests could have their pictures taken—inside the whale's mouth! For a higher fee, guests would actually eat a meal inside the whale's mouth while seated at a dinner table. Quite a few souvenir photos were purchased as a result of this floating odyssey. The traveling spectacle came to an end in the late summer of 1891, when the whale's barge sank on Lake Ontario on its way to an appearance at the New York State Fair.

The five companies of the 4th Regiment set up camp at Tolchester Beach for a week in July 1893. Dubbed Camp Frank Brown, to honor Maryland's resident governor, the men performed various military drills and maneuvers. Several drills conducted could not be executed in the company's armory, including changes in the front, deployments on the march, and the dress parade. The men would also have time to participate in a few athletic events during the week, including a baseball game.[9] Under Eliason's direction, Tolchester expanded a bit each year, prompting the eager crowds to return to see what new attraction had been added. An early roller coaster, the Great Pike's Peak Route or Bust (or Pike's Peak, for short), which featured a twisting figure-eight layout, was in operation by 1895. (Newspaper articles indicate that Tolchester had a gravity railroad in place by the 1890 season.[10])

About 2500 excursionists enjoyed the first Presbyterian Day at Tolchester in June of 1894. The large contingent was made up of congregations from several Presbyterian churches in Baltimore and the surrounding area. Messages from President Grover Cleveland and Vice-President Stevenson were read to the crowd during an afternoon of several speeches. The two had been extended invitations to attend the gathering, but their busy schedules would not accommodate it.[11]

Improvements for the 1896 season included additional pavilions and picnic booths, lengthening of the Pike's Peak layout, a baseball field, a pavilion at the end of the wharf, and the construction of a porch around the hotel. Also, eight hundred bathing suits were purchased for those wishing to wade in the cool bay waters. The steamer *Louise* was overhauled as well. New electric lighting was added and a searchlight was placed in her new pilothouse.[12]

More than 5000 people took part in the Tolchester Fair in August of 1896. This three-day late-season event offered a wide variety of Eastern Shore products to view, on display in the Excursion Building. These included watermelons, pumpkins, peaches, pears, corn and other garden produce. Ladies could see various needlework items, while the men could investigate the latest in farming devices and machines. A balloon ascension and parachute drop were part of the festivities.[13] Improvements announced for the 1897 season included the Amet magniscope, which projected life-size moving pictures. This attraction was placed in a newly erected building on the park grounds. Also, a quarter-mile bicycle track was built within the confines of the horse track's infield.[14]

A suit was brought against the owner of the Pike's Peak concession, William Potts, in 1897. A man sought $10,000 in damages stemming from a personal injury he suffered while riding in a car on the Pike's Peak railway in August of 1895. When the gentleman was noticed to be absent from the car when it returned to the station, a search was conducted, and he was found unconscious in one of the ride's tunnels, with a head wound. It could not be determined how exactly the injury occurred, and, no one witnessed the injury. No faults or defects along the ride's course could be linked to the mishap. A court of appeals found in favor of Mr. Potts in June 1898.[15]

Other early attractions awaiting anxious fun seekers included the Switchback Railway, another early roller coaster that, according to some sources, was in place by 1893. It was later sometimes referred to as the Hula Zula (the sign at the station entrance and on the side of the ride's tunnels advertised "See Hu-la and Zu-la" for a period of time). A shooting range, bowling alley, dance hall, Razzle Dazzle, miniature railroad, and bingo parlor were on hand to entertain the masses. In 1899, the Tolchester Line purchased the Sassafras River Steamboat Company, adding two steamers to the fold, the *Sassafras* and the *Kitty Knight.*

Several improvements were in evidence for the summer of 1899. In April, the *Emma Giles* transported carpenters and a load of lumber, rails, and cross ties to Tolchester Beach. These were the materials needed to build the new miniature train ride. This attraction, containing up to 10 passenger coaches holding two people each, debuted that season. The train could reach a top speed of 12 miles an hour. Also, it was noted that "an interesting addition has been made in the tunnel of the Switchback Railway, representing lovers very much engrossed in love making."[16] (Tunnels would play a key role in promoting early amusement attractions like a scenic railway or old mill ride to young couples. They afforded an opportunity for a quick kiss in public, albeit in the dark.) Also, the carousel was renovated, and new tunes were purchased for the carousel's band organ, which was thought to be one of the best south of Coney Island. A total of thirty songs, 10 on each of the three rolls, played ragtime, patriotic, and military marches.[17]

July of 1899 saw the beach host a gathering of the United Confederate Veterans. A target shooting contest at the shooting gallery and other games were arranged for the day's program. A drill and dress parade finished up an enjoyable day. It was noted that the day's events were kicked off by the "Gorilla" Band, which was made up of a dozen veterans who "drew forth discordant strains from all imaginable kinds of toy musical instruments. For the peace of mind of their hearers, the leader of the band announced the name of each piece before it was played. As might be expected, the selections were all of Southern airs."[18]

Several improvements were in place for the 1900 season. A larger steam engine was purchased for the miniature railroad, and the Switchback Railway's course was lengthened again with some additional scenery. The hotel's dining room was expanded to accommodate a larger number of guests, and several family booths were added to the park grounds.[19] Nearly 4,000 visitors crowded the *Louise* and *Sassafras* for the opening day of Tolchester's 23rd season.[20] Other improvements were made, including renovations to Pike's Peak to make the ride higher, as well as adding two new cars to the miniature train. In June of 1901, Baltimore resident William J. Glover, Jr., swam from Tolchester Beach to River View Park, a distance of at least 24 miles in a difficult current. It took over 16 hours to complete the tiring trip.[21] His arrival was met by 4000 cheering guests at River View.

A new hotel was constructed for the 1903 season, and the wharf expanded to accommodate up to three steamers at once.[22] One of the largest crowds to enjoy Tolchester's peaceful setting during the 1905 season was the June 15 gathering of the Ancient Order of Hibernians, as well as two church groups that descended on the beach. These large excursions attracted 4500 guests, and provided the largest number of bathers seen at the beach up to that point for the summer.[23] New amusements including a gymnasium were added to the park grounds that summer.

At this time, Captain Eliason, who was now president and general manager of the Tolchester Company, remarked on his given title of "Captain." "Why I couldn't take out the papers the law requires before it grants that title. It's true I went out day in and day out with the excursionists for over twenty years, and now when there's an especially big crowd I go along, but not as captain. As a matter of fact, I hardly know port side from starboard. I've filled every post except that of stewardess, engineer, and captain; but my chief occupation has been to look after the crowds. And the people got so accustomed to seeing me around, that they kind of got into the habit of calling me Captain, and the name hangs on."[24] During this same conversation, Eliason was quizzed about his secret to success in the excursion business. His response was to "cater to the women and children": "Any man who starts out to cater to the men is a fool; men are never satisfied. If they go to a first-class hotel, and you give them turkey they will say why wasn't it duck? Make the excursions for the women and children and you're all right in the excursion business."[25]

Three new large archways greeted boat passengers at the wharf entrance for the 1906 season. Other improvements included new cement paths and additional pavilions. A large funhouse, the House of Trouble, debuted as well.[26] A much-beloved miniature train ride, powered by "Jumbo" the steam locomotive, named for the famous circus elephant, was also erected. Built at Baltimore's Baldwin Locomotive Works, it carried thousands of kids over a quarter-mile layout, complete with tunnel, over the next several decades. (Leonard Ward, the engineer for some 25 years, noted that 500 pounds of coal would be burned on a busy day to keep Jumbo moving.[27]) Concession owner William Potts was sued in October of that year by a man who claimed that his son was injured by steam escaping from his carrousel.[28] Another diversion to enjoy was the Queen Anne and Kent County Fair that was held at Tolchester starting in the late 1890s, and ran for several years, until it was closed, along with the race track, in 1914.[29]

The Tolchester Line eventually encompassed a fleet of six steamers and a ferry boat that sailed from Pier 16 at Light Street in the Baltimore harbor. These included the steamers *Louise*, which could hold 2500 passengers, *Emma Giles*, *Susquehanna*, *Annapolis*, and *Tolchester*. The *Louise* was estimated to have carried over 12 million passengers from 1882 to 1925 for the Tolchester Line. The *Emma Giles* was built in 1887 and carried passengers until 1932. The *Susquehanna* could hold around 1000 passengers and completed its runs to Tolchester in 1923. The *Annapolis* was commissioned in 1899 as the *Sassafras* and was in operation into the 1930s. The journey to Tolchester from the harbor was approximately 23 miles. As many as 20,000 patrons visited the resort on summer weekends. Sunday school picnics were very popular throughout the years.

One of the park's more thrilling rides was the Coney Island Tickler. The Tickler (invented and built by W.F. Mangels) was a standard ride at several amusement parks in the early part of the 20th century. Added at Tolchester for the 1908 season, it consisted of circular cars that were released at the top of a large inclined plane. The surface of the plane was covered by various railings, which served as jarring obstacles, helping to slow the cars' descent. Essentially, riders experienced the unique sensation of being the ball in a pachinko or pinball machine.

The landmark excursion pavilion was built for the 1909 season at a cost of about $11,000. Designed with an Italian villa in mind, the three-story structure consisted of two large towers and wide verandas. Many chairs, rockers, and benches were scattered throughout the structure to offer comfortable resting places for excursionists. A lunch counter on the first floor also sold candy and sodas. A successful 1909 season prompted management to consider extensive improvements, including new amusement devices for the following summer. Sadly, William Potts, now the director of the Tolchester Steamboat Company, passed away at the age of 73 in July 1910. A travel buff by nature, he and his wife had taken an around the world cruise just one year earlier on the steamship *Cleveland.* He was the owner of most of the amusement concessions at Tolchester.[30]

Improvements were made to the wharf in the spring of 1911. An observatory tower and lighthouse were added at the end of the pier, while the ornamental arch was added at the shore end of the pier.[31] The steamer *Louise* was overhauled in the offseason, with new carpets and electric fixtures, in addition to extensive painting.[32] Fresh paint was evident at the beach, and new walking paths and flower beds were added. Poor weather limited the Kent, Queen Anne, and Cecil County Fair to just one day of operation during fair week of September 1911. More than 5000 visitors crowded the Tolchester grounds following four days of rain, and were able to enjoy the booths and games of chance.[33] A more thrilling roller coaster, the Whirlpool Dips, was built in time for the 1913 opening at a cost of $15,000. This ride lasted until the park's closing in the early 1960s. Many a Baltimorean still remembers the jarring, twisting ride. Other improvements for 1913 included a building that served up crab lunches, and bungalows constructed on the bluff overlooking the bay. Various lighting features were added as well for nighttime activities, including a 20,000 candlepower lamp that was installed in the wharf tower to help illuminate the pier after dark.[34]

Given the popularity of salt-water bathing, accommodating the large masses with suitable bathhouse facilities was a constant challenge for Tolchester's management, similar to Bay Shore's ongoing dilemma. In a somewhat humorous letter to the editor in July 1913, the writer bemoaned the predicament of renting a bathing suit:

> After arriving at Tolchester we had dinner at the hotel, and thought we would like to take a swim, and proceeded to the beach for this purpose. The writer bought three tickets, and upon presenting them to the attendant were told that we would have to wait for a while for bathing suits, and after a short while, the suits were forthcoming, but we were informed that they could not supply us with a bathhouse, and that we would have to use small buckets for our clothes and undress and dress in the adjoining public bathhouse, in which there were 20 to 30 persons, dressing and undressing, ranging in ages from 10 and upward. The bathing suits supplied us were of such a size that they would have fit the largest fat woman in any sideshow or freak museum, absolutely buttonless, leaving the wearer at the will of the waves or wind. After taking the swim under these pleasant conditions, we returned to the public bathhouse, where not the slightest degree of privacy exists. We asked the attendant for a towel, and he handed us a disease cloth, which, if the company had used to clean the flues

of its steamers with the same, could not have been much dirtier. Upon our refusing to accept same, we were consigned to a region much warmer than Tolchester, but possibly with a little less dust, and we were compelled to dry ourselves with our handkerchiefs.[35]

Additional amusements that appeared at Tolchester included pony and goat cart rides, the Whip, Ferris wheel, Dodgems, and an exciting Chutes ride that offered the brave a long slide into the water. The T.L. Stine Company of Baltimore installed and owned several of Tolchester's rides and attractions. The 1914 season was ushered in with a special excursion to Tolchester aboard the newly renovated steamer *Louise*. The company officers and stockholders joined excited Baltimoreans for the special trip. Strawberry ice cream and cake were served to all passengers. Improvements at the beach included a new bathhouse, complete with 800 private lockers.[36] With the increasing popularity of the automobile, greater numbers of Eastern Shore residents began to frequent Tolchester. Ferry service was initiated soon, with one of the side-wheel steamers reconfigured to carry vehicles. In later years, a double-ended ferry, the *Express*, was purchased and placed in service to ferry passenger cars from Baltimore.[37]

Nearly 1500 excursionists would take the pleasant trip down the bay on the steamer *Louise* on opening day for the 1915 season. The ship had fresh paint throughout, with new electric lighting and an enlarged dance hall. Visitors marveled at the flower beds and well-kept hedges. At 5:30 p.m. during the directors' special dinner, the park grounds

The Pike's Peak or Bust attraction was an early figure–8 roller coaster (courtesy Historical Society of Baltimore County).

Very early view of Tolchester's popular shooting gallery. Many shooting contests were held here over the years (Maryland Historical Society, Item PP128.73).

were illuminated for the first time by electric lights, including the wharf and entrance arch.[38]

Tolchester opened for its 45th season on June 2, 1917. The cost of the round-trip to Tolchester aboard the steamer *Louise* increased from a quarter to 35 cents, to help offset rising maintenance costs. Three trips were offered daily, leaving the harbor at 8:30 a.m., 2:00 p.m. and 6:40 p.m.[39]

In May of 1921, the management of the various beach resorts within the state responded to those pushing moral reforms related to the latest in swimwear. At Bay Shore, for example, swimmers could opt to use socks rather than full-length stockings. At Tolchester Beach, "the fair bather could dispense with stockings, but she mustn't show the dimples on her knees." William H. Hudson, secretary of the Tolchester Company, went on to elaborate that "the privilege of stockingless bathing was contingent upon the length of the skirt reached below the knee stockings might be omitted without affront to the proprieties. But should it fail to reach that point, then something must come up to meet and atone for its brevity. Girls who would disport themselves in the water with ankles untrammeled are advised to be forewarned and secure skirts of ample size to allow for a shrinkage which might doom them to wear stockings all season."[40]

The 1920s and 1930s would prove to be financially difficult times for Tolchester. The steamboat line received annual subsidies to keep the operation active during this period, but still it did not always turn a profit.[41] Sadly, Captain William C. Eliason, the father of Tolchester Beach, passed away on April 25, 1921. His estate was appraised at over $37,000, according to the inventory of estate that was filed in the Orphans Court in August later that year.[42] Ride builder and concession owner T.L. Stine passed away

A view of an early roller coaster, the Switchback Railway. This attraction was providing guests with a scenic trip through the park by 1896.

The Steamer *Emma Giles* was built in 1887 and ferried millions of Bay passengers until 1932 (courtesy Tolchester Beach Revisited Museum).

Another view of Tolchester's Switchback Railway. It was also referred to as the Hula-Zula for a time. "See Hu-La and Zu-la" was the slogan displayed at the ride's station entrance and on a midcourse tunnel (courtesy Historical Society of Baltimore County).

Excursion ticket, 1939.

suddenly in January of 1923. Herbert G. Stine assumed control of the Stine Company and operated the Tolchester interests over the next several years. In January of 1929, he sold the rowboat concession to Oscar Leverton and A.L. Warner. Over the next two years, he subsequently sold the Swing, Popcorn, and wheel privileges to the same gentlemen. Tolchester Beach celebrated its 50th anniversary during the 1929 season. However, mostly minor upgrades would be made to the beach in the depression years, as

A lifeboat drill is underway here on the *Francis Scott Key*, docked at the Tolchester Pier in this August 1941 slide.

ANNEX HOTEL   TOLCHESTER BEACH, MD.

View of the Tolchester Hotel.

A c. 1940s view of the *Bear Mountain* moored at Tolchester's pier.

funds were tight. Additional picnic benches would be added, spread about the wooded areas and ravines, with the various park structures upgraded with the occasional fresh coat of paint.

Several bleak seasons were experienced in the early 1930s. The Tolchester Line received grants from the state in the amount of $25,000 during the 1932 and 1933 seasons. However, they operated at a deficit both years.[43] The competing Claiborne-Annapolis Ferry Company also received similar subsidies over these two years, and it showed a net income of $20,000 more than the subsidy. The ferry company's stockholders were paid handsome dividends, which raised the ire of state politicians, who soon called for an end to be put to the annual subsidies for the privately owned ferry companies. It was suggested by some that Maryland's state road system absorb the ferry lines.[44] The Tolchester Improvement Company went into receivership in 1936; $19,000 was bid for the park. The whole enterprise, including the Light Street pier, ships (*Emma Giles* and *Express*), and the property at Tolchester Beach, were eventually sold to a bond holders committee for $66,000 on September 22, 1936.[45]

In June of 1937, the new Tolchester Lines announced plans to resurrect ferry service from Baltimore to Tolchester, which would begin on June 13. Verbal approval from the public service commission was granted to the new line to operate the new service at the end of June. The steamer *Tolchester* made two and three round-trips daily hauling both passengers and freight. Plans were also underway to purchase a ferry to transport autos across the bay. The Tolchester Lines was headed by Benjamin Bowling (B.B.) Wills, president, and W.H. Kirkwood, treasurer. Final approval from the public service commission was received within a week's time. The commission also granted permission for the new company to issue $62,500 in capital stock and another $60,000 in bonds.[46] Wills was no stranger to the excursion business, having gotten his start a few years earlier by offering steamboat trips down the Potomac River to Chapel Point, an amusement park in Southern Maryland.

The park was the occasional site of political gatherings over the years. Mayor Jackson drew 1000 supporters to an outing that summer to promote his run for governor. A June 1938 *Baltimore American* article offering details on the new season recognized Captain Fred Kolb as the skipper of the *Tolchester*, and Joe Clemons as the manager of the Tolchester Hotel.[47] Additional amusements and picnic tables were added that summer. Improvements to the beach for the 1939 season included a new roller skating rink, which also was home to skating exhibitions and roller hockey games, and a new baseball diamond equipped for night games.[48] On May 15, 1941, while being prepped at the Light Street pier for the upcoming excursion season, the aging steamer *Tolchester* caught fire. The large blaze engulfed nearby piers and threatened to spread to nearby structures in the harbor before being brought under control. B.B. Wills soon arranged for the steamer *Mohawk,* and then the *Francis Scott Key,* to handle the crowds for the Tolchester run.[49]

The Tolchester Line came under fire in July of 1941 when news of a stampede at the Tolchester Beach pier late on a Sunday night was reported. Upon receiving many complaints of the conditions at the pier incident, where women and children were trampled and two men arrested, the public service commission ordered the company to revise its schedules and provide a second boat to be ready on standby. The situation unraveled when the steamer *Mohawk* ferried close to 1100 passengers on the afternoon trip to Tolchester. The captain planned to transport back some of the guests who had taken the 8:45 a.m. trip earlier in the day. However, due to a rainstorm, many passengers would not disembark when the ferry arrived at Tolchester, leaving little room to take on new passengers for the return trip. At 5:00 p.m. only one boat arrived back at Tolchester, and only a few of what was believed to be a crowd of 700 were allowed to board the vessel for the trip back to Baltimore. Those remaining on the pier had to wait until 10:45 when the *Mohawk* finally arrived, forty-five minutes past its scheduled time. The large queue of people became further frustrated when they could not board until 11:00 p.m. and the mass pushed forward at once when a single gate ramp was opened. In the ensuing panic, many had to be carried on board the ship, as a result of fainting or injury.[50] Tolchester's counsel, Victor Cook, would provide a positive report to the commission within two weeks of the incident, and noted that the company's schedule changes appeared to work to everyone's satisfaction on the most recent Sunday, when crowds were large.

Many long-time Baltimore residents can still fondly recall a day at Tolchester Beach. Jo Ruth relates "the whole neighborhood would pack up picnic baskets and head to the harbor. As kids, we'd sometimes get free passes from the man that delivered the beer to the local corner tavern. Getting there was half the fun. There was dancing on board. We all crowded the rail and departure gate, ready to race down the pier to grab a picnic table." Mad dashes to place a picnic basket on a table were considered to be the rule to stake your claim to a picnic site. She remembers her favorite activities were swimming in the Chesapeake Bay and riding (and re-riding) the roller coaster.

A July 1943 newspaper article detailed Captain William Elliott's observances on the differences of the picnicking habits of families. The traditional family picnic-basket lunch had started to give way to folks who preferred to pick and choose their food at the park, buying 15-cent hot dogs, beer at a quarter a bottle, and sandwiches and candy bars. It was evident that the beachgoers had more disposable income.[51] However, the war years brought rationing and other rules for citizens to abide by. Excursionists boarding steamers for Tolchester, for example, had to check their cameras with the ship's purser, as there was a government-imposed ban on taking pictures in any harbor that was deemed vital. Those who ignored the ban in the port of Baltimore were nabbed by the authorities.[52] Excursionists sailing from Baltimore and local Kent county traffic to Tolchester dropped off significantly during these years. Whereas a typical 4th of July celebration would in the past attract up to 1000 automobiles crowding the resort's parking lot, it was reported that just one vehicle was present for the 1943 holiday. Pleasure-driving restrictions just did not allow for families to take a casual drive to Tolchester for a day's outing.[53]

In late July of 1943, the Baltimore War Price and Rationing Board denied the Tolchester Line's request for 250,000 gallons of fuel oil for their *Bear Mountain* ferry. A representative for the board stated that the *Francis Scott Key* had sufficient means to carry excursionists and freight on the Tolchester run: "The company wants to triple its load of excursionists, using fuel oil which was so precious here last winter that we doled it out to householders for necessary home heat at the rate of twenty-five and fifty gallons." The Tolchester Line countered with the claim that it was turning away 500 to 2500 passengers a day because the *Francis Scott Key* could not accommodate the influx of travelers: "Many of these people are war workers who use the boat to make bus connections to their homes at Betterton, Rock Hall, and Chestertown."[54]

Tolchester's owners did not have any funds to add new attractions during these years either. G.G. Huppman managed Tolchester during the 1940s. He would benefit from a ban handed down from the Office of Defense Transportation in 1945. The ban essentially shut down all chartered streetcar service, which forced many churches and schools to adjust their scheduled annual picnics to the local amusement parks. Many organizations opted to utilize the boat service and take their groups for picnics at Tolchester.[55]

The 1948 season opened with two ships making the Tolchester run from Pier 16. The 225-foot *Bear Mountain* (piloted by Capt. Sam "Steamboat" Harrington) and the *Francis Scott Key* carried nearly two thousand schoolchildren from five local Catholic schools on the season's opening weekend.[56] The *Tolchester II* took its maiden voyage to Tolchester Beach in 1949. This steamer was previously known as the *City of Philadelphia* and the *Liberty Belle*. This would be the third ship coined *Tolchester;* it replaced the *Bear Mountain,* which was put to work ferrying excursionists on the Potomac River.[57] *Tolchester II* sported four decks, including a restaurant and dance floor, and could handle up to 2400 guests.

In April of 1950, the Tolchester Lines transferred their Pier 16 property to the city for a total of $56,000. The city was engaged in an ongoing Light Street improvement project and needed this valuable waterfront property.[58] The company began departures from Pratt Street's Pier 3 the following season. A fire in June of 1952 leveled Pennyland and damaged several structures, including the shooting gallery, ice cream stand, and the funhouse. The park offices suffered damage as well. The nearby bumper car pavilion, bowling alleys, and a soft drink stand were spared.[59]

The competing Wilson Line and Tolchester Lines signed an agreement in March 1957 to team up to offer a different excursion schedule on the bay. As part of the deal, the *Bay Belle* would sail each morning from Baltimore to Tolchester before sailing north to Betterton. Towards the end of the day, the vessel would stop again at Tolchester before heading back to the Baltimore Harbor. The *Tolchester II* would be utilized for special charter trips.[60] The joint agreement lasted for just one season, however.

In July of 1957, Wilson Excursion Lines received permission from the public service commission to transfer its assets, including Tolchester Beach and the SS *Bay Belle*, to the Wilson-Tolchester Steamship Company (no relation to the Wilson Lines). The acquiring firm, a subsidiary of the Baltimore & Annapolis Railroad Company, reportedly paid a total of $475,000 in this transaction.[61] The firm was headed by Bruce Wilson and long-time Tolchester employee John Moylan. *Tolchester II* would be leased to a concern that converted it into a gambling ship on the Virginia side of the Potomac

Tolchester's classic Pretzel dark ride. These attractions were a staple at many traditional amusement parks from roughly the 1930s through the early 1970s (courtesy Tolchester Beach Revisited Museum).

Great view of the Excursion house and the hotel from the Tolchester pier.

A c. 1950s postcard view of the miniature train with engineer Leonard Ward at the helm, with ever-present kids waiting for a ride.

River, in a short-lived business venture. The *Belle* would continue the Tolchester run, and also sailed to Betterton Beach and continued its runs to Tolchester until the park's final season. Attractions to enjoy during the 1950s included the "scooter" boats on the lake, Pretzel ride-in-the-dark, Custer Cars, Chutes ride, Swan boats, bumper cars, and roller skating. The site of the scooter-boat lake replaced the obsolete Switchback Railway attraction, which offered little thrills when finally removed from the park in 1949.

With the approach of the 1960s, it had become increasingly difficult to maintain the beachside resort. The aging Whirlpool Dips was in poor shape and prompted the park owners to briefly shut down the ride in July 1959, prior to a Department of Labor

Above and Opposite: Wilson-Tolchester Steamship Company group outing ad (courtesy Tolchester Beach Revisited Museum).

inspection initiated by patrons' complaints of the coaster's roughness.[62] It would be removed later that year.

In early 1960, the Wilson-Tolchester Steamship Company filed a lawsuit against the former owners of the *Bay Belle* and Tolchester Beach. Just a short two years after acquiring the enterprise, the Wilson-Tolchester Steamship Company tried to enact a provision in the sale agreement to sell the *Bay Belle* back to the original owner. The former owners claimed that the repurchase was contingent upon the vessel being in good operating condition. The ship's logs showed that the *Bay Belle* had run aground in June of 1959, and had also struck a submerged object later that summer.[63] During the federal lawsuit, in the Spring of 1960, the *Bay Belle* was inspected in dry dock and was found to have a cracked propeller shaft. By this time, the Wilson-Tolchester Steamship Company had leased a new vessel owned by the Maryland Port Authority,

A view of the venerable Whirlpool Dips roller coaster. This thriller operated for many decades at Tolchester (courtesy Tolchester Beach Revisited Museum).

the *Port Welcome*. Company official Bruce P. Wilson denied that the new vessel would compete with the *Bay Belle*, as the *Port Welcome* was expected to run daily cruises to Philadelphia and did not possess nearly the capacity of the *Bay Belle*.[64]

In April 1961, Joseph Goldstein, president of Wilson Lines, Inc., purchased the troubled Wilson Steamship Company, including Tolchester Beach, with the hopes of returning the resort to its early look of the 1890s. His initial plans included restoring the entrance pavilion and the quickly aging hotel. The Goldstein family also operated the Marshall Hall Amusement Park, which was situated across from George Washington's Mount Vernon on the Potomac River. The carousel was to be kept at Tolchester also. This coveted attraction was built in 1911 by the Herschell-Spillman Company and first operated at Baltimore's Electric Park. This antique model, containing a giraffe, llama, roosters, and ostrich, had operated at the beach since 1922. Goldstein had envisioned reestablishing passenger boat service to Tolchester once again. In doing so, the beach's old slogan would be resurrected: "Bring your lunch and forget your trouble, out in the deep blue sea. Wonderful tonic and salt air for the babies."[65]

Sadly, Goldstein's vision was not achieved, and the amusement park would not operate for the 1962 season. The park's hotel was condemned and torn down. In May of 1962, after over a century of steamboat excursions, it was announced that the Chesa-

A view of the miniature train pulled by "Jumbo" rounding a curve on the railroad's sprawling layout (courtesy Tolchester Beach Revisited Museum).

peake Bay steamer era had ended. Financial problems experienced by the Wilson Lines forced Goldstein's company to close down Tolchester Beach and the steamboat excursions. The defunct company owed the city of Baltimore $3,500 in rent on Pier 1, where the idle *Bay Belle* quietly sat.[66] October 20, 1962, marked the auction of the 52-acre Tolchester Beach; Baltimore auctioneer A.J. Billig was on hand to urge bidders along. Alan E. MacNicol, of Wilmington, Delaware, purchased the park for the mortgage holders for the sum of $75,000.[67] Property improvements detailed in the trustees' sale included the 16-room hotel, framed cottage, café, railroad pavilion, bandstand, beach houses, caretaker's home, and a large pier.

Shortly after the park's auction, former Maryland governor Theodore McKeldin strongly suggested in a letter to Governor Tawes that the state acquire Tolchester Beach for inclusion in Maryland's system of state parks: "I am aware of your concern for the preservation of open spaces along the seaboard as the great cities along the coast press constantly closer to each other with the steady construction of housing developments, industrial plants, and shopping centers. It seems to me that Tolchester Beach would be one of the ideal places to insure, through state ownership, against usage for residential or commercial purposes. It is true that Maryland now has a very fine system of parks, but much of the acreage is in Western Maryland … too little along our bay and ocean shores."[68] Despite these pleas, Tolchester would not become part of the state's park system.

A local contractor, David Bramble, purchased Tolchester Beach from a holding company in November of 1969. Bramble, who owned adjoining bay-front property, disclosed plans to build a new pier and marina for use by local fishermen and boaters. Treasured pieces of Tolchester would make their way to various places after the closure. The antique carousel was awarded to an individual as payment of a debt owed by the park. The horses were sold off piecemeal by the new owner. The miniature train, Little Jumbo, was sold prior to the park's auction to

Tolchester ticket.

Alva Price of Galena, Maryland. It then operated at White Crystal Beach, Maryland, for about five years. In the late 1960s, it was sold to the Toy Train Museum in Harpers Ferry, West Virginia, purchased in the mid–1970s by the Red Caboose Motel in the railroad town of Strasburg, Pennsylvania. The former owner of the motel, Don Denlinger, sold it to undisclosed parties in 1992.

A Worton, Maryland, farmer, Walter B. Harris, also managed to save various pieces of his beloved Chesapeake resort. The Harris family acquired the band shell and has utilized the turtle-shaped building that the Whip operated in as a dining hall at their Echo Hill Outdoor School. The ticket house from the goat ride was put to use on their private beach.[69] Bill Betts managed to acquire one of the passenger cars from the Toy Train Museum, and it is now on display at the Tolchester Beach Revisited Museum. A visit to this museum is highly recommended. It sits just a few miles down the road from the Tolchester Beach site, and the walls are covered with photos from the almost-forgotten amusement park. It will surely bring back fond memories for those who were fortunate enough to visit this special place.

Chapter Notes

Chapter 1

1. "A Chesapeake Bay Resort," *Baltimore Sun* (July 14, 1880).
2. "Excursions to Bay Ridge," *Baltimore Sun* (June 18, 1881).
3. "The Excursion Season," *Baltimore Sun* (May 12, 1883).
4. "Bay Ridge Excursion Controversy," *Baltimore Sun* (June 24, 1884).
5. "Bay Ridge Improvements," *Baltimore Sun* (September 20, 1884).
6. "Fighting for a Landing," *Baltimore Sun* (May 15, 1886).
7. "The Excursion Season," *Baltimore Sun* (June 21, 1886).
8. "Improvements Made by the Bay Ridge Company," *Baltimore Sun* (May 24, 1889).
9. "Saturday's City News," *Baltimore Sun* (July 28, 1890).
10. "A Through Line Now," *Baltimore Sun* (July 2, 1890).
11. "A Catholic Reunion," *Baltimore Sun* (June 30, 1891).
12. "The Bay Ridge Cases," *Baltimore Sun* (August 3, 1882).
13. Jane Wilson McWilliams and Carol Cushard Patterson, *Bay Ridge on the Chesapeake: An Illustrated History* (1986), 90.
14. Daniel Nelson, Theodore Hudson, and Ted Chase, *Highland Beach: The First 100 Years* (Highland Beach Historical Commission, 1993).
15. "The People's Outings," *Baltimore Sun* (June 12, 1893).
16. "Suit About a Merry-Go-Round," *Baltimore Sun* (April 6, 1894).
17. "Veterans at Bay Ridge," *Baltimore Sun* (August 2, 1894).
18. McWilliams and Patterson, *Bay Ridge on the Chesapeake*, 93.
19. "Improvements at Bay Ridge," *Baltimore Sun* (March 16, 1896).
20. "Christian Endeavorers," *Baltimore Sun* (July 15, 1896).
21. "McGinity the Champion," *Baltimore Sun* (June 30, 1897).
22. "Bay Ridge Improvements," *Baltimore Sun* (November 24, 1898).
23. "Bay Ridge," *Baltimore Sun* (May 26, 1899).
24. "Bay Ridge Excursions," *Baltimore Sun* (June 10, 1899).
25. "Steamer *Columbia* Sold," *Baltimore Sun* (July 18, 1899).
26. McWilliams and Patterson, *Bay Ridge on the Chesapeake*), 97.
27. "Bay Ridge Sold," *Baltimore Sun* (April 4, 1900).
28. "Chautauqua Now Open," *Baltimore Sun* (May 31, 1900).
29. "Topics in New York," *Baltimore Sun* (June 6, 1900).
30. McWilliams and Patterson, *Bay Ridge on the Chesapeake*, 144.

Chapter 2

1. "Plans for Bay Shore Park," *Baltimore Sun* (February 21, 1906).
2. "Bay Side Park Ready May 1," *Baltimore Sun* (March 12, 1906).
3. "Bayshore Park Will Open Today," *Baltimore News-American* (August 11, 1906), p. 16.
4. "Work on Bay Shore Park," *Baltimore Sun* (June 19, 1906).
5. "Bay Shore Park Unfinished," *Baltimore Morning Sun* (July 4, 1906), p. 12.
6. "Bayshore Park Will Open Today," *Baltimore News-American* (August 11, 1906), p. 6.
7. "Bay Shore to Open," *Baltimore Sun* (August 5, 1906).
8. Ibid.
9. "A Journey of Exploration to Beautiful Bay Shore," *Baltimore Sun* (May 26, 1907).
10. "Public Aroused," *Baltimore Sun* (August 13, 1906).
11. "Mr. Fitzsimmons to Run It," *Baltimore Morning Sun* (May 6, 1906), p. 8.
12. "Improving Bay Shore Park," *Baltimore Sun* (March 21, 1907).
13. "Real Estate Transactions," *Baltimore Sun*, March 27, 1907).

14. "The Good Old Go-Round," *Washington Post*, date unknown.

15. "Bay Shore Opens Tomorrow," *Baltimore Sun* (May 22, 1907).

16. "Getting to, and Home Again from, Bay Shore," *Baltimore Evening Sun* (March 7, 1978).

17. "Bay Shore Will Open Today," *Baltimore Sun* (May 28, 1908).

18. "Summer Amusements for All," *Baltimore Sun* (July 13, 1909).

19. "'Life-Saving' Dogs at Bay Shore," *Baltimore Sun* (July 27, 1909).

20. "Some of the Season's New Attractions at the Trolley Parks," *Baltimore Sun* (May 9, 1909), p. 13.

21. "Bay Shore Park Opens," *Baltimore Sun* (May 25, 1910).

22. "Bay Shore Park Opens," *Baltimore Sun* (May 28, 1911).

23. "Bay Shore Park Opens," *Baltimore Sun* (May 29, 1914).

24. "Dies from Carousel Injury," *Baltimore Sun* (June 4, 1915).

25. "Thrown from Carousel," *Baltimore Sun* (August 24, 1917).

26. "Criticism of the United Railways and the Company's Reply," *Baltimore Sun* (July 25, 1916).

27. "Why More to Bay Shore," *Baltimore Sun* (May 15, 1918).

28. "Bay Shore," *Baltimore Sun* (June 27, 1920).

29. Bay Shore Park ad, *Baltimore Sun* (May 30, 1920).

30. Display ad, *Baltimore Sun* (May 28, 1921).

31. "Excitement for All at the C. & P. Outing," *Baltimore Sun* (August 16, 1921).

32. "New Beach at Bay Shore," *Baltimore Sun* (May 27, 1922).

33. "Atlantic City and Coney Say 'No,' but Baltimore Welcomes Her," *Baltimore Sun* (June 12, 1922).

34. "Water Exhibition Draws Big Crowd," *Baltimore Sun* (July 30, 1923).

35. "'Horseshoe Floating Chairs' New at Baltimore Park," *New York Clipper* (May 31, 1924).

36. "Bay Shore Park," *Baltimore Sun* (May 24, 1924).

37. "Bay Shore Ship Line Is Organized Here," *Baltimore Sun* (May 29, 1924).

38. "I Remember … the Great International Air Race," *Baltimore Sun* (December 28, 1958).

39. "'Horseshoe Floating Chairs' New at Baltimore Park," *New York Clipper* (May 31, 1924).

40. Amusement Park Listings, *Billboard*, 1933 season.

41. "Fire Destroys Shore Ferry Line Steamer," *Baltimore Sun* (January 5, 1928).

42. Bay Shore ad, *Baltimore Sun* (May 29, 1930).

43. Bay Shore Park ad, *Baltimore Sun* (May 29, 1931).

44. "A.A.U. Distance Swim Meet Is Won by Bay Shore Club," *Baltimore Sun* (August 24, 1931).

45. "The Street Car Looks Down the Track," *Baltimore Sun* (May 21, 1933).

46. Ibid.

47. "Bay Resorts Are Ready," *Baltimore Sun* (June 13, 1937).

48. Fr. Kevin A. Mueller, *Bay Shore Park: Fun on the Chesapeake* (2001), 53.

49. "Bay Shore Reopens," *Baltimore Sun* (May 26, 1940).

50. "Bay Shore Midway Destroyed by Fire," *Baltimore Sun* (May 25, 1941).

51. "Charles Cole Scores Knockout on Service Program at Bay Shore," *Baltimore Sun* (July 12, 1941).

52. Bay Shore ad, National Association of Amusement Parks, Pools, and Beaches (NAAPPB), 1943 Handbook.

53. "Opinions and Forecasts by Leading Operators," NAAPPB 1945 Handbook.

54. "10,000 at Legion Day Celebration," *Baltimore Sun* (August 11, 1946).

55. "Will Develop Three Islands," *Baltimore Sun* (April 7, 1947).

56. "Bay Shore Park Is Fast Becoming Just a Memory," *Baltimore Evening Sun* (December 5, 1947).

57. "Mahoney Spending Millions to Improve Bay Shore Park Area," *Baltimore News-American* (May 23, 1948).

58. "Bay Island, Newest Beach Resort, to Be Ready for Opening May 30," *Baltimore Evening Sun* (April 26, 1948).

59. "New Yorker Plans to Buy Bay Islands," *Baltimore Sun* (August 5, 1933).

60. "Charley Swan Gets a New Job," *Baltimore American* (March 19, 1948).

61. "Horse at Park Shows Stunts," *Baltimore News-American* (May 29, 1949).

62. "Bay Shore Park Opening Scheduled," *News Post* (March 23, 1954).

63. "Bay Shore Park Ready for New Season," *News Post* (May 28, 1954).

64. "20 Hurt as Storm Hits Bay Shore," *News Post* (August 3, 1955).

65. "Miss Chesapeake Chosen at Bay Shore; Also a Mr.," *Baltimore Sun* (July 19, 1959).

66. "Bay Shore Park Is Doomed," *Baltimore News-American* (December, 1964).

67. "Mahoney's Last Hurrah," *Baltimore Sun* (January 14, 1981).

68. "Park's Renewal to Begin with Old Trolley Station," *Baltimore Sun* (July 18, 1993).

Chapter 3

1. *Port Welcome* Ship booklet, 1965.

2. "Better Days for Betterton," *Baltimore Evening Sun* (date unknown), p. 1.

3. "Unitarianism in America" (library Web site), "Enoch Pratt (1808–1896); sold nails and mule shoes early in his career, before moving into the trans-

portation, insurance, and banking industries. He was considered to be one of the leading philanthropists in Baltimore's history."

4. "Sassafras River Boats," *Baltimore Sun* (August 5, 1899).

5. "Betterton Bayside Land Company," *Baltimore Sun* (March 5, 1907).

6. H. Chandlee Forman, *The Rolling Year on Maryland's Upper Eastern Shore* (Easton, MD: H. Chandlee Forman, 1985).

7. "Crowd Is Expected at Betterton on Labor Day," *Baltimore Sun* (August 31, 1913).

8. "Betterton Inundated," *Baltimore Sun* (August 5, 1915).

9. "Chesapeake Bay Shores Delightful Retreats for Vacationists," *Baltimore Sun* (June 24, 1917).

10. "Kent County to Build Permanent Highways," *Baltimore Sun* (January 15, 1922).

11. "Betterton Shoot Will Start Today," *Baltimore Sun* (July 8, 1924).

12. "New Features at Betterton," *Baltimore Sun* (June 19, 1927).

13. "Betterton Has Lure for Fishermen," *Baltimore Sun* (June 3, 1928).

14. "Betterton Resort," *Baltimore News-American* (November 14, 1965).

15. "Betterton Expands," *Baltimore Sun* (June 12, 1938).

16. "Betterton, MD, Builds New Pier," *Baltimore Sun* (June 16, 1940).

17. "On the *Bay Belle*, in the Moonlight: River Romance," *Evening Sun* (July 30, 1946).

18. "City to Have One Excursion Boat," *Evening Sun* (February 17, 1956).

19. "Betterton Challenge to History Buffs," *News-American* (June 11, 1967).

20. Ibid.

21. "3-Alarm Fire Destroys Old Kent County Hotel," *Baltimore Sun* (January 9, 1972).

22. "Betterton Cruises," *Baltimore Sun* (July 22, 1973).

23. "Betterton Changing from Resort to Residential," *Baltimore Sun* (July 2, 1978).

24. "Future of Betterton, 'Jewel of the Chesapeake,' Shines Brightly," *Baltimore Sun* (April, 14, 1989).

Chapter 4

1. "Liberty Heights Park—Baltimore's Million Dollar Playground Opens Tonight," *Baltimore Sun* (August 13, 1919).

2. "Carlin Plans Park," *Baltimore Sun* (April 11, 1919).

3. Morris Radoff, *The Old Line State: A History of Maryland*. Library of American Lives (Annapolis, Hall of Records Commission, State of Maryland, 1971), chapter on John J. Carlin, 583–585.

4. "Baltimore Gets a Kick Out of Carlin—and Carlin Reciprocates," *Baltimore News-American* (March 13, 1949).

5. "To Open Big Dance Hall," *Baltimore Sun* (May 20, 1917).

6. "Baltimore Gets a Kick Out of Carlin," *Baltimore News-American* (March 13, 1949).

7. "Liberty Heights Park," *Baltimore Sun* (August 13, 1919).

8. "Liberty Heights Park Is Newest Baltimore Amusement Resort—To Be Completed Next Season," *Billboard Magazine* (September 13, 1919).

9. "Mr. Hershey's Dandy Candyland," *Washington Post*, date unknown.

10. "Building the Mountain Speedway at Carlin's Park," *Sun Magazine* (September 3, 1978).

11. Liberty Heights Park ad, *Baltimore Sun* (May 30, 1920).

12. Classified ad, *Baltimore Sun* (June 27, 1920).

13. "Promotion and Publicity Stunts," Proceedings of the 12th Annual Meeting of the National Association of Amusement Parks (NAAP) (December, 1938).

14. "Show Opens Tomorrow," *Baltimore Sun* (September 25,1921).

15. "J.J. Carlin Off to Houston," *Baltimore Sun* (October 29, 1921).

16. "Baltimore Welcomes Battleship Maryland," *Washington Post* (October 7, 1921).

17. "To Push Work at Carlin's," *Baltimore Sun* (May 14, 1922).

18. "The Sheik at Carlin's," *News-American* (July 30, 1972).

19. "Light Opera Summer Season Is Well Under Way at Carlin's Arena," *Baltimore Sun* (July 8, 1923).

20. "Carlin's Fight Arena Opens," *News-American* (June 3, 1924).

21. "Two Amusement Parks to Open in City Today," *Baltimore Sun* (April 11, 1925).

22. "Coronation of 'King Toots I' Marks Climax of Boys' Week," *Baltimore Sun* (May 2, 1925).

23. "Carnival Queen Test Is Popular," *The Times* [Baltimore] (September 9, 1925).

24. "Draws Excellent Pre-Season Business," *Billboard* (May 8, 1926).

25. "Carlin's Park, Baltimore," *New York Clipper* (August 3, 1923).

26. "Draws Excellent Pre-Season Business," *Billboard* (May 8, 1926).

27. "Blaze at Carlin's Wrecks Building," *Baltimore Sun* (September 15, 1927).

28. "Carlin's Fire Lights Up City," *Baltimore Sun* (February 18, 1928).

29. "Renovated Carlin's Park Offers New 'Thrillers,'" *Baltimore Sun* (April 7, 1929).

30. "Today Season Begins at Carlins," unknown (April 6, 1929).

31. Richard Munch, *Legends of Terror* (Amusement Park Books, 1982).

32. "Today Begins Season at Carlin's," unknown (April 6, 1929).

33. "Rollo, Synthetic Elephant, Afire as Park Begins Summer Season," *Baltimore Sun* (April 6, 1930).

34. "'The Sheik' at Carlin's," *Baltimore News-American* (July 30, 1972).

35. "Ice Rinks Set for Big Season," *Baltimore Sun* (December 2, 1932).

36. "Carlin's Open for Summer," *Baltimore Sun* (May 21, 1933).

37. "Green Palace Under Ban for Amusements," *Baltimore Sun* (April 1, 1934).

38. "Carlin's Joyland Will Reopen Today," *Baltimore Sun* (April 21, 1935).

39. "Carlin's Park Reopens for Summer Season," *Baltimore Sun* (April 26, 1936).

40. "Mr. Carlin's String of Horses Groomed for Spring Workout," *Baltimore Sun* (March 4, 1937).

41. "Carlin Plans to Rebuild," *Billboard* (October 9, 1937).

42. "To Oppose Wooden Carlin's Buildings," *Baltimore Sun* (October 1, 1937).

43. "Carlin's Park Celebrating Twentieth Anniversary," *Jeffersonian* (June 10, 1938).

44. "Big Swimming Pool Installed at Carlin's," *Catholic Review* (July 15, 1938).

45. "New Arena," *Baltimore News-Post* (November 11, 1938).

46. "Carlin's Park Opens," *Baltimore Sun* (April 27, 1941).

47. "Theater Burns at Carlin's," *Evening Sun* (April 17, 1944).

48. "14 Hurt in Crash of Roller Coasters," *Washington Post* (June 14, 1945).

49. Carlin's Park ad, NAAPBB, 1945 Manual and Guide Book.

50. "Concert Stoppage in Baltimore Laid to Beer Shortage," *Washington Post* (July 29, 1946).

51. "Swim and Beach Party Slated at Carlin's Park," *Baltimore Sun* (July 29, 1947).

52. Classified ad, *Baltimore Sun* (May 23, 1948).

53. "Button Boy," *Baltimore Sun* (August 2, 1949).

54. "Carlin's Park Bandit Gets Over $2,000," *Baltimore Sun* (July 22, 1951).

55. "Carlin's to Have Showboat Salon, Big-Time Revue," *News-American* (May 3, 1936).

56. Obituary, John J. Carlin, *Baltimore Sun* (May 28, 1954).

57. "Carousel Case Award Is $5,174," *Baltimore Sun* (January 23, 1959).

Chapter 5

1. "5,000 Watch Joe Louis in Final Spar Session," *Baltimore Sun* (August 13, 1951).

2. 1953 NAAPPB Buyer's Guide, "Permanent Outdoor Attractions."

3. "Huge Crowd Jams Area of Jazz Concert," *Baltimore Sun* (July 13, 1956).

4. "Beach Owners to Be Warned," *Baltimore Sun* (July 21, 1956).

5. "All-Day Party Ends in Arrests," *Baltimore Sun* (June 26, 1964).

6. "Alton Seeks Shows Permit Law," *Baltimore Sun* (June 29, 1973).

7. "Beach to Be Sold for Condominiums," *Baltimore Sun* (November 9, 1982).

Chapter 6

1. "A New Railroad," *Baltimore Sun* (October 3, 1899).

2. "Chesapeake Beach Today," *Baltimore Sun* (June 9, 1900).

3. "Chesapeake Beach's Sad Tale," *Baltimore Sun* (October 8, 1975).

4. Robert Cartmell, *The Incredible Scream Machine: A History of the Roller Coaster* (Bowling Green, OH: Bowling Green State University Popular Press/Amusement Park Books, 1987).

5. "Monte Carlo on Bay," *Baltimore Sun* (October 31, 1900).

6. Ibid.

7. "Big Game Is Delayed," *Baltimore Sun* (December 11, 1900).

8. "Monte Carlo on Bay," *Baltimore Sun* (October 31, 1900).

9. "Dreamland Is Sold," *Baltimore Sun* (December 11, 1912).

10. "The Town of Chesapeake Beach," unknown (September 23, 1954).

11. *A Souvenir Book of Chesapeake Beach, MD*, 1971 reprint of c. 1912 booklet.

12. "Let's Go Down the Bay," *Baltimore Sun* (May 13, 1914).

13. "Chesapeake Beach Opens," *Baltimore Sun* (June 13, 1915).

14. "Beach Resort Raided," *Baltimore Sun* (July 16, 1916).

15. "Gala Day for Soldiers," *Baltimore Sun* (July 28, 1918).

16. "Seaside Park Plans Season," *Washington Post* (May 4, 1930).

17. "New Devices," *Washington Post* (April 20, 1930).

18. "Seaside Park," *Washington Post* (June 15, 1930).

19. "Seaside Park," *Washington Post* (June 1, 1930).

20. "A Ship-to-Shore Railroad," *Sun Magazine* (July 9, 1955).

21. "Seaside Park Offers Music as a Feature," *Washington Post* (June 7, 1931).

22. "Seaside Park, on Bay, Opens with a Bang!" *Washington Post* (May 22, 1932.)

23. Ibid.

24. "Al Fresco Circus Early Attraction for Seaside Park," *Washington Post* (July 23, 1933).

25. "No Riders, but Trains Are Missed," *Baltimore Sun* (date unknown).

26. "Many from District Enjoy 'Fourth' at Old-Time Bay Resort," *Washington Star* (date unknown).

27. Untitled, *Baltimore Sun* (June 11, 1939).

28. "Chesapeake Beach Gets PWA Funds," *Baltimore Sun* (November 8, 1939).

29. *"Bay Belle," Baltimore Sun* (May 29, 1941).

30. "The Town of Chesapeake Beach," unknown (September 23, 1954).

31. "Trains and Boardwalk Gone, but 'Good Old Days' Return," *Baltimore Sun* (June 25, 1953).

32. "Chesapeake Beach Park Now Open," *Baltimore News-Post* (June 24, 1955).

33. "Once-Famed Hotel Burns," *Baltimore News-American* (May 2, 1967).

34. "Chesapeake Beach Carousel Purchased by Area Dealer in Carousels," *Mid-Atlantic Antique Journal* (March 1973).

35. Dentzel, *3-Row Carousel at Chesapeake Beach*, Report to the Maryland Park and Planning Commission (Frederick Fried, New York: September 16, 1973).

36. "About Antiques," *Enquirer-Gazette* (Thursday, May 2, 1974).

Chapter 7

1. "A Lion Got Loose in Electric Park," *Baltimore Sun* (August 14, 1949).

2. "Electric Park," *Baltimore Sun* (July 11, 1896).

3. "Mr. Ford's New Venture," *Baltimore Sun* (June 8, 1896).

4. "The World of Sport," *Baltimore News* (January 31, 1899).

5. "Summer Amusements," *Baltimore Sun* (June 29, 1902).

6. "5 Cents to Electric Park," *Baltimore Sun* (May 29, 1903).

7. "Fire at Electric Park," *Baltimore Sun* (January 7, 1904).

8. "Concerts at Electric Park," *Baltimore Sun* (May 22, 1904).

9. Ibid.

10. "Electric Park Vaudeville," *Baltimore News-American* (May 28, 1905).

11. "Changes at Electric Park," *Baltimore Sun* (April 22, 1905).

12. "Irish Day at Electric Park," *Baltimore Sun* (June 4, 1905).

13. "Lion Loose at Electric Park," *Baltimore Sun* (August 14, 1905).

14. "Mr. Fenneman's Plans," *Baltimore Sun* (January 7, 1906).

15. Robert K. Headley, *Motion Picture Exhibition in Baltimore* (Jefferson NC: McFarland, 2007).

16. "To Be Like Coney Isle," *Baltimore Sun* (May 18, 1906).

17. "Electric Park May 28," *Baltimore Sun* (May 6, 1906).

18. "Bill at Electric Park," *Baltimore Sun* (July 15, 1906).

19. *Variety* (August 11, 1906).

20. "At Work on Big Show," *Baltimore Sun* (September 2, 1906).

21. "Shows of the War Path," *Baltimore Sun* (January 17, 1907).

22. "I Remember When ... My Hair Was a Park Attraction," *Baltimore Sun* (June 3, 1956).

23. "Electric Park Opened," *Baltimore Sun* (May 28, 1907).

24. "Concerts at Electric Park," *Baltimore Sun* (May 5, 1907).

25. *Billboard* (May, 1908).

26. "Bill at Electric Park," *Baltimore Sun* (June 2, 1907).

27. "Fair at Electric Park," *Baltimore Sun* (September 16, 1907).

28. "To Build a Luna Park Here," *Baltimore Sun* (October 30, 1907).

29. "Parks and Fairs," *Variety* (February 8, 1908).

30. "Parks and Fairs," *Variety* (May 2, 1908).

31. "Like a Coney Island," *Baltimore Sun* (April 18, 1908).

32. "Like a Coney Island," *Baltimore Sun* (June 5, 1908).

33. "Electric Park Open," *Baltimore Sun* (June 7, 1908).

34. "Lively at Electric Park," *Baltimore Sun* (June 2, 1908).

35. "I Piloted That Electric Park Shoot-the-Chute," *Sun Magazine* (December 8, 1963).

36. Ibid.

37. "Lively at Electric Park," *Baltimore Sun* (June 2, 1908).

38. "I Piloted That Electric Park Shoot-the-Chute," *Sun Magazine* (December 8, 1963).

39. "To Build Two Airships," *Baltimore Sun* (June 25, 1906).

40. "50 Years Ago," *Baltimore Sun* (August 23, 1959).

41. "Electric Park's Season," *Baltimore Star* (May 8, 1909).

42. "Electric Park Attractions," *Baltimore Sun* (July 7, 1908).

43. "Electric Park Enjoined," *Baltimore Sun* (June 21, 1908).

44. "Electric Park in New Garb," *Baltimore Sun* (May 23, 1909).

45. "From Baltimore's Family Album," *Baltimore Sun* (August 11, 1936).

46. "Electric Park's Season," *Baltimore Star* (May 8, 1909).

47. "Bills at the Theatres and Parks," *Baltimore Sun* (July 11, 1909).

48. "Bills at the Theatres and in the Parks," *Baltimore Sun* (June 6, 1909).

49. "Bills at the Summer Parks," *Baltimore Sun* (July 25, 1909).

50. "Electric Park Opens May 28," *Baltimore Sun* (May 15, 1910).

51. Headley, *Motion Picture Exhibition*.

52. "Earthquake at Electric Park," *Baltimore Sun* (August 15, 1911).

53. "At Electric Park," *Baltimore Sun* (May 28, 1911).

54. "Attractions in American Cities for Season of 1911," *Billboard* (May 13, 1911).

55. "Mr.Fenneman Out of Electric Park," *Baltimore Sun* (June 8, 1911).

56. "Fenneman Cuts Throat," *Baltimore Sun* (August 7, 1914).

57. "August Fenneman Dead," *Baltimore Sun* (December 24, 1917).

Chapter 8

1. "The Never-Never Land That Came True," *Maryland Motorist* (May-June, 1956).

2. "Enchanted Forest Will Open August 15," *Baltimore News-Post* (August 10, 1955).

3. "Storybook Summers," *Maryland Life Magazine* (July/August 2005).

4. "Kids Can Picnic with Miss Muffet," *Washington Post* (June 3, 1956).

5. "How About a Visit with Mother Goose," *Washington Post* (September 9, 1956).

6. "He Turns Children's Fantasies into Reality," *Baltimore Sun* (May 15, 1960).

7. "Figures Moved to Farm," *Howard County Sun* (February 10, 2005).

8. "Thefts Plague Howard Park," *Baltimore Sun* (September 1, 1977).

9. "Rekindling a Fairy Tale Dream in Howard," *Baltimore Sun* (December 1, 2003).

10. Ibid.

11. "Big Pumpkin Enchants Again," *Howard County Sun* (September 5, 2004).

12. "Figures Moved to Farm," *Howard County Sun* (February 10, 2005).

Chapter 9

1. "Merry Volksfest Opens," *Baltimore Sun* (August 29, 1916).

2. "I Remember … the Music and Fellowship of Volksfests," *Baltimore Sun Magazine* (June 23, 196?).

3. "Germans Raise U.S. Flag," *Baltimore Sun* (September 1, 1914).

4. "I Remember … the Music and Fellowship of Volksfests," *Baltimore Sun Magazine* (June 23, 196?).

5. "Frederick Road Park," *New York Clipper* (September 7, 1923).

6. "Monastery Parish Picnic," *Baltimore Sun* (July 7, 1915).

7. "German Athletes Out Today," *Baltimore Sun* (July 3, 1916).

8. "15,000 Hibernians Celebrate," *Baltimore Sun* (August 19, 1919).

9. "20,000 Children Greet Mayor at Amusement Park," *Baltimore Sun* (June 6, 1922).

10. "Five Firemen Hurt in Blaze at Park," *Baltimore Sun* (April 3, 1923).

11. "Frederick Rd. Park Sold for $500,000," *Baltimore Sun* (May 18, 1923).

12. George P. Smith, *Report to the Directors of the Recreation Service Corporation* (October 4, 1923, courtesy of Philadelphia Toboggan Coasters/Tom Rebbie).

Chapter 10

1. "Gwynn Oak Park," *Baltimore Sun* (July 2, 1894).

2. "Gwynn Oak Park," *Baltimore Sun* (July 25, 1894).

3. "Tournament at Gwynn Oak," *Baltimore Sun* (September 26, 1894).

4. "Street Railway Deal," *Baltimore Sun* (December 8, 1894).

5. "Traction Company," *Baltimore Sun* (February 7, 1895).

6. "Palace Trolley Cars," *Baltimore Sun* (March 19, 1895).

7. "Gwynn Oak Park," *Baltimore Sun* (March 29, 1895).

8. "Trolley Outgrowths," *Baltimore Sun* (July 24, 1895).

9. Gwynn Oak Park ad, *Baltimore Sun* (July 4, 1896).

10. "Street Railway Extension," *Baltimore Sun* (August 9, 1898).

11. Gwynn Oak Park ad, *Baltimore Sun* (July 21, 1899).

12. "Royal Arcanum's Anniversary," *Baltimore Sun* (June 21, 1900).

13. "The Street Railway System of Baltimore," *Street Railway Review* (August 15, 1901).

14. "At Gwynn Oak Park," *Baltimore Sun* (May 31, 1904).

15. "Improvements for Gwynn Oak," *Baltimore Sun* (March 30, 1906).

16. "Gwynn Oak's 50th Birthday Unheeded by Holiday Throng," *Baltimore Sun* (June 1944).

17. "Red Men to Have Reunion," *Baltimore Sun* (July 7, 1907).

18. "Vaudeville at Gwynn Oak," *Baltimore Sun* (July 7, 1907).

19. "The Stage—Gwyn Oak Park," *Baltimore Sun* (May 22, 1910).

20. Gwynn Oak ad, *Baltimore Sun* (May, 1910).

21. "Attractions in American Cities for Season of 1911," *Billboard* (May 13, 1911).

22. "Balloonist Owens at Gwynn Oak," *Baltimore Sun* (June 18, 1912).

23. "Carnival on the Lake," *Baltimore Sun* (August 16, 1912).

24. "Hiawatha at Gwynn Oak," *Baltimore Sun* (July 3, 1913).

25. "Maryland Feasting and Vaudeville at Gwynn Oak," *Baltimore Sun* (June 12, 1913).

26. "Open-Air Tango Season On," *Baltimore Sun* (May 29, 1914).

27. "Gwynn Oak Park," *Baltimore Sun* (July 16, 1916).

28. Gwynn Oak Park ad, *Baltimore Sun* (May 21, 1921).

29. "Gwynn Oak's 50th Birthday Unheeded By Holiday Throng," *Baltimore Sun* (June, 1944).

30. Display ad, *Baltimore Sun* (May 21, 1922).

31. "Citizens to Urge City to Buy Gwynn Oak," *Baltimore Sun* (April 30, 1930).

32. "Gwynn Oak's 50th Birthday Unheralded by Holiday Throng," *Baltimore Sun* (June, 1944).

33. "United Not Expected to Seek Beer License," *Baltimore Sun* (May 23, 1934).

34. "Retail Grocers Plan Their Annual Picnic," *Baltimore Sun* (August 19, 1394).

35. "15,000 Take Part in German Picnic," *Baltimore Sun* (September 3, 1934).

36. "Obituary—John D. Farson," *Baltimore Sun* (December 27, 1935).

37. "Gwynn Oak Park Opening on Saturday," *Baltimore Sun* (May 17, 1936).

38. "German Day Followed by 2 'Hangovers,'" *Baltimore Sun* (September 14, 1937).

39. "New Attractions Listed as Gwynn Oak Opens," *Baltimore Sun* (May 21, 1939).

40. "Fire Demon Plays Havoc in County Over Weekend," *Jeffersonian* (November 3, 1939).

41. Classified ad, *Baltimore Sun* (July 4, 1942).

42. "Park Roller Coasters Earned Their Winter Rest," *Baltimore Sun* (October 10, 1943).

43. "Perfect Spring Sunday Coaxes Thousands to Various Parks," *Baltimore Sun* (May 15, 1944).

44. 1945 NAAPPB Buyer's Guide, "Permanent Outdoor Amusements," index.

45. "Gwynn Oak to Begin 54th Year," *Baltimore News-Post* (Spring, 1948).

46. Gwynn Oak Park ad, *Baltimore Sun* (May 5, 1956).

47. "'All Nations Day' Fete Scheduled Tomorrow," *Baltimore Sun* (September 8, 1951).

48. "25,000 at Second Annual All Nations Day Festival," *Baltimore Sun* (September 8, 1952).

49. "3 Policemen, 6 Detectives Injured in Dance Hall Fight," *Baltimore Sun* (December 29, 1958).

50. "Gwynn Oak to Be Integrated Aug. 28," *Baltimore Sun* (July 20, 1963).

51. Balto. Integration Calm," *Amusement Business* (September 14, 1963).

52. "Ferris Wheel Rage Reaches Gwynn Oak; Boy, 14, Starts," *Baltimore Sun* (August 24, 1964).

53. "Wheel Rider Breaks Record," *Baltimore Sun* (July 5, 1970).

54. "30 at Gwynn Oak Hurt as Fireworks Fall into Crowd," *Evening Sun* (June 1, 1965).

55. "Gwynn Oak Park to Begin 75th Year," *News-American* (April 11, 1971).

56. "Gwynn Oak Park Allowed to Open," *Baltimore Sun* (June 3, 1972).

57. "80-Year-Old Gwynn Oak Park to Close," *Baltimore Sun* (Summer, 1974).

58. "Fire Destroys Ballroom at Gwynn Oak," *Baltimore Sun* (late February, 1975).

59. "Gwynn Oak Owners Agree to Raze Park by July 1," *News-American* (March 4, 1976).

60. "Amusement Park Site Going Public," *Evening Sun* (June 22, 1977).

61. "County Buys Gwynn Oak Park," *News-American* (June 21, 1977).

Chapter 11

1. "A Chesapeake Bay Resort," *Baltimore Sun* (July 14, 1880).

2. "Eagles in Country Home," *Baltimore Sun* (May 13, 1901).

3. "Outdoor Summer Resorts," *Baltimore Sun* (May 25, 1901).

4. "Hollywood Park Opens Saturday," *Baltimore Sun* (May 21, 1902).

5. "Excitement on Back River," *Baltimore Sun* (July 3, 1902).

6. William J. Kelley, *Brewing in Maryland from the Colonial to the Present Times* (Self-published, 1965).

7. "Fire Wipes Out Old Hollywood River Resort," *Baltimore Sun* (March 21, 1921).

8. "Building Hotel at Back River," *Baltimore Sun* (October 1, 1906).

9. "At Hollywood on Sunday Among the Plain People," *Baltimore Sun* (June 16, 1907).

10. Ibid.

11. "Police Invade Resorts," *Baltimore Sun* (June 15, 1908).

12. "Summer Disorder Begins," *Baltimore Sun* (April 13, 1909).

13. "To Develop Hollywood," *Baltimore Sun* (March 8, 1910).

14. "Hollywood to Open Tomorrow," *Baltimore Sun* (May 21, 1911).

15. "Amusement Parks," *Billboard* (April 22, 1911).

16. "Goeller's License Suppressed," *Baltimore Sun* (Feb 29, 1912).

17. "Will Close Hollywood Park," *Baltimore Sun* (March 7, 1912).

18. "Hollywood Park Opens," *Baltimore Sun* (May 14, 1912).

19. "Injunction Against Goeller," *Baltimore Sun* (May 30, 1912).

20. "Resorts Wide Open; Two Raids Made," *Baltimore Sun* (July 21, 1913).

21. "Goeller's as Example," *Baltimore Sun* (August 10, 1913)

22. "Thrown from Coaster," *Baltimore Sun* (August 16, 1913).

23. "Said to Want Goeller's," *Baltimore Sun* (August 3, 1913).

24. "14 'Cops' Suspended," *Baltimore Sun* (August 12, 1913).

25. "Suit Over 'Hell's Kitchen,'" *Baltimore Sun* (August 15, 1913).

26. "To Investigate Beating of Men," *Baltimore Sun* (May 19, 1914).

27. Hollywood Park ad, *Baltimore Sun* (July 17, 1914).

28. Hollywood Park Grand Opening ad, *Baltimore Sun* (May 8, 1915).

29. "Hollywood Park," *Baltimore Sun* (May 9, 1915).

30. "2 Shot at Hollywood," *Baltimore Sun* (May 15, 1915).

31. "Joseph Oronson: A Wonderful Teller of Yarns," *Essex Times* (August 3, 1972).

32. "Teeners, Don't Read This Stuff," *Baltimore News-Post* (March 3, 1958).

33. "Big Booze Farewell," *Baltimore Sun* (May 1, 1918).

34. "Hollywood Ends Career, Goeller Beats Law to It," *Baltimore Sun* (c. 1922).

35. Hollywood Park ad, *Baltimore Sun* (June 5, 1920).

36. "Fire Wipes Out Old Hollywood River Resort," *Baltimore Sun* (March 21, 1921).

37. "Teeners, Don't Read This Stuff," *Baltimore News-Post* (March 3, 1958).

38. "Liquor, Auto and Still Seized in Three Raids," *Baltimore Sun* (October 1, 1921).

39. "Police System Scored by County Grand Jury," *Baltimore Sun* (October 1, 1921).

40. "Hollywood Park to Stay Shut, He Says," *Evening Sun* (April 13, 1922).

41. Obituary—Joseph Goeller, *Baltimore Sun* (June 4, 1940).

Chapter 12

1. "For Luna Park Here," *Baltimore Sun* (January 28, 1910).

2. "Luna Park Company Incorporated," *Baltimore Sun* (February 4, 1910).

3. David W. Francis and Diane Demali Francis, *Luna Park: Cleveland's Fairyland of Pleasure* (Amusement Park Books, 1996).

4. "Ground Broken for Park," *Baltimore Sun* (March 2, 1910).

5. "To Remove Massive Poplar," *Baltimore Sun* (March 12, 1910).

6. "Lightning Hits Coaster," *Baltimore Sun* (May 25, 1910).

7. "Fire Wrecks Luna Park," *Baltimore Sun* (July 6, 1910).

8. "Luna Park Reopens," *Baltimore Sun* (July 7, 1910).

9. "Luna Park Opens Today," *Baltimore Sun* (May 20, 1911).

10. "Receivers for Luna Park," *Baltimore Sun* (August 2, 1911).

11. "'Judy' Wrecks Her Car," *Baltimore Sun* (May 4, 1913).

12. "Wild Animals at Elks' Fete," *Baltimore Sun* (May 9, 1913).

13. "Paragon Park Opens," *Baltimore Sun* (May 31, 1913).

14. "Biplane Lands in Valley," *Baltimore Sun* (May 14, 1913).

15. "Special Bill at Paragon Park," *Baltimore Sun* (July 3, 1913).

Chapter 13

1. "Bay Shore Park Just a Memory, to Follow in Steps of River View," *Evening Sun* (August 20, 1947).

2. "Coney Island of the South," *Sunday Sun Magazine* (August 31, 1952).

3. "Western Electric—25 Years of Achievement in Baltimore," *Western Electric Newsletter*, c. 1954.

4. "Improvements at Point Breeze," *Baltimore Sun* (April 22, 1895).

5. "A Sunday Outing," *Baltimore Sun* (June 24, 1895).

6. "Summer Shows," *Baltimore Sun* (May 31, 1898).

7. "Point Breeze Improvements," *Baltimore Sun* (March 19, 1898).

8. "Mr. Kernan's Enterprise," *Baltimore Sun* (March 21, 1899).

9. "Removing a Carrousel," *Baltimore Sun* (July 1, 1899).

10. "An Attractive Resort," *Baltimore Sun* (May 21, 1900).

11. "Summer Amusements," *Baltimore Sun* (June 30, 1900).

12. "Outdoor Summer Resorts," *Baltimore Sun* (May 25, 1901).

13. "River View Season Closes," *Baltimore Sun* (September 19, 1904).

14. "Notes from the Courts," *Baltimore Sun* (November 26, 1904).

15. "Orders Railway and Camels," *Baltimore Sun* (June 29, 1905).

16. "Park Improvements at Baltimore," *Street Railway Review* (May 13, 1905).

17. "River View as It Will Be Next Summer," *Baltimore Sun* (January 21, 1906).

18. "Attractions at River View," *Baltimore Sun* (May 27, 1906).

19. "River View a Maze of Lights," *Baltimore Sun* (July 15, 1906).

20. "Many Enjoy River View Park," *Baltimore Sun* (May 20, 1906).

21. "Civil War in 'Tone Picture,'" *Baltimore Sun* (June 30, 1907).

22. "Open to Children," *Baltimore Sun* (August 14, 1907).

23. "Elks to Have Outing," *Baltimore Sun* (May 24, 1908).

24. "Mr. M.J. Fitzsimmons Out," *Baltimore Sun* (October 26, 1908).

25. "I Remember ... Thrills at Old River View Park," *Sunday Sun Magazine* (July 7, 1963).

26. "Bills at the Summer Parks," *Baltimore Sun* (July 25, 1909).

27. "Some of the Season's New Attractions at the Trolley Parks," *Baltimore Sun* (May 9, 1909).

28. Ibid.,13.

29. "Bills at the Theatres and in the Parks," *Baltimore Sun* (June 6, 1909).

30. "Fire Wrecks River View," *Baltimore News-American* (October 1, 1909).

31. "Days of Old—When Coney Island of South Was Popular as Riverview," *Baltimore-American* (September 23, 1951).

32. "River View Park Streetcar Restored," *Sun Magazine* (May 25, 1969).

33. "River View Park," *Sunday Sun* (May 28, 1963)

34. "Summers at Riverview Park," unknown (May 7, 1972).

35. Ibid.

36. "Attractions in American Cities for Season of 1911," *Billboard* (May 13, 1911).

37. "Resort Owners Accused," *Baltimore Sun* (August 30, 1913).

38. "River View Park," *Baltimore Sun* (May 30, 1915).

39. "River View Park," *Baltimore Sun* (May 7, 1916).

40. "River View Park," *Baltimore Sun* (May 21, 1916).

41. "Killed on Racer Dip," *Baltimore Sun* (June 26, 1916).

42. River View Park ad, *Baltimore Sun* (August 19, 1917).

43. "Big Time at River View," *Baltimore Sun* (August 4, 1918).

44. "10-Cent Fare to River View Stands," *Baltimore Sun* (August 7, 1918).

45. "Soldier Ban Modified," *Baltimore Sun* (June 7, 1919).

46. "River View Opens Next Saturday," *Baltimore Sun* (April 25, 1920).

47. "Parks Piers and Beaches—Park Notes," *Billboard* (September 13, 1919).

48. "Two Hurt in Accidents at Amusement Park," *Baltimore Sun* (April 25, 1920).

49. "Italian Societies on Picnic," *Baltimore Sun* (August 16, 1922).

50. "Gets $5,000 for Son's Death," *Baltimore Sun* (January 23, 1923).

51. "River View Park Opens Gates for 1924 Season," *Baltimore Sun* (April 20, 1924).

52. "Labor Day Outing Attended by 10,000," *Baltimore Sun* (September 8, 1925).

53. "Call Cops as 700 Clamor for 75 jobs," *Baltimore Sun* (c. December 1929).

54. "The Little Locomotive," *Baltimore Sun* (November 12, 1950)

Chapter 14

1. "Nabob of Summer Time," *Baltimore Sun* (July 19, 1905).

2. "Tolchester Beach Goes Back to 1877," *Baltimore Sun* (date unknown).

3. "Local Matters," *Baltimore Sun* (June 25, 1877).

4. "Steamboat Summer Excursions," *Baltimore Sun* (June 20, 1881).

5. "The Excursion Season," *Baltimore Sun* (May 12, 1883).

6. "The Excursion Season," *Baltimore Sun* (June 8, 1885).

7. "Chesapeake Excursions," *Baltimore Sun* (June 23, 1887).

8. "The Improvements at Tolchester," *Baltimore Sun* (May 30, 1889).

9. "A Military Camp," *Baltimore Sun* (July 17, 1893).

10. "Washington Visitors Go to Tolchester," *Baltimore Sun* (June 12, 1890).

11. "Presbyterian Day," *Baltimore Sun* (June 30, 1894).

12. "Tolchester Improvements," *Baltimore Sun* (May 11, 1896).

13. "Tolchester Fair Opened," *Baltimore Sun* (August 28, 1896).

14. "Tolchester Improvements," *Baltimore Sun* (May 10, 1897).

15. "Court of Appeals," *Baltimore Sun* (June 29, 1898).

16. "Tolchester Beach Opens," *Baltimore Sun* (June 2, 1899).

17. "New Tunes for Carrousels," *Baltimore Sun* (May 5, 1899).

18. "Old Soldiers at Play," *Baltimore Sun* (July 15, 1899).

19. "The Tolchester Season," *Baltimore Sun* (May 9, 1900).

20. "Tolchester Beach Opened," *Baltimore Sun* (June 5, 1900).

21. "Baltimore Man Took a Long Swim," *Baltimore Sun* (June 26, 1901).

22. "Tolchester Season Opens," *Baltimore Sun* (May 29, 1903).

23. "Big Day at Tolchester," *Baltimore Sun* (June 16, 1905).

24. "Nabob of Summer Time," *Baltimore Sun* (July 19, 1905).

25. Ibid.

26. "Tolchester Open Again," *Baltimore Sun* (June 1, 1906).

27. "A Maryland Mecca," *Baltimore Sun* (June 27, 1961).

28. "Carrousel Owner Sued," *Baltimore Sun* (October 2, 1906).

29. "Tolchester Beach Goes Back to 1877," *Baltimore Sun* (date unknown).

30. "Mr. Williams A. Potts Dead," *Baltimore Sun* (July 18, 1910).

31. "Old Tolchester Is Opened," *Baltimore Sun* (May 28, 1911).

32. "Many Go on Excursions," *Baltimore Sun* (May 21, 1911).

33. "Big Crowd at Tolchester," *Baltimore Sun* (September 2, 1911).

34. "Old Tolchester Opens," *Baltimore Sun* (May 30, 1913).

35. "Complaints of the Bathing Suits and Tolchester Towels…," *Baltimore Sun* (July 28, 1913).

36. "Tolchester in Bloom," *Baltimore Sun* (May 30, 1914).

37. "Tolchester Beach Goes Back to 1877," *Baltimore Sun* (date unknown)

38. "Tolchester Opens," *Baltimore Sun* (May 29, 1915).

39. "Tolchester Beach Opens," *Baltimore Sun* (June 3, 1917).

40. "Dimples on Fair Bathers' Knees Must Be Covered, Edict at Nearby Beaches," *Baltimore Sun* (May 23, 1921).

41. "Tolchester Sold at 1-Bid Auction," *Baltimore Sun* (October 21, 1962).

42. "Eliason Personalty $37,467," *Baltimore Sun* (August 19, 1921).

43. "Ferry Earns $20,000 More Than Subsidy," *Baltimore Sun* (January 8, 1935).

44. Ibid.

45. "Tolchester Sold at 1-Bid Auction," *Baltimore Sun* (October 21, 1962).

46. "Tolchester Ferry Firm Given P.S.C. Approval," *Baltimore Sun* (July 3, 1937).

47. "Tolchester Is Ready for Busy Season," *Baltimore American* (June 12, 1938).

48. "Tolchester Beach Opens Decoration Day," *Baltimore Sun* (May 21, 1939).

49. Brian J. Cudahy, *Twilight on the Bay: The Excursion Boat Empire of B.B. Wills* (Tidewater, 1998).

50. "Tolchester Line Gets P.S.C. Order," *Baltimore Sun* (July 25, 1941).

51. "Down the Harbor and Back to 1890," *Baltimore Sun* (July 23, 1943).

52. Ibid.

53. Ibid.

54. "Tolchester Boat Denied Fuel Oil," *Baltimore Sun* (July 28, 1943).

55. "Ban On Chartered Streetcars Brings Many Picnic Changes," *Baltimore Sun* (July 22, 1945).

56. "Tolchester Is Put Back on the Map by Arrival of First 1800 Youngsters," *Evening Sun* (June 15, 1948).

57. "Pier Transfer Is Scheduled," *Baltimore Sun* (April 5, 1950).

58. Ibid.

59. "Tolchester Park Partially Burned," *Baltimore Sun* (date unknown).

60. Cudahy, *Twilight on the Bay*.

61. "Wilson Line Plans Sale," *Baltimore Sun* (July 18, 1957).

62. "State Will Go on Ride If Coaster Runs Again," *Evening Sun* (July 24, 1959)

63. "Former *Bay Belle* Owner Faces Repurchase Suit," *Evening Sun* (January 7, 1960).

64. "*Bay Belle* in Drydock," *Baltimore Sun* (April 26, 1960).

65. "Wave a Sad Good-By to Tolchester Park," *Evening Sun* (October 20, 1962).

66. "Bay Steamboat Excursions End; Tolchester Is Closed," *Baltimore Sun* (May 5, 1962).

67. "Tolchester Sold at 1-Bid Auction," *Baltimore Sun* (October 21, 1962).

68. "Md. Should Take Over Tolchester for Park, McKeldin Urges," *Evening Sun* (October 28, 1962).

69. "If Ghosts Like Amusement, There's Tolchester Beach," *Baltimore Sun* (July 28, 1968).

Bibliography

Newspaper Articles

"A.A.U. Distance Swim Meet Is Won by Bay Shore Club." *Baltimore Sun*, August 24, 1931.

"About Antiques." [Waldorf MD] *Enquirer-Gazette*, May 2, 1974.

"Acrobats at River View." *Baltimore Sun*, July 7, 1908.

"Ah, Tolchester." *Baltimore Sun*, May 6, 1962.

"Al Fresco Early Attraction for Seaside Park." *Washington Post*, July 23, 1933.

"All Aboard for Tolchester." *Baltimore Sun*, May 31, 1908.

"All-Day Party Ends in Arrests." *Baltimore Sun*, June 26, 1964.

"'All Nations Day' Fete Scheduled Tomorrow." *Baltimore Sun*, September 8, 1951.

"All Nations Fete Readied." *Baltimore Sun*, August 28, 1954.

"All Sorts of Novel Attractions Will Greet the Visitor to the New Electric Park." *Baltimore Sun*, May 17, 1908.

"Alton Seeks Shows Permit Law." Unknown, June 29, 1973.

"Alton to Propose Curbs on Outdoor Rock Concerts." *Baltimore Sun*, June 29, 1973.

"Amusement Park Remains Thrill-Seekers Paradise." *Baltimore Sun*, July 17, 1971.

"Amusement Park Site Going Public." *Baltimore Evening Sun*, June 22, 1977.

"Amusement Parks Open." *Baltimore Sun*, May 2, 1920.

"Amusement Parks Open 1922 Season." *Sunday Sun*, April 16, 1922.

"Amusement Parks Ready." *Baltimore Sun*, April 1923.

"Amusements This Week." *Baltimore Sun*, July 19, 1904.

"Amusements This Week." *Baltimore Sun*, June 4, 1905.

"Another Fire at Gwynn Oak." *Baltimore Sun*, February 28, 1975.

"Arcanumites at Gwynn Oak." *Baltimore Sun*, June 22, 1906.

"Archbishop Tells Priests to Get Picket Permission." *Baltimore Sun*, July 10, 1963.

"Arthur B. Price, 72, Ex-Council Head, Dies." *Baltimore Sun*, December 10, 1957.

"At Electric Park." *Baltimore Sun*, May 28, 1911.

"At Gwynn Oak Park." *Baltimore Sun*, May 31, 1904.

"At Gwynn Oak Park." *Baltimore Sun*, July 31, 1938.

"At Gwynn Oak Park." *Baltimore Sun*, September 11, 1938.

"At Gwynn Oak Park." *Baltimore Sun*, July 27, 1941.

"At Hollywood on Sunday Among the Plain People." *Baltimore Sun*, June 16, 1907.

"At Tolchester and Betterton." *Baltimore Sun*, June 20, 1926.

"At Work on Big Show." *Baltimore Sun*, September 2, 1906.

"Atlantic City and Coney Say 'No,' but Baltimore Welcomes Her." *Baltimore Sun,* June 12, 1922.

"Attack on Chesapeake Beach." *Baltimore Sun*, July 27, 1918.

"Attempt Is Made to Burn Down Pavilion." *Baltimore Evening Sun*, February 1925.

"Attraction at Gwynn Oak." *Baltimore Sun*, August 24, 1941.

"Attractions at Bay Shore Park." *Baltimore Sun*, June 30, 1912.

"Attractions at River View." *Baltimore Sun*, June 3, 1906.

"Attractions at River View." *Baltimore Sun*, July 18, 1917.

"An Attractive Resort." *Baltimore Sun*, May 21, 1900.

"Auctioneer's Gavel May Silence Gwynn Oak's Calliope." *Baltimore Sun*, June 4, 1974.

"B. and O. Men at Tolchester." *Baltimore Sun*, July 15, 1910.

"The Baby Incubators at New Electric Park." *Baltimore Sun*, June 7, 1908.

"Back and Middle Rivers." *Baltimore Sun*, May 20, 1899.

"Back River People Protest." *Baltimore Sun*, January 17, 1917.

"Balloonist Owens at Gwynn Oak." *Baltimore Sun*, June 18, 1912.

"Baltimore Around the Clock." *Baltimore Evening Sun*, June 10, 1937.

"Baltimore Man Took a Long Swim." *Baltimore Sun*, June 26, 1901.

"Baltimore Transit Company to Honor Six Old Employees." *Baltimore Sun*, June 29, 1936.

"Baltimore Welcomes Battleship *Maryland*." *Washington Post*, October 7, 1921.

"Ban on Chartered Streetcars Brings Many Picnic Changes." *Baltimore Sun*, July 22, 1945.

"The Battle of Port Arthur." *Baltimore Sun*, June 30, 1907.

"*Bay Belle*." *Baltimore Sun*, May 29, 1941.

"*Bay Belle* Case Now Before PSC." *Baltimore Sun*, July 25, 1957.

"*Bay Belle* in Drydock." *Baltimore Sun*, April 26, 1960,

"Bay Island, Newest Beach Resort, to Be Ready for Opening May 30." *Baltimore Evening Sun*, April 26, 1948.

"Bay Resorts Are Ready." *Baltimore Sun*, June 17, 1934.

"Bay Resorts Are Ready." *Baltimore Sun*, June 13, 1937.

"Bay Ridge." *Baltimore Sun*, May 26, 1899.

"The Bay Ridge Cases." *Baltimore Sun*, August 3, 1882.

"Bay Ridge Excursion Controversy." *Baltimore Sun*, June 24, 1884.

"Bay Ridge Excursions." *Baltimore Sun*, June 10, 1899.

"The Bay Ridge Fracas." *Baltimore Sun*, August 2, 1881.

"Bay Ridge Improvements." *Baltimore Sun*, September 20, 1884.

"Bay Ridge Improvements." *Baltimore Sun*, November 24, 1898.

"Bay Ridge Sold." *Baltimore Sun*, April 4, 1900.

"Bay Shore." *Baltimore Sun*, June 19, 1919.

"Bay Shore." *Baltimore Sun*, June 27, 1920.

"Bay Shore." *Baltimore Sun*, June 26, 1921.

"The Bay Shore Bath Houses." *Baltimore Sun*, July 28, 1917.

"Bay Shore Club Applies for Sanction for Meets." *Baltimore Sun*, July 21, 1923.

Bay Shore display ad. *Baltimore Sun*, May 29, 1931.

"Bay Shore in New Dress." *Baltimore Sun*, May 26, 1912.

"Bay Shore Midway Destroyed by Fire." *Baltimore Sun*, May 25, 1941.

"Bay Shore Opens Tomorrow." *Baltimore Sun*, May 22, 1907.

"Bay Shore Park." *Baltimore Sun*, July 16, 1916.

"Bay Shore Park." *Baltimore Sun*, May 24, 1924.

"Bay Shore Park Attractive." *Baltimore Sun*, June 29, 1913.

"Bay Shore Park Closed After 16 Years." Unknown, June 15, 1964.

"Bay Shore Park Is Doomed." *Baltimore News-American*, December 29, 1964.

"Bay Shore Park Is Fast Becoming Just a Memory." *Baltimore Evening Sun*, December 5, 1947.

"Bay Shore Park Just a Memory, to Follow in Steps of River View." *Baltimore Evening Sun*, August 20, 1947.

"Bay Shore Park Open." *Baltimore Sun*, August 11, 1906.

"Bay Shore Park Open." *Baltimore Sun*, May 28, 1911.

"Bay Shore Park Opening Scheduled." *Baltimore News-Post*, March 23, 1954.

"Bay Shore Park Opens." *Baltimore American*, May 30, 1954.

"Bay Shore Park Opens." *Baltimore Sun*, August 12, 1906.

"Bay Shore Park Opens." *Baltimore Sun*, May 25, 1910.

"Bay Shore Park Opens." *Baltimore Sun*, May 29, 1914.

"Bay Shore Park Opens Sunday." *News-American*, May 2, 1947.

"Bay Shore Park Unfinished." *Baltimore Sun*, July 4, 1906.

"Bay Shore Park Will Open Today." *News-American*, August 11, 1906.

"Bay Shore Park Wins Favor of Baltimoreans." *Baltimore Sun*, June 14, 1936.

"Bay Shore Popular as Ever." *Baltimore Sun*, May 29, 1908.

"Bay Shore Preparing for Big Swim Meet." *Baltimore Sun*, July 8, 1930.

"Bay Shore Ready for New Season." *Baltimore News-Post*, May 28, 1954.

"Bay Shore Reopens." *Baltimore Sun*, May 26, 1940.

"Bay Shore Ship Line Is Organized Here." *Baltimore Sun*, May 29, 1924.

"Bay Shore Storm Is False Alarm." *News-American*, August 21, 1950.

"Bay Shore to Open." *Baltimore Sun*, August 5, 1906.

"Bay Shore Will Open Today." *Baltimore Sun*, May 28, 1908.

"Bay Side Park Ready May 1." *Baltimore Sun*, March 12, 1906.

"Bay Steamboat Excursions End; Tolchester Is Closed." *Baltimore Sun*, May 5, 1962.

"Beach Owners to Be Warned." *Baltimore Sun*, July 21, 1956.

"Beach Resort Raided." *Baltimore Sun*, July 16, 1916.

"Beach to Be Sold for Condominiums." *Baltimore Sun*, November 9, 1982.

"Beach's Banner Day." *Baltimore Sun*, August 30, 1901.

"Beautifying Electric Park." *Baltimore Sun*, March 10, 1907.

"Belmont Changes Hands." *Baltimore Sun*, June 1, 1907.

"Benefit Carnival Given at Carlin's." *Baltimore Sun*, May 26, 1923.

"Better Days for Betterton." *Baltimore Evening Sun*, date unknown.

"Betterton Bayside Land Company." *Baltimore Sun*, March 5, 1907.

"Betterton Beach." *Baltimore News-American*, November 14, 1965.

"Betterton Beach Draws Devoted City Tourists." *Baltimore Sun*, April 23, 1978.

"Betterton Challenge to History Buffs." *Baltimore News-American*, June 11, 1967.

"Betterton Changing from Resort to Residential." *Baltimore Sun*, July 2, 1978.

"Betterton Cruises." *Baltimore Sun*, July 22, 1973.

"Betterton Expands." *Baltimore Sun*, June 12, 1938.

"Betterton Has Lure for Fishermen." *Baltimore Sun*, June 3, 1928.

"Betterton Inundated." *Baltimore Sun*, August 5, 1915.

"Betterton Is All Set." *Baltimore Sun*, June 15, 1941.

"Betterton Is Close By." *Baltimore Sun*, July 22, 1924.

"Betterton, MD, Builds New Pier." *Baltimore Sun*, June 16, 1940.

"Betterton on the Bay." *Baltimore Sun*, August 1, 1943.

"Betterton Opening." *Baltimore Sun*, May 27, 1951.

"Betterton Ready for Fishing and Fun." *Baltimore Sun*, June 18, 1944.

"Betterton Season Near." *Baltimore Sun*, May 7, 1950.

"Betterton Shoot Will Start Today." *Baltimore Sun*, July 8, 1924.

"Betterton Very Luring in Summer." *Baltimore Sun*, June 24, 1923.

"Betterton … Where the Bay Begins." *News American Sunday*, June 26, 1966.

"Bid Booze Farewell." *Baltimore Sun*, May 1, 1918.

"Big Crowd at Electric Park." *Baltimore Sun*, July 5, 1910.

"Big Crowd at Tolchester." *Baltimore Sun*, September 2, 1911.

"Big Day at Tolchester." *Baltimore Sun*, June 16, 1905.

"Big Days Return to Tolchester Beach." *Baltimore Sun*, June 12, 1938.

"Big Game Is Delayed." *Baltimore Sun*, December 11, 1900.

"Big Pumpkin Enchants Again." *Howard County (MD) Sun*, September 5, 2004.

"Big Swim Meet for Bay Shore." *Baltimore Sun*, August 3, 1926.

"Big Swimming Pool Installed at Carlin's." *Catholic Review*, July 15, 1938.

"Big Time at River View." *Baltimore Sun*, August 4, 1918.

"Big Tree Falls, Destroys Stage." *Baltimore Sun*, August 29, 1962.

"Big Year Expected at Betterton." *Baltimore Sun*, May 8, 1955.

"Bill at Electric Park." *Baltimore Sun*, June 2, 1907.

"Bill at Electric Park." *Baltimore Sun*, July 9, 1907.

"Bill Would Permit Drive-In Theater at Carlin's Park." *Baltimore Sun*, April 30, 1957.

"Bills at the Summer Parks." *Baltimore Sun*, July 25, 1909.

"Bills at the Theatres and in the Parks." *Baltimore Sun*, June 6, 1909.

"Bills at the Theatres and Parks." *Baltimore Sun*, July 4, 1909.

"Bills at the Theatres and Parks." *Baltimore Sun*, July 11, 1909.

"Bills at the Theatres and the Summer Parks." *Baltimore Sun*, August 1, 1909.

"Blaze at Carlin's Wrecks Building." *Baltimore Sun*, September 15, 1927.

"Bodies Sought as Auto Jumps Span." *Baltimore News-Post*, date unknown.

"Bouts Booked for This Week in New Arena." *Baltimore Sun*, December 11, 1938.

"Boy Injured in Fall from Racer-Dip." *Baltimore Sun*, June 28, 1925.

"Boy Scout Coroboree Held at Gwynn Oak Park." *Baltimore Sun*, May 22, 1932.

"Boy Seriously Injured on Amusement Device." *Baltimore Sun*, June 20, 1924.

"Building Hotel at Back River." *Baltimore Sun*, October 1, 1906.

"Building the Mountain Speedway at Carlin's Park." *Baltimore Sun Magazine*, September 3, 1979.

"Business Men at Beach." *Baltimore Sun*, July 17, 1919.

"Busy at Tolchester Beach." *Baltimore Sun*, April 2, 1910.

"Button Boy." *Baltimore Sun*, August 2, 1949.

"By Rail Route to Bay." *Baltimore Sun*, June 15, 1907.

"By Trolley to Bay Ridge." *Baltimore Sun*, January 8, 1907.

"Call Cops as 700 Clamor for 75 Jobs." *Baltimore News-American*, c. 1929.

"Calvert Interests at Gwynn Oak." *Baltimore Sun*, July 27, 1909.

"Cannstatter Festival Open." *Baltimore Sun*, September 7, 1920.

"Captain Eliason Admits It, but Puts Part of the Blame on the Passengers." *Baltimore Sun*, June 25, 1920.

"Captain Eliason 'Hoodooed.'" *Baltimore Sun*, April 28, 1911.

"Carlin Plans Park." *Baltimore Sun*, April 11, 1919.

"Carlin's Amusement Park Damaged by $15,000 Fire." *Baltimore Sun*, July 5, 1926.

"Carlin's Arena Is Ruled Safe Enough to Use." *Baltimore Sun*, January 25, 1939.

"Carlin's Fight Arena Opens June 13." *Baltimore News-American,* June 3, 1924.

"Carlin's Fire Lights Up City." *Baltimore Sun*, February 18, 1928.

"Carlin's Joyland Will Reopen Today." *Baltimore Sun*, April 21, 1935.

"Carlin's Open for Summer." *Baltimore Sun*, May 21, 1933.

"Carlin's Park Bandit Gets Over $2,000." *Baltimore Sun*, July 22, 1951.

"Carlin's Park Building Is Damaged by Blaze." *Baltimore Sun*, January 16, 1932.

"Carlin's Park Is Fairyland." *Baltimore Sun*, June 26, 1921.

"Carlin's Park Marks 8th Birthday." *Baltimore News-American*, Aug 10, 1927.

"Carlin's Park Opens." *Baltimore Sun*, April 27, 1941.

"Carlin's Park Reopens." *Baltimore Sun*, April 26, 1936.

"Carlin's Park Sports Arena Is Held Unsafe." *Baltimore Sun*, January 13, 1939.

"Carlin's to Have Showboat Salon, Big-Time Revue." *Baltimore News-American,* May 3, 1936.

"Carnival at Industrial Park." *Baltimore Sun*, May 28, 1905.

"Carnival on the Lake." *Baltimore Sun*, August 16, 1912.

"Carnival Queen Test Is Popular." *The Times* [Baltimore], September 9, 1925.

"Carousal at Bay Ridge Totally Destroyed by Fire." *Baltimore Sun*, July 28, 1890.

"Carousel Case Award Is $5,174." *Baltimore Sun*, January 23, 1959.

"Carrousel Owner Sued." *Baltimore Sun*, October 2, 1906.

"Carr's Beach Fans Share Their Fondest Memories." *Frederick (MD) News Post*, March 19, 2007.

"Carus at Electric Park." *Baltimore Sun*, June 3, 1906.

"Catholic Day at Beach." *Baltimore Sun*, July 16, 1949.

"A Catholic Reunion." *Baltimore Sun*, June 30, 1891.

"A Celebration Abandoned." *Baltimore Sun*, July 5, 1898.

"Changes at Electric Park." *Baltimore Sun*, April 22, 1905.

"Charles Cole Scores Knockout on Service Program at Bay Shore." *Baltimore Sun*, July 12, 1941.

"Charley Swan Gets a New Job." *News-American*, March 19, 1948.

"Chautauqua Beach Is Open." *Baltimore Sun*, June 18, 1901.

"Chautauqua Now Open." *Baltimore Sun*, May 31, 1900.

"A Chesapeake Bay Resort—Bay Ridge." *Baltimore Sun,* July 14, 1880.

"Chesapeake Bay Resorts Prepared for Season." *Baltimore Sun*, June 11, 1933.

"Chesapeake Beach Carousel Purchased by Area Dealer in Carousels." *The Mid-Atlantic Antique Journal*, March, 1973.

"Chesapeake Beach Gets PWA Funds." *Baltimore Evening Sun*, November 8, 1939.

"Chesapeake Beach, On Bay." *Baltimore Sun*, June 25, 1916.

"Chesapeake Beach on the Bay Is a Nearby Resort." *Baltimore Sun*, June 23, 1918.

"Chesapeake Beach Opens." *Baltimore Sun*, June 13, 1915.

"Chesapeake Beach Park Now Open." *Baltimore-News-Post*, June 24, 1955.

"Chesapeake Beach R.R. to Make Improvements." *Baltimore Sun*, November 17, 1922.

"Chesapeake Beach's Sad Tale." *Baltimore Sun*, October 8, 1975.

"Chesapeake Chautauqua." *Baltimore Sun*, May 10, 1900.

"Chesapeake Excursions." *Baltimore Sun*, June 23, 1887.

"Children Flock to Park." *Baltimore Sun*, June 9, 1922.

"Children to Romp in Storybook Land." *Washington Post*, July 21, 1957.

"Christian Endeavorers." *Baltimore Sun*, July 15, 1896.

"Citizens to Urge City Buy Gwynn Oak." *Baltimore Sun*, April 30, 1930.

"City to Have One Excursion Boat." *Baltimore Evening Sun*, February 17, 1956.

"Civil War in 'Tone Picture.'" *Baltimore Sun*, June 30, 1907.

"Clang, Clang, Clang Went the Trolley, Down to Bay Shore." *Baltimore Evening Sun* (Jacques Kelly column). Date unknown.

"Complaints of the Bathing Suits and Tolchester Towels." *Baltimore Sun*, July 28, 1913.

"Concert Stoppage in Baltimore Laid to Beer Shortage." *Washington Post*, July 29, 1946.

"Concerts at Bay Shore Park." *Baltimore Sun*, June 7, 1907.

"Concerts at Bay Shore Park." *Baltimore Sun*, June 18, 1912.

"Concerts at Bay Shore Park." *Baltimore Sun*, July 12, 1914.

"Concerts at Electric Park." *Baltimore Sun,* May 22, 1904.

"Concerts at Electric Park." *Baltimore Sun,* May 5, 1907.

"Concerts at Electric Park." *Baltimore Sun*, August 22, 1911.

"Condo-Hotel-Marina Project Planned at Carr's Beach." *Baltimore Sun*, November 9, 1982.

"Coney Island of the South." *Baltimore Sun Magazine*, August 31, 1952.

"Contractor Buys Tolchester Park." *Baltimore Sun*, November 15, 1969.

"Coronation of "King Toots I" Marks Climax of Boys' Week." *Baltimore Sun*, May 2, 1925.

"County Buys Gwynn Oak Park." *Baltimore News-American*, June 21, 1977.

"Court of Appeals." *Baltimore Sun*, June 29, 1898.

"Criticism of the United Railways and the Company's Reply." *Baltimore Sun*, July 25, 1916.

"Crowd at Gwynn Oak's Opening." *Baltimore Sun*, May 28, 1911.

"Crowd Falls into Water When Boardwalk Collapses." *Baltimore Sun*, July 14, 1921.

"Crowd Is Expected at Betterton on Labor Day." *Baltimore Sun*, August 31, 1913.

"Crowds at River View." *Baltimore Sun*, July 19, 1904.

"Cruises Galore Offered in Maryland." *Baltimore Sun*, July 31, 1966.

"Cruising to Brown's Grove." *Baltimore Sun*, October 23, 1978.

"Dance at Betterton." *Baltimore Sun*, November 23, 1902.

"Dancing at Electric Park." *Baltimore Sun*, May 24, 1904.

"The Day at Bay Shore." *Baltimore Sun*, July 5, 1908.

"Days of Old—When 'Coney Island of South' Was Popular as Riverview." *Baltimore American*, September 23, 1951.

"Deal Island Boat Swiftest of Schooners." *Baltimore Sun*, June 17, 1928.

"Defenders' Day of Baltimore." *Baltimore Sun*, September 13, 1877.

"Defends Bay Shore Rates." *Baltimore Sun,* March 18, 1913.

"Develo at Bay Shore Park." *Baltimore Sun*, August 7, 1910.

"Dies from Carousel Injury." *Baltimore Sun*, June 4, 1915.

"Dies of Injuries Received at Park." *Baltimore Evening Sun*, June 20, 1924.

"Dimples on Fair Bathers' Knees Must Be Cov-

ered, Edict at Nearby Beaches." *Baltimore Sun*, May 23, 1921.

"Diving Girls at Gwynn Oak Park." *Baltimore Sun*, July 23, 1911.

"Do You Remember? Part I, In the Good Old Frivolous Days There Were Many Amusement Parks." *Baltimore Evening Sun*, July 19, 1961.

"Do You Remember? Part II, Electric Park Had Sulky Races; Lion Broke Loose." *Baltimore Evening Sun*, July 20, 1961.

"Do You Remember? Part III, Valentino Mobbed Here." *Baltimore Evening Sun*, July 21, 1961.

"Dr. Wharton as Coacher." *Baltimore Sun*, July 15, 1893.

"Down the Harbor and Back to 1890." *Baltimore Sun*, July 25, 1943.

"Down the Spillway." *Baltimore Sun*, September 16, 1954.

"Dreamland for Chesapeake Beach." *Baltimore Sun*, May 10, 1909.

"Dreamland Is Sold." *Baltimore Sun*, December 11, 1912.

"Dreamland Passengers Sue." *Baltimore Sun*, August 10, 1913.

"Dreamland Trips Begin." *Baltimore Sun*, June 27, 1909.

"Eager to Get Outdoors." *Baltimore Sun*, May 14, 1906.

"Eagles in Country Home." *Baltimore Sun*, May 13, 1901.

"Eagles on the Wing." *Baltimore Sun*, May 12, 1902.

"Earthquake at Electric Park." *Baltimore Sun*, August 15, 1911.

"80-Year-Old Gywnn Oak Park to Close." *Baltimore Sun*, Summer 1974.

"Electric Park." *Baltimore Sun*, July 11, 1896.

"Electric Park." *Baltimore Sun*, June 12, 1900.

"Electric Park Attractions." *Baltimore Sun*, July 7, 1908.

"Electric Park Company Sued." *Baltimore Sun*, September 23, 1909.

"Electric Park Deal Closed." *Baltimore Sun*, September 2, 1910.

"Electric Park Enjoined." *Baltimore Sun*, June 21, 1908.

"Electric Park in New Garb." *Baltimore Sun*, May 23, 1909.

"Electric Park Is Well Attended." *Baltimore Sun*, Spring 1911.

"Electric Park May 28." *Baltimore Sun*, May 6, 1906.

"Electric Park Next." *Baltimore Sun*, May 20, 1914.

"Electric Park Open." *Baltimore Sun*, June 7, 1908.

"Electric Park Opened." *Baltimore Sun*, May 27, 1907.

"Electric Park Opened." *Baltimore Sun*, May 28, 1907.

"Electric Park Opens May 28." *Baltimore Sun*, May 15, 1910.

"Electric Park Opens Tonight." *Baltimore Sun*, May 27, 1907.

"Electric Park Popular." *Baltimore Sun*, July 5, 1908.

"Electric Park to Be Sold." *Baltimore Sun*, May 11, 1906.

"Electric Park to Open." *Baltimore Sun*, May 27, 1906.

"Electric Park to Open Tomorrow." *Baltimore Sun*, May 21, 1909.

"Electric Park Vaudeville." *Baltimore Sun*, May 28, 1905.

"Electric Park's Season." *Star*, May 8, 1909.

"Eliason Personalty $37,467." *Baltimore Sun*, August 19, 1921.

"Elks to Have Outing." *Baltimore Sun*, May 24, 1908.

"Enchanted Forest." *Howard County (MD) Sun*, September 5, 2004.

"Enchanted Forest Will Open Aug. 15." *Baltimore News-Post*, August 10, 1955.

"Excitement for All at the C. & P. Outing." *Baltimore Sun*, August 16, 1921.

"Excitement on Back River." *Baltimore Sun*, July 3, 1902.

"The Excursion Season." *Baltimore Sun*, May 12, 1883.

"The Excursion Season." *Baltimore Sun*, June 8, 1885.

"The Excursion Season." *Baltimore Sun*, June 21, 1886.

"Excursion Season on in Earnest." *Baltimore Sun*, June 15, 1913.

"Excursion to Bay Ridge." *Baltimore Sun*, June 18, 1881.

"Excursions." *Baltimore Sun*, July 27, 1857.

"Excursions To-day." *Baltimore Sun*, August 15, 1878.

"Faints After Looping Loop." *Baltimore Sun*, July 30, 1907.

"Fair at Electric Park." *Baltimore Sun*, September 16, 1907.

"Falls Down Racer Dip." *Baltimore Sun*, September 18, 1922.

"Farm Rewrites Happy Ending for Park Pieces." *Baltimore Sun*, August 12, 2005.

"Favorite Summer Resorts." *Baltimore Sun*, June 23, 1883.

"Fenneman Cuts Throat." *Baltimore Sun*, August 7, 1914.

"Ferris Wheel Rage Reaches Gwynn Oak." *Baltimore Sun*, August 25, 1964.

"Ferry Earns $20,000 More Than Subsidy." *Baltimore Sun*, January 8, 1935.

"15,000 Take Part in German Picnic." *Baltimore Sun*, September 3, 1934.

"Fifteenth Annual Report to the Stockholders of the United Railways." *Baltimore Sun*, April 9, 1914.

"50 Years Ago." *Baltimore Sun*, August 23, 1959.

"Fighting for a Landing." *Baltimore Sun*, May 15, 1886.

"Figures Moved to Farm." *Howard County (MD) Sun*, February 10, 2005.

"Fire Demon Plays Havoc in County Over Weekend." *Baltimore Jeffersonian*, November 3, 1939.

"Fire Destroys Ballroom at Gwynn Oak." *Baltimore Sun*, November 20, 1939.

"Fire Destroys Ballroom at Gwynn Oak." *Baltimore Sun*, February 1975.

"Fire Destroys Shore Ferry Line Steamer." *Baltimore Sun*, January 5, 1928.

"Fire Not to Delay Opening of Park." *News-American*, April 3, 1923.

"Fire Sweeps Park on Frederick Road." *Baltimore Sun*, April 16, 1925.

"Fire Sweeps River View." *Baltimore Sun*, October 1, 1909.

"Fire Wipes Out Old Hollywood River Resort." *Baltimore Sun*, March 21, 1921.

"Fire Wrecks Luna Park." *Baltimore Sun*, July 6, 1910.

"Fire Wrecks River View." *Baltimore News-American*, October 1, 1909.

"Fire Wrecks Theater at Frederick Road Amusement Park." *Baltimore Sun*, July 14, 1923.

"Firm Buys Park, Steamer; Plans Tolchester Cruises." *Baltimore Evening Sun*, unknown.

"Firm Eyes Bay Shore, Report." *Baltimore News-American*, January 18, 1947.

"5 Cents to Electric Park." *Baltimore Sun*, May 29, 1903.

"Five Firemen Hurt in Blaze at Park." *Baltimore Sun*, April, 1923.

"Five Hurt by Tiny Train." *Baltimore Sun*, June 26, 1916.

"5 Persons Sue Price, Park." *Baltimore Evening Sun*, September 7, 1954.

"5,000 Watch Joe Louis in Final Spar Session." *Baltimore Sun*, August 13, 1951.

"Fleet Workboats to Race Near City." *Baltimore Sun*, May 25, 1928.

"Flood's Park—Initial Performances at Open-Air Theater at Curtis Bay." *Baltimore News-American*, May 8, 1906.

"Follow Rt. 40 to New World." *Baltimore News-American*, August 6, 1976.

"For Luna Park Here." *Baltimore Sun*, January 28, 1910.

"Former Bay Belle Owner Faces Repurchase Suit." *Baltimore Evening Sun*, January 7, 1960.

"Four Injured on 'Bug' Ride at Carlin's Park." *Sunday Sun*, July 23, 1938.

"14 'Cops' Suspended." *Baltimore Sun,* August 12, 1913.

"14 Hurt in Crash of Roller Coasters." *Washington Post,* June 14, 1945.

"Fourth of July Excursions." *Baltimore Sun,* July 3, 1877.

"Frederick Rd. Park Sold for $500,000." *Baltimore Sun,* May 18, 1923.

"Frederick Road Park Scene of Another Fire." *Baltimore Sun,* May 5, 1925.

"From Baltimore's Family Album." *Baltimore Evening Sun,* Aug 11, 1936.

"From Baltimore's Family Album" (Bay Ridge). *Baltimore Evening Sun,* March 8, 1937.

"From Baltimore's Family Album" (Bay Ridge). *Baltimore Evening Sun,* March 23, 1937.

"Fun and Fireworks." *Baltimore Sun,* July 6, 1896.

"Fun to Be Found at Home." *Baltimore Sun,* June 22, 1924.

"Furnace Causes New Fire Scare at Park." *Baltimore Evening Sun,* date unknown.

"Future of Betterton, 'Jewel of the Chesapeake,' Shines Brightly." *Baltimore Sun,* April 14, 1989.

"Gala Day for Soldiers." *Baltimore Sun,* July 28, 1918.

"The Gay Season Open at Riverview Park." *Baltimore Sun,* May 20, 1917.

"A General Holiday." *Baltimore Sun,* May 30, 1896.

"German Athletes Out Today." *Baltimore Sun,* July 3, 1916.

"German Day Followed by 2 'Hangovers.'" *Baltimore Sun,* September 14, 1937.

"Germans Raise U.S. Flag." *Baltimore Sun,* September 1, 1914.

"Gets $5,000 in Son's Death." *Baltimore Sun,* January 23, 1923.

"Getting to, and Home Again from, Bay Shore." *Baltimore Evening Sun,* March 7, 1978.

"Ghost Resort Grasps at Hope of New Life." *Baltimore Sun,* March 27, 1983.

"Given $2,400 for Injuries." *Baltimore Sun,* February 17, 1925.

"Go On the *Bay Belle* with Me, This Saturday?" *Baltimore Evening Sun,* June 7, 1977.

"Goeller Case a Mixed One." *Baltimore Sun,* August 10, 1905.

"Goeller's as Example." *Baltimore Sun,* Aug 10, 1913.

"Goeller's Liscense Suppressed." *Baltimore Sun,* February 29, 1912.

"Good Music at River View." *Baltimore Sun,* July 12, 1908.

"Green Palace Under Ban for Amusements." *Baltimore Sun,* April 1, 1934.

"Ground Broken for Park." *Baltimore Sun,* March 2, 1910.

"Gwynn Oak: A Haunting Walk Down Memory Lane." *Baltimore News-American,* July 7, 1974.

"Gwynn Oak a Sylvan Gem." *Baltimore Sun,* May 26, 1912.

"Gwynn Oak Charms." *Baltimore Sun,* May 20, 1923.

"Gwynn Oak Dying, but ... the Memory Lingers On." *Baltimore News-American,* June 10, 1976.

"Gwynn Oak Named in Suit." *Baltimore Sun,* October 29, 1954.

"Gwynn Oak Park." *Baltimore Sun,* July 1, 1894.

"Gwynn Oak Park." *Baltimore Sun,* July 25, 1894.

"Gwynn Oak Park." *Baltimore Sun,* March 29, 1895.

"Gwynn Oak Park." *Baltimore Sun,* May 26, 1899.

"Gwynn Oak Park." *Baltimore Sun,* July 16, 1916.

Gwynn Oak Park ad. *Baltimore Sun,* July 4, 1896.

Gwynn Oak Park ad. *Baltimore Sun,* July 21, 1899.

"Gwynn Oak Park Allowed to Open." *Baltimore Sun,* June 3, 1972.

"Gwynn Oak Park Auctioned." *Baltimore Evening Sun,* June 26, 1974.

"Gwynn Oak Park Brings $415,000." *Baltimore Sun,* June 26, 1974.

"Gwynn Oak Park Crumbles, but Memories Grow Strong." *Baltimore News-American,* September 8, 1974.

"Gwynn Oak Park Opening." *Baltimore Sun,* May 16, 1909.

"Gwynn Oak Park Opening on Saturday." *Baltimore Sun,* May 17, 1936.

"Gwynn Oak Park Opens." *Baltimore Sun,* May 23, 1909.

"Gwynn Oak Park Owners Agree to Raze Park by July." *Baltimore News-American,* March 4, 1976.

"Gwynn Oak Park Proves Elusive." *Baltimore Sun,* July 5, 1963.

"Gwynn Oak Park Purchase Voted." *Baltimore Sun,* June 21, 1977.

"Gwynn Oak Park Stirs Thoughts of Childhood." *Baltimore Sun,* July 15, 1971.

"Gwynn Oak Park to Begin 75th Year." *Baltimore News-American,* April 11, 1971.

"Gwynn Oak Park Weathers Crisis After 1963 Integration." Unknown, c. 1964.

"Gwynn Oak to Be Integrated Aug 28." *Baltimore Sun,* July 20, 1963.

"Gwynn Oak to Begin 54th Year." *Baltimore News-Post,* Spring 1948.

"Gwynn Oak's 50th Birthday Unheeded by Holiday Throng." *Baltimore Sun,* May 8, 1944.

"The Handling of Excursion Crowds at Tolchester." *Baltimore Sun,* July 21, 1916.

"Happily Ever After Is on the Farm." *Baltimore Sun,* February 10, 2005.

"He Turns Children's Fantasies into Reality." *Baltimore Sun,* May 15, 1960.

"Heirs Settle Ownership of Carlin's Park." *Baltimore News-American*, Feb 1, 1955.

"Held for the Grand Jury." *Baltimore Sun*, June 20, 1902.

"Hiawatha at Gwynn Oak." *Baltimore Sun*, July 3, 1913.

"High Wire Feats at Gwynn Oak." *Baltimore Sun*, June 30, 1912.

"Highlights on Carlin's fire." *Baltimore Evening Sun*, September 30, 1937.

"The Historical Significance of Gwynn Oak." *Baltimore Sun,* July 2, 1976.

"History of the Steamboat on the Chesapeake." *Baltimore Sun*, March 22, 1908.

"Hitting at Bay Resorts." *Baltimore Sun*, June 16, 1890.

"Hockey Team Left without Home; Fire Routs 50." *Baltimore Evening Sun*, January 23, 1956.

"Holdup at Hollywood." *Baltimore Sun*, August 5, 1904.

"Hollywood Ends Career—Goeller Beats Law to It." *Baltimore Sun*, c. 1922.

"Hollywood Opens Sunday." *Baltimore Sun*, April 11, 1903.

"Hollywood Park." *Baltimore Sun*, May 26, 1900.

"Hollywood Park." *Baltimore Sun*, May 9, 1915.

Hollywood Park Grand Opening ad. *Baltimore Sun*, May 8, 1915.

"Hollywood Park Opened." *Baltimore Sun*, April 13, 1903.

"Hollywood Park Opens Saturday." *Baltimore Sun*, May 21, 1902.

"Hollywood Park Raided." *Baltimore Sun*, March 2, 1909.

"Hollywood Park to Stay Shut." *Baltimore Sun*, April 13, 1922.

"Hollywood Park's Season Opens." *Baltimore Sun*, May 13, 1913.

"Hollywood to Open Tomorrow." *Baltimore Sun*, May 21, 1911.

"Horse at Park Shows Stunts." *Baltimore American*, May 29, 1949.

"How About a Visit with Mother Goose?" *Washington Post*, September 9, 1956.

"How Independence Day Will Be Celebrated." *Baltimore Sun*, July 2, 1881.

"Huge Crowd Jams Area of Jazz Concert." July 13, 1956.

"Hurled from Racer-Dip." *Baltimore Sun*, July 27, 1909.

"Hurt in Haunted Castle." *Baltimore Sun*, July 13, 1920.

"Hurt in Scenic Railway." *Baltimore Sun*, May 30, 1910.

"I Remember … a Childhood Day at Magical Tolchester Beach." *Baltimore Sun Magazine*, August 22, 1971.

"I Remember … a Wrong-Way Race at Electric Park." *Baltimore Sun*, April 4, 1965.

"I Remember … Christened the *Emma Giles*." *Baltimore Sun*, September 25, 1949.

"I Remember … Gwynn Oak Park in Its Heyday." *Baltimore Sun Magazine*, March 28, 1976.

"I Remember … Monuments Made of Fruit." *Baltimore Sun*, September 11, 1955.

"I Remember … Picnics at Gwynn Oak Park and Tolchester." *Baltimore Sun*, June 14, 1970.

"I Remember … Riding the Red Rockets to the Point." *Baltimore Sun*, April 28, 1963.

"I Remember … the Great International Air Race at Bay Shore Park." *Baltimore Sun*, December 28, 1958.

"I Remember … Thrills at Old Riverview Park." *Sunday Sun Magazine*, July 7, 1963.

"I Remember When … a Lion Got Loose in Electric Park." *Baltimore Sun*, August 14, 1949.

"I Remember When … I Piloted That Electric Park Shoot-the-Chute." *Baltimore Sun Magazine*, December 8, 1963.

"I Remember When … My Hair Was a Park Attraction." *Baltimore Sun*, June 3, 1956.

"I Remember When … Park Circle Was Both Park and Circle." *Baltimore Sun Magazine*, May 5, 1968.

"Ice Rinks Set for Big Season." *Baltimore Sun*, December 2, 1932.

"If Ghosts Like Amusement, There's Tolchester Beach." *Baltimore Sun*, July 29, 1968.

"Improvements at Bay Ridge." *Baltimore Sun*, March 16, 1896.

"Improvements at Point Breeze." *Baltimore Sun*, April 22, 1895.

"The Improvements at Tolchester." *Baltimore Sun,* May 30, 1889.

"Improvements at Tolchester." *Baltimore Sun*, April 3, 1899.

"Improvements at Tolchester." *Baltimore Sun*, September 8, 1909.

"Improvements for Gwynn Oak." *Baltimore Sun*, March 30, 1906.

"Improvements Made by the Bay Ridge Company." *Baltimore Sun*, May 24, 1889.

"Improving Bay Shore Park." *Baltimore Sun*, March 21, 1907.

"Improving Electric Park." *Baltimore Sun*, May 20, 1906.

"In the Fun House, Timing Was Everything." *Baltimore Evening Sun*, October 18, 1977.

"In the Good Old Frivolous Days There Were Many Amusement Parks." *Baltimore Evening Sun*, July 19, 1961.

"Injunction Against Goeller." *Baltimore Sun*, May 30, 1912.

"Integration Aids Business at Gwynn Oak." Unknown, September 13, 1963.

"Irish Day at Electric Park." *Baltimore Sun*, June 4, 1905.

"Italian Societies on Picnic." *Baltimore Sun*, August 16, 1922.

"Jackson Quizzed on Coliseum." *Baltimore News-American*, Jan 5, 1939.

"Jail Term for Goeller in Addition to Big Fine." *Baltimore Sun,* January 31, 1922.

"Jerked from Racer Dip." *Baltimore Sun*, August 5, 1917.

"J.J. Carlin Off for Houston." *Baltimore Sun*, October 29, 1921.

"Joseph Oronson: A Wonderful Teller of Yarns." *Baltimore Essex Times*, August 3, 1972.

"A Journey of Exploration to Beautiful Bay Shore." *Baltimore Morning Sun,* May 26, 1907.

"'Judy' Wrecks Her Car." *Baltimore Sun.* May 4, 1913.

"A July Outing." *Baltimore Sun*, September 17, 1911.

"Kent and Queen Anne's Fair," *Baltimore Sun*, August 26, 1903

"Kent County Farmers to Hold Annual Picnic at Tolchester Beach." *Baltimore Sun,* August 3, 1942.

"Kent County to Build Permanent Highways." *Baltimore Sun*, January 15, 1922.

"Kent Farmer's Day Picnic to Be Held at Tolchester." *Baltimore Sun*, August 3, 1925.

"Kernan's Hollywood Park." *Baltimore Sun*, August 4, 1900.

"Kids Can Picnic with Miss Muffet." *Washington Post*, June 3, 1956.

"Kids of 3 or 83 Will Love the Enchanted Forest." *Washington Post*, April 15, 1956.

"Killed on Racer Dip." *Baltimore Sun*, June 26, 1916.

"Labor Day Outing Attended by 10,000." *Baltimore Sun*, September 8, 1925.

"Let's Go Down the Bay." *Baltimore Sun*, May 13, 1914.

"Let's Go Mentally, to Carlin's." *Baltimore Evening Sun*, date unknown.

Letters to the Editor, "Gwynn Oak Park." *Baltimore Sun*, June 14, 1930.

"Liberty Heights Park Opens Tonight." *Baltimore Sun*, August 13, 1919.

"'Life-Saving' Dogs at Bay Shore." *Baltimore Sun*, July 27, 1909.

"Light Opera Summer Season Is Well Under Way at Carlin's Arena." *Baltimore Sun,* July 8, 1923.

"Lightning Hits Coaster." *Baltimore Sun*, May 25, 1925.

"Like a Coney Island." *Baltimore Sun*, April 18, 1908.

"Lion Loose at Electric Park." *Baltimore Sun*, August 14, 1905.

"Liquor, Auto and Still Seized in Three Raids." *Baltimore Sun*, October 1, 1921.

"Lithuanians Hold Bay Shore Picnic." *Baltimore Sun*, August 28, 1944.

"The Little Locomotive." *Baltimore Sun*, November 12, 1950.

"Lively at Electric Park." *Baltimore Sun*, June 2, 1908.

"Lively Outing Youngsters Enjoyed." *Baltimore Sun*, August 7, 1949.

"Local Matters." *Baltimore Sun*, June 25, 1877.

"Louis to Referee Moore-Henry Tiff." *Cumberland (MD) Evening Times*, June 25, 1952.

"Luna Park Company Incorporated." *Baltimore Sun*, February 4, 1910.

"Luna Park Is Opened." *Baltimore Sun*, May 31, 1910.

"Luna Park Is Opened." *Baltimore Sun*, Spring 1911.

"Luna Park Opens Today." *Baltimore Sun*, May 20, 1911.

"Luna Park Opens Tonight." *Baltimore Sun*, May 30, 1910.

"Luna Park Reopens." *Baltimore Sun*, July 7, 1910.

"Mahoney Sells Shore Park to Dealer." *Baltimore Evening Sun*, April 28, 1950.

"Mahoney Spending Millions to Improve Bay Shore Park Area." *Baltimore American*, May 23, 1948.

"Mahoney's Last Hurrah." *Baltimore Sun.* January 14, 1981.

"Making Money and a Difference." Unknown.

"Making Ready Resort Joys for Week-Ender." *Baltimore Sun*, March 23, 1913.

"Many Enjoy River View Park." *Baltimore Sun*, May 20, 1906.

"Many from District Enjoy 'Fourth' at Old-Time Bay Resort." *Washington Star*, July 4, c. early 1960s.

"Many Go on Excursions." *Baltimore Sun*, May 21, 1911.

"Many New Features." May 8, 1906.

"Many to Leave City Today." *Baltimore Sun*, July 4, 1911.

"Many Ways to Celebrate." *Baltimore Sun*, July 4, 1899.

"Marches and Merriment," *Baltimore Jewish Times*, date unknown.

"Maryland Feasting and Vaudeville at Gwynn Oak." *Baltimore Sun*, June 12, 1913.

"Maryland Legislature." *Baltimore Sun*, March 7, 1850.

"A Maryland Mecca." *Baltimore Sun,* June 27, 1961.

"Md. Should Take Over Tolchester for Park, McKeldin Urges." *Baltimore Evening Sun*, October 23, 1962.

"May Extend the W., B. and A." *Baltimore Sun*, May 1, 1909.

"Mayor Ends White Picnics." *Baltimore Sun*, June 14, 1922.

"Mayor Rides in Donkey Cart." *Baltimore Sun*, June 23, 1910.

"McGinity the Champion." *Baltimore Sun*, June 30, 1897.

"Memories Remain at Skeleton Called Gwynn Oak." *Baltimore Evening Sun*, June 2, 1975.

"Merchants at River View." *Baltimore Sun*, September 11, 1908.

"Merry Volksfest Opens." *Baltimore Sun*, August 29, 1916.

"A Military Camp." *Baltimore Sun*, July 17, 1893.

"Miniature Race Car Meet Held at Carlin's." *Baltimore Sun*, September 8, 1942.

"Miniature Train Derailed, 3 Held." *Baltimore Sun*, August 31, 1955.

"Miss Chesapeake Chosen at Bay Shore; Also a Mr...." *Baltimore Sun*, July 19, 1959.

"Miss Miller at Electric Park." *Baltimore Sun*, August 7, 1910.

"Mr. Carlin's String of Horses Groomed for Spring Workouts." *Baltimore Sun*, March 4, 1937.

"Mr. Fenneman Out of Electric Park." *Baltimore Sun*, June 8, 1911.

"Mr. Fenneman's Plans." *Baltimore Sun*, January 7, 1906.

"Mr. Fitzsimmons to Run it." *Baltimore Sun*, May 6, 1906.

"Mr. Ford's New Venture." *Baltimore Sun*, June 8, 1896.

"Mr. Kernan's Enterprise." *Baltimore Sun*, March 21, 1899.

"Mr. M.J. Fitzsimmons Out." *Baltimore Sun*, October 26, 1908.

"Mr. William A. Potts Dead." *Baltimore Sun*, July 18, 1910.

"Monastery Parish Picnic." *Baltimore Sun*, July 7, 1915.

"Monte Carlo on Bay." *Baltimore Sun*, October 31, 1900.

"Moose Carnival Week Begins." *Baltimore Sun*, August 17, 1915.

"More Leaps to the Moon." *Baltimore Sun*, August 25, 1907.

"Motor Horns Sound the Bay-boats' Knell." *Baltimore Sun*, March 6, 1932.

"Moving by Electricity." *Baltimore Sun*, August 22, 1889.

"Nabob of Summer Time." *Baltimore Sun*, July 19, 1905.

"Nature Reasserts Claim." *Baltimore Sun*, May 24, 1995.

"Negro Family Integrates Gwynn Oak in Brief Visit." *Baltimore Sun*, August 29, 1963.

"Neptune Regatta at Bay Ridge." *Baltimore Sun*, August 21, 1893.

"New Act at Electric Park." *Baltimore Sun,* June 8, 1906.

"New Amusement Park Is Planned." *Baltimore News-American*, April 7, 1919.

"New Amusements at River View." *Baltimore Sun*, May 28, 1905.

"New Arena—Fight, Mat Building Rising at Carlin's." *Baltimore News-Post*, November 11, 1938.

"New Arrangement for the Sassafras Route." *Baltimore Sun*, August 18, 1855.

"New Attractions Listed as Gwynn Oak Opens." *Baltimore Sun*, May 21, 1939.

"New 'Barn' Comes to Enchanted Forest." *Washington Post*, July 8, 1956.

"New Bay Shore Bus Line to Open." *Baltimore American*, May 28, 1949.

"New Bay Shore Opening Slated Memorial Day." *Baltimore News-Post*, May 22, 1956.

"New Beach at Bay Shore." *Baltimore Sun*, May 27, 1922.

"The New Chautauqua." *Baltimore Sun*, June 4, 1900.

"New Devices." *Washington Post*, April 20, 1930.

"New Electric Park." *Baltimore Sun*, May 9, 1909.

"A New Excursion Resort." *Baltimore Sun*, March 9, 1880.

"New Features at Betterton." *Baltimore Sun*, June 19, 1927.

"New Gwynn Oak Park." *Baltimore Sun,* September 12, 1937.

"A New Railroad." *Baltimore Sun*, October 3, 1899.

"New Steel Plant Extension Seen in Land Deals." *Baltimore News-American*, January 18, 1947.

"New Tunes for Carrousels." *Baltimore Sun,* May 5, 1899.

"New Yorker Plans to Buy Bay Islands." *Baltimore Sun*, August 5, 1933.

"Newsboys and Bootblacks at Tolchester." *Baltimore Sun*, June 18, 1892.

"Nickelodeon to Be Opened at Carlin's." *Baltimore News-American*, April 29, 1953.

"No Riders, but Trains Are Missed." Unknown, July, 1935.

"Notes from the Courts." *Baltimore Sun*, November 26, 1904.

"Now Holds Industry." *Baltimore News-American,* c. early 1960s.

"Old Bay Ridge." *Baltimore News-Post*, September 26, 1942.

"Old River View Opens." *Baltimore Sun*, May 12, 1911.

"Old Soldiers at Play." *Baltimore Sun*, July 15, 1899.

"Old Tolchester Beach to Be Modern Resort." *Baltimore News-Post*, October 26, 1961.

"Old Tolchester Is Opened." *Baltimore Sun*, May 28, 1911.

"Old Tolchester Opens." *Baltimore Sun*, May 30, 1913.

"On a Beach ... Tolchester Redevelops." *Washington Post*, December 22, 1969.

"On Picnic to River View." *Baltimore Sun*, August 26, 1910.

"On the *Bay Belle*, in the Moonlight: River Romance." *Baltimore Evening Sun*, July 30, 1946.

"Once-Famed Hotel Burns." *Baltimore News-American*, May 2, 1967.

"100 Newsboys on an Outing." *Baltimore Sun*, July 2, 1896.

"$150,000 Suits in 3 Drownings." *Baltimore News-Post*, November 6, 1951.

"Open-Air Tango Season On." *Baltimore Sun*, May 29, 1914.

"Open at Electric Park." *Baltimore Sun*, September 9, 1906.

"Open to Children." *Baltimore Sun*, August 14, 1907.

"Orders Railway and Camels." *Baltimore Sun*, June 29, 1905.

"Orders Sports Arena Inspected." *News-American*, Jan 6, 1939.

"Outdoor Summer Resorts." *Baltimore Sun*, May 25, 1901.

"Palace Trolley Cars." *Baltimore Sun*, March 19, 1895.

"Paragon Park Is Opened." *Baltimore Sun*, April 27, 1915.

"Paragon Park Opens." *Baltimore Sun*, May 31, 1913.

"Paragon Park Was Dark." *Baltimore Sun*, May 14, 1913.

"Park Opens Seasons." *Baltimore Sun*, May 19, 1940.

"Park Roller Coasters Earned Their Winter Rest." *Baltimore Sun*, October 10, 1943.

"Parks and Bay Resorts." *Baltimore Sun*, July 22, 1889.

"Park's Renewal to Begin with Old Trolley Station." *Baltimore Sun*, July 18, 1993.

"Parks to Open for Summer." *Baltimore Sun*, May 25, 1913.

"Passion Play Pictures." *Baltimore Sun*, May 29, 1899.

"The People's Outings." *Baltimore Sun*, June 12, 1893.

"Perfect Spring Sunday Coaxes Thousands to Various Parks." *Baltimore Sun*, May 15, 1944.

"Picnics and Excursions." *Baltimore Sun*, June 14, 1887.

"Picnics at Gwynn Oak." *Baltimore Sun*, July 5, 1908.

"Pier Transfer Is Scheduled." *Baltimore Sun*, April 9, 1950.

"Plans for Bay Shore Park." *Baltimore Sun*, February 21, 1906.

"The Playground That Went to Work." Unknown publication, February 1969.

"Point Breeze Improvements." *Baltimore Sun*, March 19, 1898.

"Police Hit 'Decent' Citizens at Outing." *Baltimore Sun*, June 26, 1964.

"Police Invade Resorts." *Baltimore Sun*, June 15, 1908.

"Police Negligence Blamed for Fire." *Baltimore Evening Sun*, April 16, 1925.

"Police Probing Park Train Derailing." *Baltimore Evening Sun*, August 12, 1954.

"Police System Scored by County Grand Jury." *Baltimore Sun*, October 1, 1921.

"Police Will Not Molest Park Amusement Devices." *Baltimore Sun*, July 6, 1920.

"Popular Resorts Open." *Baltimore Sun*, May 30, 1915.

"A Postoffice at Bay Ridge." *Baltimore Sun*, July 2, 1885.

"Presbyterian Day." *Baltimore Sun*, June 30, 1894.

"PSC O.K.'s Sale of *Bay Belle*." *Baltimore Sun*, July 26, 1957.

"P.S.C. to Consider Bay Ferry Proposal." *Baltimore Sun*, June 12, 1937.

"Public Arroused [*sic*]." *Baltimore Sun*, August 13, 1906.

"Quite a Commotion." *Baltimore Sun*, July 4, 1961.

"Races at Tolchester Beach." *Baltimore Sun*, July 24, 1887.

"Races Feature Picnic of Telephone Company Employees at Bay Shore." *Baltimore Sun*, July 25, 1927.

"Racing Wheelmen Out." *Baltimore Sun*, June 27, 1904.

"The Rain Did Come." *Baltimore Sun*, July 26, 1890.

"Rassling Site to Be Retained." *Baltimore Sun*, April 3, 1934.

"Razing of Gwynn Oak Park Due Soon." *Baltimore Evening Sun*, March 4, 1976.

"Real Estate Deals and Building News." *Baltimore Sun*, August 24, 1925.

"Receivers for Luna Park." *Baltimore Sun*, August 2, 1911.

"Receivership Asked for Carlin's Park." *Baltimore News-American*, October 9, 1931.

"Receivership Asked for Carlin's Park." *Baltimore News-American*, December 5, 1933.

"Red Men to Have Reunion." *Baltimore Sun*, July 7, 1907.

"Rekindling a Fairy Tale Dream in Howard." *Baltimore Sun*, December 1, 2003.

"Removing a Carrousel." *Baltimore Sun*, July 1, 1899.

"Renovated Carlin's Park Offers 'New Thrillers.'" *Baltimore Sun*, April 7, 1929.

"Reports Crowding of Boats Corrected." *Baltimore Sun*, July 30, 1941.

"Resort Noise Is Protested." *Baltimore Sun*, July 10, 1957.

"Resort Owners Accused." *Baltimore Sun*, August 13, 1913.

"Resorts Getting in Shape." *Baltimore Sun*, April 29, 1914.

"Resorts Wide Open; Two Raids Made." *Baltimore Sun*, July 21, 1913.

"Retail Grocers Plan Their Annual Picnic." *Baltimore Sun*, August 19, 1934.

Riegger, Christian A. "I Remember … the Music and Fellowships of Volksfests." *Baltimore Sun Magazine*, June 23, 196?.

"Rink Will Open Next Week." *Baltimore News-American*, Nov 19, 1931.

"River View a Maze of Lights." *Baltimore Sun*, July 15, 1906.

"River View as It Will Be Next Summer." *Baltimore Sun*, January 21, 1906.

"River View Attractive." *Baltimore Sun*, June 25, 1905.

"River View Is Open." *Baltimore Sun*, May 9, 1915.

"River View Opens Next Saturday." *Baltimore Sun*, April 25, 1920.

"River View Opens Tomorrow." *Baltimore Sun*, May 11 1906.

"River View Park." *Baltimore Sun*, June 19, 1900.

"River View Park." *Baltimore Sun*, May 30, 1915.

"River View Park." *Baltimore Sun*, June 20, 1915.

"River View Park." *Baltimore Sun*, May 7, 1916.

"River View Park." *Baltimore Sun*, May 21, 1916.

"River View Park Open." *Baltimore Sun*, May 8, 1910.

"River View Park Opens." *Baltimore Sun*, May 5, 1918.

"River View Park Opens Gates for 1924 Season." *Baltimore Sun*, April 20, 1924.

"River View Park Opens Today." *Baltimore Sun*, May 14, 1918.

"River View Park Streetcar Restored." *Baltimore Sun Magazine*, May 25, 1969.

"River View Popular." *Baltimore Sun*, May 26, 1908.

"River View Resplendent." *Baltimore Sun*, July 1, 1906.

"River View Season Begins." *Baltimore Sun*, May 12, 1907.

"River View Season Closes." *Baltimore Sun*, September 19, 1904.

"River View Season Closes." *Baltimore Sun*, September 18, 1905.

"River View the Most Popular Baltimore Park." *Baltimore Sun*, July 21, 1921.

"River View to Open." *Baltimore Sun*, May 6, 1906.

"River View Today." *Baltimore Sun*, May 16, 1909.

"River View's New Feature Draws." *Baltimore Sun*, July 27, 1909.

"Roller Coasters Live—but Only Out of Town." *Baltimore Sun*, June 30, 1978.

"Rollo, Synthetic Elephant, Afire as Park Begins Summer Season." *Baltimore Sun*, April 6, 1930.

"Royal Arcanum's Anniversary." *Baltimore Sun*, June 21, 1900.

"The Rush for Bay Ridge." *Baltimore Sun*, July 2, 1888.

"Sacred Concert at Bay Shore." *Baltimore Sun*, July 27, 1913.

"Said to Want Goeller's." *Baltimore Sun*, August 3, 1913.

"Salt-Water Land in Great Demand, Says Realty Firm." *Washington Post*, June 13, 1926.

"The Same Old Strap-Hanger, Only More Incensed." *Baltimore Sun*, July 16, 1924.

"Sassafras River Boats." *Baltimore Sun*, August 5, 1899.

"Says Noah's Taste in Water Might Be Greatly Improved." *Baltimore Sun*, August 28, 1924.

"Scenic Railway Great." *Baltimore Sun*, September 17, 1911.

"The School Teachers." *Baltimore Sun*, July 9, 1890.

"Seaside Park." *Baltimore Sun*, June 11, 1939.

"Seaside Park." *Washington Post*, June 1, 1930.

"Seaside Park." *Washington Post*, June 15, 1930.

"Seaside Park." *Washington Post*, July 6, 1930.

"Seaside Park Now Open to Beach Lovers." *Washington Post*, May 25, 1930.

"Seaside Park Offers Music as a Feature." *Washington Post*, June 7, 1931.

"Seaside Park, on Bay, Opens with a Bang." *Washington Post*, May 22, 1932.

"Seaside Park Opens Season on Bay's Edge." *Washington Post*, May 24, 1931.

"Seaside Park Plans Season." *Washington Post*, May 4, 1930.

"Seaside Park Reached by Daily Boat Trip." *Baltimore Sun*, June 16, 1940.

"Seaside Park to Open Soon at the Beach." *Washington Post*, May 18, 1930.

"A Season of Fun but a Year of Work." *Baltimore News-American*, April 5, 1959.

"Seek Carlin's Pool for Melody and Mirth." *Baltimore Sun*, June 24, 1923.

"Services Set for Stinnett." *Baltimore Sun*, August 9, 1963.

"Seventh Heaven Suddenly Found at Gwynn Oak by 1,000 Children." *Baltimore Sun*, July 8, 1925.

"'The Sheik' at Carlin's." *Baltimore News-American*, July 30, 1972.

"A Ship-to-Shore Railroad." *Baltimore Sun Magazine*, July 9, 1955.

"The Shoot-the-Chute." *Baltimore Sun*, November 24, 1963.

"Shore Park Soon to Become Memory." Unknown. C. 1964

"Show Opens Tomorrow." *Baltimore Sun*, September 25, 1921.

"Shows of the War Path." *Baltimore Sun*, January 17, 1907.

"Soldier Ban Modified." *Baltimore Sun*, June 7, 1919.

"Some of the Season's New Attractions at the Trolley Parks." *Sunday Sun*, May 9, 1909.

"Songs and Beer Feature 57th Annual German Day." *Baltimore Sun*, September 30, 1957.

"Special Bill at Paragon Park." *Baltimore Sun*, July 3, 1913.

Spencer, Estelle. "I Remember … Bay Shore Park's Great Days." *Baltimore Sun*. May 1, 1966.

"State Will Go on Ride if Coaster Runs Again." *Baltimore Evening Sun*, July 24, 1959.

"Steamboat Summer Excursions." *Baltimore Sun*, June 20, 1881.

"Steamer *Columbia* Sold." *Baltimore Sun*, July 18, 1899.

"Steamer *Louise* Passes from Bay after 43 Years." *Baltimore Sun*, February 1, 1925.

"Steel Pier on Bay Shore." *Baltimore Sun*, October 20, 1905.

"The Stage—Gwynn Oak Park." *Baltimore Sun*, May 22, 1910.

"The Street Car Looks Down the Track." *Baltimore Sun*, May 21, 1933.

"Street Railway Deal." *Baltimore Sun*, December 8, 1894.

"Street Railway Extension." *Baltimore Sun*, August 9, 1898.

"Streetcar and Operator Both Retired as No. 38 Line Ends." *Baltimore Sun*, October 20, 1952.

"A Successful Opening." *Baltimore Sun*, June 9, 1896.

"Suit About a Merry Go Round." *Baltimore Sun*, April 6, 1894.

"Suit Over 'Hell's Kitchen.'" *Baltimore Sun*, August 15, 1913.

"Summer Amusements." *Baltimore Sun*, June 14, 1898.

"Summer Amusements." *Baltimore Sun*, June 12, 1900.

"Summer Amusements." *Baltimore Sun*, June 30, 1900.

"Summer Amusements." *Baltimore Sun*, July 2, 1901.

"Summer Amusements." *Baltimore Sun*, June 29, 1902.

"Summer Amusements." *Baltimore Sun*, June 21, 1904.

"Summer Amusements for All." *Baltimore Sun*, July 13, 1909.

"Summer Car to Riverview Park." *Baltimore Sun*, 1993.

"Summer Disorder Begins." *Baltimore Sun*, April 13, 1909.

"Summer Shows." *Baltimore Sun*, May 31, 1898.

"Summers at Riverview Park." Unknown, May 7, 1972.

"Swim and Beach Party Slated at Carlin's Park." *Baltimore Sun*, July 29, 1947.

"Tall Cedars Close Carnival." *Baltimore Sun*, August 10, 1921.

"Tasca Back at River View." *Baltimore Sun*, May 5, 1907.

"Teeners, Don't Read This Stuff." *Baltimore News-Post*, March 3, 1958.

"10-Alarm Blaze Razes Scores of Structures." *Baltimore Evening Sun*, September 30, 1937.

"Ten-Cent Fare to River View Stands." *Baltimore Sun*, August 7, 1918.

"10,000 at Legion Day Celebration." Baltimore Sun, August 11, 1946.

"$10,000 Is Sought In Carousel Suit." *Baltimore Evening Sun*, February 28, 1950?.

"10,000 Watch Divers." *Baltimore Sun*, August 13, 1923.

"That Park System of the Old Days." *Baltimore Sun*, March 25, 1928.

"Theater Burns at Carlin's." *Baltimore Evening Sun*, April 17, 1944.

"Theatres This Week." *Baltimore Sun*, June 3, 1906.

"Thefts Plague Howard Park." *Baltimore Sun*, September 1, 1977.

"Third Mystery Fire at Park in 60 Days." *Baltimore Sun*, March 25, 1925.

"30 at Gwynn Oak Hurt as Fireworks Fall into Crowd." *Baltimore Evening Sun*, June 1, 1965.

"Three Alarm Fire Destroys Old Kent County Hotel." *Baltimore Sun*, January 9, 1972.

"Three Persons Injured in Racer-Dips Accidents." *Baltimore Sun*, May 14, 1923.

"3 Policemen, 6 Detectives Injured in Dance Hall Fight." *Baltimore Sun*, December 29, 1958.

"A Thriller at Bay Shore." *Baltimore Sun*, July 7, 1907.

"Thriller at Bay Shore Park." *Baltimore Sun*, July 11, 1911.

"Throngs at Shore Resorts." *Baltimore Sun*, July 5, 1901.

"A Through Line Now." *Baltimore Sun*, July 2, 1890.

"Thrown from Carrousel." *Baltimore Sun*, August 24, 1917.

"Thrown from Coaster." *Baltimore Sun*, August 16, 1913.

"To Be Like Coney Isle." *Baltimore Sun*, May 18, 1906.

"To Build a Luna Park Here." *Baltimore Sun*, October 30, 1907.

"To Build Two Airships." *Baltimore Sun*, June 25, 1906.

"To Chesapeake Beach." *Baltimore Sun*, June 11, 1900.

"To Develop Hollywood." *Baltimore Sun,* March 8, 1910.

"To Investigate Beating of Men." *Baltimore Sun*, May 19, 1914.

"To Make Diversion Devices—Frederick Road Park Company to Build Plant." *Baltimore Sun*, May 19, 1923.

"To Open Big Dance Hall." *Baltimore Sun*, May 20, 1917.

"To Oppose Wooden Carlin's Buildings." *Baltimore Sun*, October 1, 1937.

"To Push Work at Carlin's." *Baltimore Sun*, May 14, 1922.

"To Reduce Park Tax." *Baltimore Sun*, March 6, 1896.

"To Remove Massive Poplar." *Baltimore Sun,* March 12, 1910.

"To Swim Is to Travel." *Baltimore Sun,* June 19, 1970.

"Today Begins Season at Carlin's." *News-American*, April 6, 1929.

"Today, Gwynn Oak Park Is Just a Quiet Park in the County." *Baltimore Evening Sun*, April 12, 1991.

"Tolchester." *Baltimore Sun*, November 13, 1936.

"Tolchester, Adieu." *Baltimore Evening Sun*, date unknown.

"Tolchester Beach." *Baltimore Sun*, May 26, 1899.

"Tolchester Beach Goes Back to 1877." Unknown.

"Tolchester Beach Marks Anniversary." *Baltimore Sun*, June 9, 1929.

"Tolchester Beach Opened." *Baltimore Sun*, June 2, 1899.

"Tolchester Beach Opened." *Baltimore Sun*, June 5, 1900.

"Tolchester Beach Opens." *Baltimore Sun*, June 3, 1917.

"Tolchester Beach Opens Decoration Day." *Baltimore Sun*, May 21, 1939.

"Tolchester Boat Denied Fuel Oil." *Baltimore Sun*, July 28, 1943.

"Tolchester Co. 32 Years Old." *Baltimore Sun*, June 24, 1909.

"Tolchester Fair Opened." *Baltimore Sun*, August 28, 1896.

"Tolchester Ferry Firm Given P.S.C. Approval." *Baltimore Sun*, July 3, 1937.

"Tolchester Has Opening." *Baltimore Sun*, June 1, 1916.

"Tolchester Hearing Set." *Baltimore Sun*, September 14, 1955.

"Tolchester Improvements." *Baltimore Sun*, May 11, 1896.

"Tolchester Improvements." *Baltimore Sun*, May 10, 1897.

"Tolchester in Bloom." *Baltimore Sun,* May 30, 1914.

"Tolchester Inspection Party." *Baltimore Sun*, April 6, 1900.

"Tolchester Is Put Back on the Map by Arrival of First 1,800 Youngsters." *Baltimore Evening Sun*, June 15, 1948.

"Tolchester Is Ready for Busy Season." *Baltimore American*, June 12, 1938.

"Tolchester Line Gets P.S.C. Order." *Baltimore Sun*, July 25, 1941.

"Tolchester Open Again." *Baltimore Sun*, June 1, 1906.

"Tolchester Opens." *Baltimore Sun*, May 30, 1909.

"Tolchester Opens." *Baltimore Sun*, May 29, 1915.

"Tolchester Park Partially Burned." *Baltimore Sun*, June 21, 1952.

"The Tolchester Season." *Baltimore Sun*, May 9, 1900.

"Tolchester Season Opens." *Baltimore Sun*, June 2, 1905.

"Tolchester Service Allowed to Operate." *Baltimore Sun*, June 30, 1937.

"Tolchester Sold at 1-Bid Auction." *Baltimore Sun*, October 21, 1962.

"Topics in New York." *Baltimore Sun*, June 6, 1900.

"Tournament at Gwynn Oak." *Baltimore Sun*, September 26, 1894.

"The Town of Chesapeake Beach." Unknown, September 23, 1954.

"Town Real Estate Firm Acquires Bay Shore." *Baltimore Sun*, May 7, 1946.

"Toys to Be Given Away." *Baltimore Sun*, August 21, 1913.

"Traction Company." *Baltimore Sun*, February 7, 1895.

"Traffic Blocks Route Until 3:30 A.M." *Baltimore Sun*, July 13, 1956.

"Trains and Boardwalk Gone, but Good Old Days Return." *Baltimore Evening Sun,* June 25, 1953.

"A Trip to Pike's Peak." *Baltimore Sun*, June 2, 1896.

"Trips 'Down the Bay' Still Draw Crowds." *Baltimore Sun*, August 11, 1940.

"Trolley Outgrowths." *Baltimore Sun*, July 24, 1895.

"Trustees Sale—Tolchester Beach." *Baltimore Sun*, October 14, 1962.

"20 Hurt as Storm Hits Bay Shore." *Baltimore News-Post*, August 3, 1955.

"25,000 at Second Annual All Nations Day Festival." *Baltimore Sun*, September 8, 1952.

"20,000 Children Greet Mayor at Amusement Park." *Baltimore Sun*, June 6, 1922.

"Two Are Injured in Falls from Racer Dips At Park." *Baltimore Sun*, July 30, 1923.

"2 Beaches Rezoned for Complex." *Baltimore Sun*, May 25, 1983.

"Two Clubs Admitted in South Atlantic." *Baltimore Sun*, July 26, 1923.

"2 Exotic Dancers Fined on Disorderly Charges." *Baltimore Sun*, July 23, 1964.

"Two File Damage Suits Against Pleasure Parks." *Baltimore Sun*, June 19, 1923.

"283 Integrationists, Many Clerics, Are Arrested at Gwynn Oak Park." *Baltimore Sun*, July 5, 1963.

"Two Hurt in Accidents at Amusement Park." *Baltimore Sun*, June 19, 1922.

"2 Shot at Hollywood." *Baltimore Sun*, May 15, 1915.

"United Employees Open Annual Outing Today." *Baltimore Sun*, July 18, 1925.

"United Not Expected to Seek Beer License." *Baltimore Sun*, May 23, 1934.

"The United Railways and Electric Company." *Baltimore Sun*, August 1, 1903.

"United Railways to Hold Annual Picnics This Week." *Baltimore Sun*, July 27, 1926.

"U.S. May Spend $32,400 to Improve Tolchester." *Baltimore Sun*, April 14, 1955.

"United to Be the Host." *Baltimore Sun*, July 26, 1909.

"United's Expense Cut 32.5 Per Cent." *Baltimore Sun*, April 30, 1933.

Untitled (Electric Park). *Baltimore Sun*, June 16, 1957.

Untitled (Riverview Park). *Baltimore News-American*, September 18, 1955.

"Vacationists Turn to Bay Shore Park." *Washington Post*, June 12, 1932.

"Varieties at Electric Park." *Baltimore Sun*, July 7, 1907.

"Variety at Gwynn Oak Park." *Baltimore Sun*, July 10, 1910.

"Variety Bill at Carlin's." *Baltimore Sun*, June 5, 1921.

"Vaudeville and Bullfight." *Baltimore Sun*, July 15, 1906.

"Vaudeville at Electric Park." *Baltimore Sun*, July 19, 1904.

"Vaudeville at Gwynn Oak." *Baltimore Sun*, July 7, 1907.

"Vaudeville at Gwynn Oak." *Baltimore Sun*, July 7, 1908.

"Vaudeville Program at Gwynn Oak Park." *Baltimore Sun*, July 15, 1917.

"Veterans at Bay Ridge." *Baltimore Sun*, August 2, 1894.

"Walbrook, Which Dared Be Suburb." *Baltimore Sun*, May 22, 1927.

"The Warships Have Arrived." *Baltimore Sun*, June 8, 1905.

"Washington Visitors Go to Tolchester." *Baltimore Sun*, June 12, 1890.

"Water Exhibition Draws Big Crowd." *Baltimore Sun*, July 30, 1923.

"Wave a Sad Good-by to Tolchester Park." *Baltimore Evening Sun*, October 20, 1962.

"We Sang 'Schnitzelbank' at Arion Park." *Baltimore Sun Magazine*, February 20, 1949.

"The Week at Gwynn Oak Park." *Baltimore Sun*, July 27, 1913.

"Were Guests at River View." *Baltimore Sun*, September 3, 1904.

"Were Princely Hosts." *Baltimore Sun*, August 25, 1905.

"Western Electric Buys 125 Acres at Riverview Park." October 28, 1928.

"Wheel Rider Breaks Record." *Baltimore Sun*, July 5, 1970.

"When Carlin's Was Liberty Heights Park." *Sunday Sun*, July 27, 1958.

"When 1 Cent's Worth of Fun Was Fun Indeed." *Baltimore Evening Sun*, date unknown.

"Where the Crowds Go to Get a Breath of Fresh Air." *Baltimore Sunday Herald*, July 3, 1904.

"Where the Roller Coaster Rumbles." *Baltimore Sun*, June 19, 1938.

"Who Razed Carrousel?" *Baltimore News-American*, December 20, 1958.

"Why More to Bay Shore?" *Baltimore Sun*, May 15, 1918.

"Wild Animals at Elks' Fete." *Baltimore Sun*, May 9, 1913.

"Will Close Hollywood Park." *Baltimore Sun*, March 7, 1912.

"Will Develop Three Islands." *Baltimore Sun*, April 7, 1947.

"Will Have New Managers." *Baltimore Sun*, April 8, 1902.

"Will Lay Double Track." *Baltimore Sun*, June 6, 1920.

"Will Rebuild Dance Hall." *Baltimore Sun*, June 18, 1921.

"Will Select Miss Bay Shore Park." *Baltimore News-Post*, July 24, 1954.

"Wilson Line Plans Sale." *Baltimore Sun*, July 18, 1957.

"Woman Killed in Fall from Racer Dip." *Baltimore Sun*, May 17, 1944.

"Work Being Rushed on Electric Park Buildings Preparatory to the Opening." *Baltimore Sun*, May 31, 1908.

"Work on Bay Shore Park." *Baltimore Sun*, June 19, 1906.

"Work on the *Columbia*." *Baltimore Sun*, June 6, 1899.

"The Workboat Races." *Baltimore Sun*, June 16, 1928.

"The World of Sport." *Baltimore News*, January 31, 1899.

"Zoo to Receive Baby Elephant." *Baltimore Sun*, September 27, 1953.

Periodical Articles

Anne Arundel County History Notes 20, no. 4 (July 1989).

"Baltimoreans Flock to New Bay Shore Park." *Baltimore*, July 1948.

Barker, Stan. "Paradises Lost." *Chicago History* 22, no. 1 (March 1993).

"Bay Shore Park Near Baltimore." *Street Railway Journal* 29 (February 23, 1907), 312–316.

Billboard. Annual Directory of Amusement Parks, Pleasure Resorts, and Summer Gardens. 1899–1955.

"Carlin's Park Celebrating Twentieth Anniversary." *Baltimore Jeffersonian*, June 10, 1938.

Crown Corker. Employee publication of the Crown Cork and Seal Company, Baltimore, MD, August 1951.

"Enchanted Forest—Story Book Land of Fairy Tales Come True." *Holiday Inn*, May 1965.

"Highland Beach—the First 100 Years." Highland Beach Historical Commission, 1993.

Jacques, Charles, Jr. *Amusement Park Journal* (1979–1987).

_____. *The Carousels of the Philadelphia Toboggan Company.* 1984.

"March on Gwynn Oak Park." *Time* magazine, July 12, 1963.

Maryland Life. "Storybook Summers: Recalling Ellicott City's Enchanted Past," July/August 2005.

NAPHA [National Amusement Park Historical Association] *News*, 1985–present.

"The Never-Never Land That Came True." *Maryland Motorist*, May-June 1956.

Scheinin, Lisa, "Racer Dips of Baltimore." *Rollercoaster* (Summer 2004), American Coaster Enthusiasts publication.

Sears, Jane. *Maryland Token and Medal Society Newsletter.* "Luna Park," "Gwynn Oak Park," and "Bay Shore Park." Dates unknown.

Books

Adams, Judith. *The American Amusement Park Industry: A History of Technology and Thrills.* Boston: Twayne, 1991.

Cartmell, Robert. *The Incredible Scream Machine: A History of the Roller Coaster.* Bowling Green, OH: Amusement Park Books and Bowling Green State University Popular Press, 1987.

Cudahy, Brian J. *Twilight on the Bay: The Excursion Boat Empire of B.B. Wills.* Centreville, MD: Tidewater, 1998.

Farrell, Michael R. *Who Made All Our Streetcars Go? The Story of Rail Transit in Baltimore.* Baltimore: Baltimore NRHS, 197).

Forman, Henry Chandlee. *The Rolling Year on Maryland's Upper Eastern Shore.* Centreville and Chestertown, MD, 1985.

Francis, David W., and Diane DeMali Francis. *Luna Park: Cleveland's Fairyland of Pleasure.* Fairview Park, OH: Amusement Park Books, 1996.

Fried, Frederick. *A Pictorial History of the Carousel.* New York: A.S. Barnes, 1964. Reprnt. Vestal, NY: Vestal Press, 1982.

Griffin, Al. *Step Right Up.* Chicago: Henry Regnery, 1974.

Jacques, Charles J., Jr. *Hersheypark.* Jefferson, OH: Amusement Park Journal Books, 2000.

Keith, Robert C. *Baltimore Harbor: A Picture History.* Baltimore: Ocean World, 1982.

Kyriazi, Gary. *The Great American Amusement Parks.* Secaucus, NJ: Citadel, 1976.

Mangels, William F. *The Outdoor Amusement Industry: From Earliest Times to the Present.* Vestal, NY: Vestal Press, 1952.

McWilliams, Jane Wilson, and Carol Cushard Patterson. *Bay Ridge on the Chesapeake: An Illustrated History.* Annapolis: Brighton, 1986.

Mueller, Father Kevin A. *Bay Shore Park: Fun on the Chesapeake.* Baltimore: Father Kevin A. Mueller, 2001.

_____. *The Best Way to Go: A History of the Baltimore Transit Company (BTC).* Baltimore: Father Kevin A. Mueller, 1997.

Munch, Richard. *Legends of Terror.* Mentor, OH: Amusement Park Books, 1982.

Warren, Mame. *Then Again, Annapolis.* Annapolis: Annapolis, 1990.

Miscellaneous

Baltimore Beaches Directory, July 1950. Prepared by the Tourist Bureau, Baltimore Association of Commerce.

"Bay Ridge History," courtesy Baltimore Streetcar Museum.

Chesapeake Beach Souvenir, 1971 reprint of souvenir guide, c.1906.

Maryland's Chesapeake Bay Resort, Betterton Beach, *Port Welcome* Ship's booklet, 1965.

Munch, Richard. Roller Coaster Directory (poster c. 1991).

National Association of Amusement Parks, Pools, and Beaches (NAAPPB). Annual Industry Handbook and Guide, 1943–1964.

Proceedings of the Annual Convention of the National Association of Amusement Parks, 1926–1932.

Riverview. Weekly newsletter, 1910.

"Western Electric: 25 Years of Achievement in Baltimore." Western Electric Company newsletter, c. 1954.

Index

Numbers in **bold italics** indicate pages with photographs.